The Politics of Social Theory

For Thomas and Amy

The Politics of Social Theory

Habermas, Freud and the Critique of Positivism

Russell Keat

a2 -1101

The University of Chicago Press

The University of Chicago Press, Chicago 60637
Basil Blackwell, Publisher, Oxford, England

Library of Congress Catalog Card Number: 81-40532

Library of Congress Cataloging in Publication Data

Keat, Russell.
  The politics of social theory.

  Bibliography: p.
  Includes index.
  1. Social sciences — Philosophy. 2. Habermas,
Jürgen. 3. Freud, Sigmund, 1856-1939. I. Title.
H61.K34 1981 300'.1 81-40532
ISBN 0-226-42875-3   AACR2
ISBN 0-226-42876-1 (pbk.)

Contents

Preface

Prefaces are for confessions and thanks, so I will do both. I became interested in Habermas's *Knowledge and Human Interests* whilst working with John Urry on our *Social Theory as Science*. Soon afterwards I spent a lot of time trying to sort out what Habermas was saying, partly through many long discussions with Linda Nicholson. My biggest thanks are to her. After the struggle for comprehension came near-conversion, followed soon by doubts. This book registers them fully, but I hope also sympathetically and constructively. Trying to come to terms with Habermas's work has been, as they say, a rewarding experience. And it was helped a lot by the publication of Brian Fay's *Social Theory and Political Practice*. Here was someone who amongst other things had succeeded in translating many of the central themes in Habermas's writings into the language of analytical philosophy, in which I continue to feel most at home. It was by using Fay's book in teaching that I began to work out more systematically where I agreed and disagreed with this conception of critical social theory, aided by the contributions of several students, especially John O'Neill.

For me, the centrepiece of *Knowledge and Human Interests* is the discussion of Freud. I had already been interested in psychoanalytic theory, mainly in the context of debates about its scientific status, and had come to think that it could best be understood, epistemologically, in terms of the theoretical realism presented in *Social Theory as Science*. I later became involved as a participant in various therapeutic groups, and it is partly through those encounters that my attitude towards Habermas's interpretation of psycho-analytic theory has emerged, one which is sceptical of the kind of unity he maintains between epistemology, theory, values, and therapeutic techniques. Further, both philosophical and personal reflection suggested a more physiological, somatic view of human existence than he seemed to adopt; but I have found it difficult to provide much in the way of a philosophical articulation of this.

Towards the end of *Social Theory as Science* we posed the question of how far the Frankfurt School's view of social theory departed from Weber's account of the place of political and moral values in social science. In effect, much of what follows can be seen to offer a view of critical social theory that stays quite close to Weber's position. I have always liked Weber's work, especially *The Protestant Ethic and the Spirit of Capitalism* and the essays in *The Methodology of the Social Sciences*. I suppose I became attached to Weber before becoming attracted to Marx, and have ever since been intellectually and politically embarrassed by this. For Weber, people say, is a bourgeois theorist; and worse still, his bourgeois commitment is most clearly expressed in his doctrine of value-freedom. I have always felt there was something wrong with this accusation, and wanted to be both Weberian and socialist. And since it is possible to hold beliefs that may in fact be incompatible, I seem to have succeeded.

The title of this book was at one time to have been 'Epistemology and Politics', which at least had the virtue of indicating its contents. What it says is that there is little if any connection between the two; or anyway, that the kinds of connections that critical theorists of the Frankfurt School have said there are, do not exist. But they are not the only Marxist (or neo-Marxist) writers who have maintained the existence of such links; it seems to me an almost obsessional feature of a lot of contemporary 'Left' theoretical work, and one that has tended to operate as a substitute for both substantive theoretical analyses of late capitalist societies, and a sustained normative critique of them. What we have often had instead is a form of 'ideology-critique' that attacks everything in sight (and not in sight) for its failure to be 'scientific' in the manner supposedly displayed by the texts of Marx (and often Freud). Not that epistemology is unimportant; but it should not displace social theory and politics.

Finally, some more thanks. To my colleagues in the Philosophy Department for their responses to numerous seminar papers on Habermas over the past few years, and especially Michael Hammond, with whom almost everything in this book (and a lot more) has been discussed; to the participants in meetings organized by the Radical Philosophy Group in Bristol, Oxford, Sussex and London; to Roy Edgley and Carolyn Stone, for their comments on drafts of various chapters; to the British Sociological Association, for the opportunity of giving a version of chapter 1 as a paper at its 1980 conference in Lancaster; and to Margaret Gudgin, Wendy Höpfl, and Ivy Thexton for typing it all more than once.

Russell Keat
University of Lancaster

Acknowledgements

I would like to thank Beacon Press of Boston, Massachusetts and Heinemann Educational Books Ltd for permission to quote from Jürgen Habermas, *Knowledge and Human Interests*, translated by Jeremy J. Shapiro, © 1971 by Beacon Press, © 1972 by Heinemann Educational Books; and George Allen and Unwin Ltd for permission to quote from Brian Fay, *Social Theory and Political Practice*, © 1975.

Introduction

The critical theory of the Frankfurt School has exercised a
major influence on debates within Marxism and the
philosophy of science over the past fifty years. Starting with
the work of the School's early members such as Max
Horkheimer and Herbert Marcuse, [1] many of its central
themes have more recently been developed and reconstructed
in the writings of Jürgen Habermas. [2] Like his predecessors,
Habermas has aimed at articulating the distinctive
epistemological character of a kind of social theory
supposedly represented in much of Marx's work: social
theory as *critique*. A critical social theory, it is argued, differs
significantly both from the positivist conception of social
science, and from the main historical alternative to this, the
hermeneutic or interpretive tradition. [3]

This book is an attempt to evaluate the claims made for a
critical social theory by the Frankfurt School, and in
particular by Habermas. So I will begin by giving a fairly
schematic account of how critical theorists have characterized
the nature of such a theory, and follow this with an outline of
the main elements in Habermas's position that I will be
examining later. But these are not intended to represent all
the major areas of his or other critical theorists' work. My
focus is deliberately restricted to certain epistemological and
ontological issues about social theory and its relationship to
political practice. So I shall not, for instance, consider the
substantive merits of Habermas's analysis of the crisis-
potentials in late capitalist societies, or of his studies on the
developmental logic of normative structures. [4]

Critical theorists' conception of a critical social theory can
best be understood by outlining their attitude towards the
positivist and hermeneutic alternatives. [5] The former is taken
to involve a belief in the possibility of a scientific
investigation of social phenomena which shares its

epistemological status with that of natural science, regarded as the paradigmatic example of human knowledge. Such a science aims at the discovery of universal laws, which enable us to predict and control physical and social processes. The truth or falsity of scientific theories depends exclusively upon their logical relationships to the empirical data provided through observation. No other criteria are relevant. In particular, scientific practice must be governed by the requirement of objectivity, of freedom from the distortions that result from the intrusion of moral or political values into science.

For positivists, normative issues are quite distinct from scientific ones, and are relevant only to decisions about how scientific knowledge is to be used. Science itself can only establish conditional predictions about the consequences of possible courses of action, but cannot justify the goals of such actions. Scientific knowledge is, in itself, politically and morally neutral. It is this claim which is the central target for critical theorists' critique of positivism. Against it they argue that the kind of practice that can be guided by a positivist social science has a specific and politically unacceptable character. Scientific knowledge, positivistically conceived, is inherently repressive, and contributes to the maintenance of a form of society in which science is one of the resources employed for the domination of one class by another, and in which the possibilities for a radical transformation towards a more rational society are blocked and concealed.

Why is it that a positivist social science is thought to have these political consequences? The attempt to formulate universal laws governing social phenomena leads to the misrepresentation as eternal or natural of what should instead be seen as historically specific and alterable. Positivism thus reinforces the reified and alienated character of (especially capitalist) social structures. Its conception of the relationship between theory and practice makes scientific knowledge necessarily manipulative, the ideal basis for a system of social control exercised by a dominant class, which can present itself as making political decisions in a purely rational, scientific manner. And by defining reason in this narrowly instrumental way, positivism undermines the intelligibility of any critique of society from the standpoint of a different conception of reason that is grounded in the human capacity for self-reflective autonomy and emancipation.

It is from this standpoint that a critical social theory is constructed, designed so as to become part of a self-reflective movement towards a more rational society. Thus critical social theory is itself to be one element contributing towards that transformation. It is therefore concerned with identifying the present possibilities for radical change towards a society in which human beings exercise fully their capacity for self-conscious control over social processes, and in which there is an absence of dominative power relationships and ideological consciousness. So the critique of existing ideologies and ideologically informed practices, such as positivist social science itself, is an important feature of critical social theory. But this critique is not purely 'theoretical': it must also specify and motivate the kinds of political action that will realize its emancipatory goal.

This conception of social theory differs too from the hermeneutic alternative to positivism. According to this, the central aim in the study of social reality is not the explanation and prediction of observable phenomena, but the interpretive understanding of meanings. Often taking the interpretation of texts as their model, hermeneutic theorists emphasize the significance of language or communicative interaction as the primary feature of the 'objects' of social theory, which thus distinguishes them from the objects of the natural sciences. Social reality is seen to consist in rule-governed, meaningful activity; and the understanding of this must involve an implicit dialogue between theorist and theorized, since the way in which the latter conceive of their own activities is itself a central part of social reality, unlike the situation in the natural sciences. Thus the criteria of validity for a hermeneutic social theory are distinct from those proposed by positivists, who mistakenly believe in the methodological unity of the sciences.

For critical theorists, however, a hermeneutic social theory is also unacceptable. Through its exclusive concern with the self-understandings of social agents it is unable to identify the existence of self-misunderstanding, of ideological consciousness. Nor can it recognize the significance of structural features of society that operate as unconscious determinants of social phenomena. Its non-critical attitude towards dominant forms of consciousness and practice conceals the way these function to maintain systematic a-symmetries of power and control. Thus interpretive social theory in effect views its objects as if they had already achieved what should instead be regarded as an as yet unrealized historical project: a society free from ideology and domination. It is this project towards which a critical social theory must be directed. And its own criteria of validity must therefore differ from those of either positivist or hermeneutic science. They must be tied to the successful outcome of social practices that are themselves partly guided by this kind of theory, and where success is defined by reference to the aim of human emancipation.

This completes my general sketch of critical theorists' views about the nature of social theory. I have made no attempt to do justice to the subtleties of formulation and argument in the writings of its major proponents, or to the important divergences between them. But this will be partly remedied by now giving a preliminary outline of Habermas's position which is, I believe, the most sophisticated and plausible development of these views.

Habermas's conception of critical social theory is articulated in the context of an overall critique of positivism which, he says,

> stands or falls with the principle of scientism, that is that the meaning of knowledge is defined by what the sciences do and can thus be explicated through the methodological analysis of scientific procedures.[6]

In place of positivism, Habermas proposes the differentiation of three forms of knowledge, of which only one, 'empirical-analytic science', represents the kind that positivists have presented as definitive of all genuine knowledge. But his analysis of empirical-analytic knowledge itself challenges the positivist conception of science as 'objective', in the sense of being both value- or interest-free, and descriptive of a subject-independent reality. Instead, Habermas argues that empirical-analytic science is constituted by, and thus presupposes, a specific human interest, the 'technical' interest. It is because of this that the theories of empirical-analytic science can, and can only, be utilized in a specific form of practice which is by no means normatively neutral, namely the instrumental control of natural or social processes.

In precisely what sense is the technical interest 'constitutive'? Habermas claims that it constitutes both the object-domain of empirical-analytic science, and the criteria of validity appropriate to assessing statements about that object-domain. The technical interest determines 'the objectivity of possible objects of experience',[7] i.e. what basic kinds of characteristics the 'object' must have, for such a science; and this object-domain consists of 'moving bodies', of 'things, events, and conditions which arc, in principle, capable of being manipulated'.[8] The criteria of validity for claims about such objects, are those of hypothetico-deductive theory-testing in experimentally reproducible conditions.

Though Habermas's conception of object-constitution is partly Kantian, he differs from Kant in at least one major respect. He argues that the necessary features of these objects of empirical-analytic science cannot be derived by transcendental arguments establishing the conditions for the possibility of knowledge for any knowing subject, but instead must be seen to result from a particular interest of the human species that is grounded in a species-universal characteristic: labour, involving instrumental feedback-controlled activity.

The two other forms of knowledge – 'historical-hermeneutic' and 'self-reflective' – are analysed by Habermas in a similar fashion, in terms of constitutive interests, species-universal characteristics, and their related object-domains and criteria of validity. Thus, in the case of hermeneutic knowledge, the object-domain consists of 'speaking and acting subjects', 'persons, utterances and conditions which in principle are structured and to be understood symbolically';[9] and its criteria of validity involve agreement upon meanings between partners in a (possibly imaginary) situation of dialogue. Its constitutive interest, the 'practical' interest, is that of successful communication, and is grounded in the human species-universal characteristic of language. It is this interest which determines the nature of hermeneutic theories' practical application, the restoration of communicative understanding between or within various groups or individuals.

Self-reflective knowledge (to which category belongs critical social theory) differs from both empirical and hermeneutic knowledge, though it involves elements that have parallels with each. Its object-domain can be seen as consisting of actions and utterances that are, in a sense to be specified further, defective or distorted. Their defective character is such that they bear some resemblance to the objects of empirical-analytic science, and may indeed often be misidentified as belonging to this domain; for they are subject to quasi-causal determinants, 'the causality of fate',[10] and cannot be understood by the interpretive procedures of hermeneutic theories. Instead they require what Habermas calls 'explanatory understanding',[11] which is neither purely causal, nor purely interpretive.

The constitutive interest of this form of knowledge, the 'emancipatory' interest, aims at the realization of autonomy through the freeing of distorted communicative activities from their quasi-causal determinants. Its criteria of validity include the successful outcome of self-reflective processes by human subjects, aided by their use of the insights provided by a critical social theory. Thus — though Habermas does not explicitly put it this way — the aim of a critical theory is, in effect, the abolition of its own object-domain, the transformation of defective actions and utterances into non-defective ones. I think it follows from this that, with the success of emancipatory knowledge, all actions and utterances will belong fully to the object-domain of hermeneutic knowledge, and (at least some forms of) self-reflective knowledge will become redundant.

In *Knowledge and Human Interests*, Habermas presents his conception of critical social theory through an analysis of the epistemological status of psychoanalysis, focusing especially on the relationship between the explanatory theory and the character of the therapeutic interaction between analyst and patient. Thus, at the outset of his discussion of Freud Habermas announces that 'Psychoanalysis is relevant to us as the only tangible example of a science incorporating methodical self-reflection'. [12]

Freud himself, he notes, regarded his theory as empirical-analytic; but Habermas argues that this is a scientistic self-misunderstanding, indeed one that introduced certain misguided elements into Freud's own work, particularly the attempt to conceptualize psychological processes in ways expressing his belief that one day psychoanalytic theory would be provided with a neurophysiological reduction. But Habermas also rejects what has been the main alternative to this positivist view of psychoanalytic theory's epistemological status, a purely hermeneutic one. This, he believes, cannot account for the significance in Freud's theoretical and therapeutic standpoint of the distortions of human activity resulting from the operation of unconscious, repressed, forces. To understand these requires a 'depth hermeneutics', providing explanatory understanding.

It will be helpful at this point to give a brief account of Habermas's interpretation of psychoanalysis; particularly as I will later be following Habermas's lead in analysing the epistemological character of critical social theory by examining the relationships between psychotherapeutic theories and practices. But it should be noted that this focus upon psychotherapy does not indicate, either for Habermas or me, that critical social theory must be exclusively psychotherapeutic in its substantive content; nor that a political practice guided by such a theory must involve some form of personal politics based upon psychotherapeutic theories or techniques. Habermas's concern with Freudian theory in this part of *Knowledge and Human Interests* is primarily epistemological, and this is how I will be presenting and assessing it.

Habermas examines three main elements in psychoanalytic theory: the structural model of ego, id, and super-ego; the theory of dream formation and interpretation; and the theory of psychosexual development, which specifies the relationships between childhood experiences and the characteristics of adults, including the sources of neurosis. In each case he argues that both the meanings of the theoretical claims and their criteria of validation must be understood by reference to the nature of the therapeutic situation, which involves a self-reflective process on the part of the patient, leading to emancipation from the quasi-causal power of the unconscious determinants of distorted actions and utterances. He thus wishes to reject a scientistic understanding of the relationship between theory and practice in psychoanalysis, according to which psychoanalytic theory is supported by empirical evidence derived from both clinical and experimental contexts, and can guide therapeutic practice by providing conditional predictions about the likely outcomes of the manipulation of causal variables in the interactions between analyst and patient.

Against this picture Habermas claims, for instance, that although the theory of psychosexual development can be used by the analyst to suggest interpretations of a patient's neurotic activity, the truth or falsity of these is not determinable in the manner appropriate to the hypotheses of an empirical-analytic science. But neither can they be assessed by the criteria appropriate to ordinary forms of hermeneutic interpretation, since the meaning of the patient's activity is at least temporarily concealed by the disguised character of unconscious wishes. The distorted communications of neurosis have to be deciphered by the kinds of procedures used by Freud for the interpretation of dreams. Through this process the power of the repressed unconscious is overcome, and the patient moves self-reflectively towards emancipation. And for Habermas this is to be seen as a movement from the realm of necessity to that of freedom.

So far, this account of Habermas's position has been drawn almost entirely from *Knowledge and Human Interests*. But there are certain features of some of his later writings which should also be noted here. In particular, the concept of distorted communication has been developed in the form of a 'theory of communicative competence' and a 'universal pragmatics', in which, amongst other things, an attempt is made to specify a number of norms presupposed by all communicative activity, such as truth and sincerity. On this basis, one can identify systematically the various kinds of possible distortions to which such activity may be subject.[13] Further, Habermas argues that the realization of these norms requires the existence of an 'ideal speech situation' which is marked by the absence of internal and external sources of coercion. And he makes use of this concept to construct both a theory of truth, and a theory of the rational foundation for the normative judgments involved in the 'practical discourse' of ethics and politics. What is true, and what is right, are defined in terms of the consensus potentially achieved by participants in this speech situation, where there are no a-symmetries of power between them, and where they are motivated solely by 'the unforced force of the better argument'.[14]

These, then, are the main elements in Habermas's position that will be examined in the following chapters. Before describing the various issues and claims that will be presented there, I will give some indication of my overall view of critical theorists's conception of the nature of social theory and its relation to politics. I share their opposition to positivism's identification of human knowledge with empirical science, to a positivist social science, and to the idea and practice of a scientific politics. But I believe there are important errors in their analysis of positivism which lead them to adopt an unacceptable view of the distinctive criteria of validity for a critical social theory. In particular, whilst sympathetic to the project of a social theory which, guided by certain values, is aimed at contributing towards the transformation of social reality, I think it is a mistake to tie the assessment of the scientific claims made by such a theory to the successful realization of those values. Further, although generally supporting the ideals of autonomy and self-reflection, I reject the view that these are to be seen as freeing human activity from the realm of causality; and I also reject the associated ontological dichotomy between humans and nature implicit in critical theory. Finally, I do not believe that the normative concepts relied upon by critical theorists, such as autonomy or emancipation, and their supposed antitheses, such as domination or control, are adequate for an understanding of the political and moral complexities of social practice.

The starting point for an assessment of critical theory must be an examination of its critique of positivism. The first two chapters are devoted to this. In them I argue that there are a number of logically distinct elements in what critical theorists have called 'positivism'. In particular, I suggest that the doctrine of value-freedom should be seen not as part and parcel of a unified positivist standpoint, but instead as an important basis for the criticism of certain other 'positivist' doctrines, especially the scientization of politics. I argue also that this doctrine, properly understood, is compatible with the construction of theories that are in various ways 'critical' of social reality, and I defend the relationship between science and values involved in this doctrine against the claim that it entails reformist or moralistic forms of political practice.

In the remaining four chapters I turn specifically to Habermas's position. I begin, in chapter 3, by criticizing his theory of knowledge-constitutive interests, arguing that he is mistaken in believing that the object-domain and criteria of validity of empirical-analytic science are constituted by a technical interest. I suggest also that this theory involves an unacceptable dichotomy between nature and humans, which both conceals the diversity of different kinds of 'natural beings', especially organic ones, and in effect 'de-naturalizes' human beings by defining them exclusively in terms of their species-*distinctive* features, especially language.

Further aspects of this dichotomy are examined and criticized in chapter 4, where I begin a discussion of Habermas's use of psychoanalysis as a model for critical social theory. I argue against his attempt to eliminate a biological conception of the instincts from psychoanalytic theory, which is reflected in his misunderstanding of Freud's concept of the id. I also defend the possibility of a neurophysiological reduction of psychoanalysis and suggest that this is compatible with the characterization of therapeutic processes as emancipatory, provided that one rejects Habermas's view that such processes involve a movement from the realm of causality. So I try to show how his concept of autonomy can be reconstructed within a deterministic framework.

In chapter 5 the relationship between the truth of psychoanalytic theory and the success of therapeutic practice based upon it is examined. I argue that Habermas's account of this is mistaken, and relies upon an oversimplified view of the logic of theory-testing in the natural sciences. In the course of this argument I also criticize Popper's attack on the scientific status of psychoanalytic theory, and Fay's attempt to show the distinctive way in which a critical social theory is related to the outcome of political practice. More generally, I emphasize the degree of logical independence that exists between the truth of theories and the effectiveness of therapeutic techniques, whilst also arguing that judgments about effectiveness presuppose normative decisions about therapeutic goals.

This theme of the normative elements in psychotherapeutic practices is continued in chapter 6. I suggest that the moral and political concepts of critical theory, and in particular Habermas's depiction of psychoanalysis as a self-reflective process aiming at autonomy, provide an inadequate basis for understanding the normative complexity of such practices. I then go on to argue that his attempt to provide a rational foundation for normative judgments is unsuccessful, partly by indicating certain problems in his theory of truth as consensus in an ideal speech situation, and partly by examining various parallels between his position and Rawls's theory of justice, pointing to difficulties facing both of these.

Finally, an explanation of my use of the phrases 'critical theory' and 'critical social theory' may be helpful. I use the latter to refer to any substantive theory about a 'social' object-domain, which is in some way constructed from a 'critical' standpoint. Psychological and economic theories, as well as sociological ones, thus potentially belong to this category. By contrast, I use 'critical theory' to refer to the (broadly) epistemological views characteristic of the Frankfurt School and its supporters, which involve claims about, for instance, the defects of positivism and positivist social science, and the proper character of the relationships between social theory and practice. Thus, according to my use of the terms, 'critical theorists' (amongst other things) advocate the construction of 'critical social theories'.

1 The Critique of Positivism

Despite the major significance attached by critical theorists to the critique of positivism, one of the few things that emerges clearly from their work on this is the absence of any clear conception of what positivism consists in. (This is a feature shared by many other critiques of positivism, an activity that has become almost obligatory amongst epistemologically sensitive social theorists over the past decade or so.) I believe it can be shown that what they call 'positivism' in fact consists of a number of distinct claims, which have quite complex logical and historical relationships to one another. My main aim here is to disentangle these, and thereby make some preliminary assessment of the success of their critique. I will begin by suggesting a certain paradox in this, which indicates the need for a more detailed analysis of the concept of positivism.

1 A PARADOX IN CRITICAL THEORISTS' CRITIQUE OF POSITIVISM

Most critical theorists appear to regard the doctrine of value-freedom as a central feature of positivism. This is true, for instance, of Horkheimer, in his early and influential article, 'The Latest Attack on Metaphysics';[1] of Marcuse, in his discussion of Comtean positivism in *Reason and Revolution*;[2] and of Habermas, in his contributions to *The Positivist Dispute in German Sociology*.[3] And for them, as for others, Weber's methodological writings represent one of the major expressions of this doctrine.[4] But when one examines these, one finds I believe that his overriding concern was to attack those who thought that political and ethical issues could be resolved by purely scientific means. He wished to reject the legitimacy of a 'scientific politics'; to dispel what he regarded as the illusory authority given to political and ethical ideals propounded in the name of 'science'. Yet it seems that, for critical theorists, the scientization of politics is also one of their main targets of criticism which, like value-freedom, they take as a key element in positivism.

For instance, according to Habermas one of the earliest articulations of this scientific conception of politics is to be found in Hobbes; and it represents a wholesale rejection of what Habermas regards as the classical tradition of politics, going back at least to Aristotle.[5] For Aristotle, claims Habermas, politics was intimately related to ethics and both were distinct from 'theory', since they could not be ascribed the status of a rigorous science. By contrast, he argues, Hobbes believed it possible to construct a science of human activity that would enable the conditions for the proper ordering of society to be rationally determined. It is this (Hobbesian) scientization of politics that forms one of the main targets of Habermas's critical work, as was also the case for many of his predecessors in the Frankfurt School.

Positivism as the advocacy of a scientific politics first became a major theoretical and practical phenomenon in early nineteenth-century Europe, especially through the writings of Saint-Simon, Comte and their followers.[6] Thus Saint-Simon, speaking of how political decisions would be made in a society organized on the basis of the 'positive sciences', had this to say:

> These questions . . . are eminently positive and answerable; decisions can only be the result of scientific demonstrations, absolutely independent of all human will, which may be discussed by all those educated enough to understand them . . . . And just as every question of social interest will then be decided as well as it can be with acquired knowledge, so will all social functions inevitably be entrusted to the men most capable of performing them in conformity with the association's general aim. Thus, in this situation the three principal disadvantages of the present political system − arbitrariness, incapacity and intrigue − will be seen to disappear all at once.[7]

Here, and throughout Saint-Simon's writings, we are presented with the ideal of a society organized upon scientific principles, and in which all social and political problems are open to a *rational* solution through the application of (social and natural) scientific knowledge.

But it is just this kind of view that Weber was concerned to reject, by insisting upon the separation of science and values emphasized by the Heidelberg School of neo-Kantians. His most important single paper on this issue, 'The Meaning of "Ethical Neutrality" in Sociology and Economics',[8] was initially written in the form of a position paper for a meeting of the committee of the German Association for Social Policy (*Verein für Sozialpolitik*) in January 1914. His argument involved a complete rejection of the dominant attitude amongst members of the Association, especially of its recognized head at that time, Gustav Schmoller. Thus Ralf Dahrendorf tells us that:

> It was Schmoller who had prescribed for the 'science of economics' not merely the tasks of 'explaining individual phenomena by their causes, of helping us understand the course of economic development, and if possible of predicting the future', but also that of 'recommending' certain 'economic measures' as 'ideals'.[9]

Weber argued that it was not possible to justify such normative claims by scientific evidence and argument alone, so the very idea of a scientific politics was epistemologically misconceived. He maintained also that once the relevance or significance of certain objects of enquiry was established, necessarily by reference to normative standpoints, it was possible to produce social scientific work whose statements could be assessed by reference to scientific, value-free criteria of validity. It is these claims which, I believe, form the central elements in his view of the place of values in social theory — the doctrine of value-freedom.

And this is why I suggest there is a paradox in the critical theorists' critique of positivism. For it seems that, at least in Weber's view, the doctrine of value-freedom represents an alternative to the ideal of a scientific politics, and is based upon an account of the relations between science and values that provides the basis for rejecting altogether that characteristic ideal of nineteenth-century positivists. Yet according to critical theorists, both value-freedom and the scientization of politics are to be seen as key features of positivism, both of which are to be rejected in favour of their own preferred critical conception of social theory.

Nor is Weber the only figure whose position suggests a difficulty of this kind in the concept of positivism. Karl Popper, and his ally in the *Positivismusstreit* of the 1960s, Hans Albert, were both taken by the proponents of critical theory (Adorno and Habermas) to represent the positivist position they wished to attack. In the course of the exchanges between them, Habermas makes it clear that he regards Popper's espousal of value-freedom, of 'the dualism of facts [*Tatsachen*] and decisions [*Entscheidangen*]', as clear proof of his positivism.[10] Popper, of course, was vehement in his resistance to this label (for quite good reasons, I believe, related to his rejection of another supposedly positivist doctrine, 'scientism', which I will discuss later). But both he and Albert were emphatic in their support for the doctrine of value-freedom, and in criticizing the critical theorists' 'dialectical' rejection of it.[11] They, unlike their opponents, clearly regarded the espousal of value-freedom as entirely compatible with the rejection of positivism.

Many other examples indicating a similar state of confusion could be given. But what I will now do is attempt to remove it, by defining a number of distinct doctrines that have been taken to be 'positivist', and exploring their logical and historical relationships.

2 POSITIVISM: THE ONE OR THE MANY?

We can identify at least four doctrines, each of which may not unreasonably be termed 'positivist'. I shall call them 'scientism', 'the positivist conception of science', 'scientific politics', and 'value-freedom'. In this section I shall first define them, and then examine the logical relations between them. This will make it possible to understand precisely what is involved in a 'positivist' social science and thus, by contrast, what the supposedly non-positivist character of a critical social theory consists in.

'Scientism' is the view that science alone represents a genuine form of human knowledge. As Habermas puts it, scientism 'means science's belief in itself: that is, the conviction that we can no longer understand science as *one* form of possible knowledge, but rather must identify knowledge with science'.[12] It is important to note that scientism involves not merely a distinction between science and non-science, but the relegation of the latter to an inferior status, even to cognitive meaninglessness or nonsense. Typical examples of such pseudo-knowledge, for advocates of scientism, have been religion, metaphysics, 'ideology', and the normative discourse of politics and ethics − unless any of these can be suitably interpreted or reconstructed as scientific claims.

As a philosophical position, scientism has a long history, with the 'logical positivism' of the Vienna Circle providing one of its most influential recent expressions.[13] And one of the reasons why Popper has persistently maintained that he is not a positivist, is his rejection of this feature of logical positivism. From very early on, he argued that the Vienna Circle were mistaken in dismissing the non-scientific as meaningless. What was needed was a principle for demarcating science from non-science, but which did not thereby distinguish sense from nonsense.[14] It should also be noted that a standard objection to scientism has been that it is, in effect, self-refuting, since the statement of the doctrine does not conform to the criteria of legitimate knowledge specified by it. In particular, it is argued that scientism is itself a philosophical, epistemological doctrine, and not a scientific one. This, I take it, is one of Habermas's major criticisms of scientism, expressed in his pointed remark: 'that we disavow reflection *is* positivism'.[15] (Defenders of scientism may, however, argue that this objection can be met if logical analysis is included within the category of genuine knowledge, and epistemology then understood as involving this form of analysis.)

By itself, scientism says rather little without some further account of what scientific knowledge consists in. One such account is provided in the second of the four doctrines, 'the positivist conception of science'. According to this, science aims at the explanation and prediction of observable phenomena by showing that these are instances of universal laws that apply in all regions of space and time. The truth or falsity of statements intended to express such laws is determined solely by their logical relationships to other, non-universal statements that describe particular observable 'data'. Statements of scientific laws may contain 'theoretical' terms, which do not refer to what is directly observable; but they are not to be understood as referring to unobservable items. Rather, their meanings must be specified (if only incompletely) via statements whose descriptive terms are exclusively observational. Further, the relationships that exist between phenomena display no form of necessity, of either a logical or non-logical kind: these relationships involve only universal regularities of occurrence between logically distinct items.[16]

As with scientism, the positivist conception of science has a long history.[17] Many of its elements can be found, for instance, in the writings of Berkeley and Hume; of Comte, associated with his 'law' of the three stages of human thought; and of Ernst Mach, who adopted it in his critical reconstruction of Newtonian science, eliminating from it such 'metaphysical' concepts as absolute space and time, force (except as a theoretical concept definable in terms of mass and momentum), and any idea of causality as consisting in something 'more' than regular relationships. Science, according to this view, must be kept free of metaphysics; and this is achieved by, amongst other things, eliminating the unobservable from its ontology.

It is more difficult to define precisely the third 'positivist' doctrine, the advocacy of a scientific politics. This is partly because many of its proponents, such as Saint-Simon, have hardly had the merit of philosophical clarity or sophistication. But it is, I think, well captured in the following passage from Fay's *Social Theory and Political Practice*:

> it is thought that if it were to be the case that political decisions would be made on the basis of technical application of social scientific knowledge, then the character of political argument

would drastically alter. The point here is that, at least in the ideal, the disagreements that arise in engineering or medicine are not expressed in terms of personal value or wishes, nor are they debated on the basis of the power or position which the disputants have in the social order to which they belong, nor settled in terms of subtlety of exposition or rhetorical power; rather, the issues are tangible, measurable, and testable, and debates about them are conducted in such a way that it is these objective features accessible to all which decide the matter at hand . . . . If politics were to become an applied science, it is argued, its conjectural, arbitrary, emotional and personal elements would drop out, and its arguments and decisions would assume the same neutral characteristics as those of engineering . . . . In political arguments there would be, as there are in scientific arguments, reliable public standards of ascertainable truth, and therefore the possibility of a universally recognizable decisive solution to a particular problem. It is in this way that a social science would be able to eliminate the 'anarchy of opinion' which characterizes modern political thinking.[18]

So here the ideal is the use of scientific knowledge to provide rational solutions to all problems concerning the organization of society, and to free such decisions from influences of a non-scientific (and thus supposedly non-rational) kind. But it would seem that the possibility of doing this is denied by proponents of the final 'positivist' doctrine, value-freedom. According to them, it is essential to separate the realms of science and political or moral values. This separation has at least two dimensions. First, the criteria of validity for scientific theories involve no reference to the acceptance or rejection of particular moral or political commitments: whether a theory is true or false can be determined independently of such normative standpoints. Second, it is not possible to support political or moral judgments solely by means of scientific knowledge; so people may agree on the relevant scientifically establishable claims, yet legitimately disagree about the desirability of what is advocated in such judgments.

The doctrine of value-freedom, defined in this way, has been accepted by many philosophers and social theorists who in other respects have often had little else in common. Hume, Kant, Mill and Weber can all be seen to subscribe to it, despite the considerable differences between them on other epistemological and normative issues. As I will suggest later, this is one reason for the complexity of the history of positivism – which is, in fact, not so much one history but many histories. But before exploring this I will outline what are, for my purposes, the most important logical relationships between these positivist doctrines.

First, scientism and the positivist conception of science do not entail each other. The latter can be maintained without acceptance of the former, since it is possible to adopt the positivist view of what scientific knowledge consists in without also believing that science is the only form of knowledge. Thus science may be conceived positivistically, and in this way distinguished from, say, religion or morality, without these being regarded as meaningless, epistemologically defective, non-rational, or suchlike. Indeed, historically, the positivist conception of science has sometimes been adopted by those who have wished to 'protect' the legitimacy of religion or metaphysics against the claims of science.[19]

Conversely, scientism does not entail a positivist view of science, since this view may well be rejected in favour of another, whilst it is still maintained that science has a monopoly on human knowledge. It will be useful here to note briefly some of the alternatives to a positivist account of science. First, a rough distinction can be made between 'realist' and 'instrumentalist' views, according to whether science is thought to provide statements about some theory-independent 'real world', or is instead regarded as a device or instrument that may serve certain purposes such as technical control or predictive power.[20] The former view involves adopting some form of correspondence theory of truth, whilst the latter involves either rejecting the idea of truth as characterizing the contents of scientific theories, and substituting instead some idea of 'usefulness', or adopting a pragmatic definition of truth itself. But it is important to note that a realist view of the cognitive status of scientific theories may be associated with the claim that the main goal of scientific enquiry is to serve human practical purposes; for it may be argued that the best way of achieving this is to produce theories that are true in a realist sense. (This, I think, was Bacon's position.)

The positivist conception of science, as I have defined it, is a realist one — although some versions of it come very close to instrumentalism.[21] But there are also non-positivist forms of realism. In particular, there is the position often called 'theoretical realism', which differs from positivism mainly in not restricting scientific ontology to the domain of what is observable. For theoretical realists, scientific theories typically make claims about the nature and existence of unobservable items: so the positivists' attempt to define theoretical terms in an observational vocabulary is seen to be misconceived. Further, theoretical realism involves rejection of the positivist analysis of causality as regularity, and replaces this with some concept of natural, non-logical necessity.[22]

A second useful dichotomy for locating various conceptions of scientific knowledge is that between empiricists and rationalists. The former regard scientific theories as ultimately testable by reference to the compatibility of its claims with 'the evidence of the senses', perceptual observation. By contrast, rationalists see the truth or falsity of theories as determinable by *a priori* knowledge, in roughly the way that mathematical or logical statements are. The major difficulty for rationalists has been to find some way of non-arbitrarily choosing between different internally consistent theories, and showing just how they relate to the non-logical world. For empiricists, the main problem has been in identifying a form of perceptual information that is reasonably certain, free from problematic theoretical presuppositions, and related to the statements of scientific theories in such a way that it can be used to determine their truth or falsity. These difficulties for rationalist and empiricist philosophers of science have yet to be resolved.[23] But I believe that positivist and theoretical realist accounts of science are both empiricist — though some advocates of the latter would no doubt dispute this claim.

So the significance of the doctrine of scientism depends partly on what view is taken of the nature of scientific knowledge, the positivist conception being but one possibility, which can itself be adopted without commitment to scientism. I will now examine the relations between both these positions and, in turn, scientific politics and value-freedom.

Neither scientism nor the positivist view of science entail the possibility of a scientific politics, since both are consistent with the claim that political decisions cannot be made solely by reference to scientific knowledge. Advocates of scientism who accept this claim must believe therefore that political life cannot be fully rational, since it requires answers to questions that are not scientifically resolvable, and thus not 'knowable'. By contrast, proponents of the positivist conception of science who reject the possibility of a scientific politics need not regard politics as inherently non-rational, since they may accept that science is not the only form of human knowledge or rational enquiry.

The relations between this conception of science and the doctrine of value-freedom is a little more complex. It is clear that the latter does not entail the former, since the separation of science and values implies no particular view of what scientific knowledge consists in. But the positivist view of science is consistent with regarding normative judgments as scientifically establishable, and thus with a denial of the second of the two elements of value-freedom that I specified. However, since this conception of science requires that scientific theories are assessed only by reference to empirical observation, it does entail the first element of value-freedom, the insistence that scientific criteria of validity are independent of normative commitments.[24]

The claims I have made about the logical relationships between these four doctrines can be summarized as follows (where 'S', 'PS', 'SP', and 'V-F' represent respectively scientism, the positivist view of science, scientific politics, and value-freedom; and '→' and '↛' represent 'entails' and 'does not entail'):

1 (a) S↛PS	3 (a) V-F↛S
(b) PS↛S	(b) V-F↛PS
2 (a) S↛SP	(c) PS→first element of V-F
(b) PS↛SP	(d) PS↛second element of V-F

This is not a complete list, of course, but it specifies the main relationships that are necessary for analysing critical theorists' critique of positivism. But before going on to show how this critique fails to recognize these relationships, we need to consider one further doctrine, advocacy of a positivist social science. According to this, it is possible to develop a science of society that conforms to the positivist conception of science. However, this could be denied by proponents of that conception, since it might be argued that social phenomena cannot be studied in a scientific manner at all; and this is a position that defenders of scientism could also consistently adopt. Positivist social science stands in the same relationship to scientism, scientific politics, and value-freedom as does the positivist view of science (1 (a) and (b); 2 (b); 3 (b)-(d) above). But it also rules out the claim that social theory involves a different form of knowledge to the one specified in that view of science. In particular, it is opposed to advocates of a hermeneutic social science, who argue that this distinctively non-empiricist, and thus non-positivist form of knowledge is necessarily involved in the understanding of social reality.

3 HOW NOT TO CRITICIZE POSITIVISM

I will now provide some illustrations of how critical theorists, in their critique of positivism, have ignored or misunderstood the character of the logical relationships between the various positivist doctrines I have identified. I begin with a characteristic passage from one of Horkheimer's early papers, where he attacks positivism (at this point calling it 'empiricism') by claiming that there is a

> crucial point which empirical science fails to note, namely, the common interest and the idea of a truly human existence. Empiricism declares that such ideas arise from the confusion of personal desires, moral beliefs, and sentiments with science; it regards the strict separation of values from science to be one of the most important achievements of scientific thought. Empiricism further contends that other aims may be set alongside the will to freedom and that it is not the task of science to decide which of these is right. [25]

Here there is a definite confusion between scientism,

positivist science, and value-freedom. To claim that the values of 'freedom' or 'a truly human existence' (whatever they may mean – for here we have an example of the highly abstract, undifferentiated character of many critical theorists' normative concepts) cannot be established by a positivist science, is not thereby to deny the possibility and legitimacy of defending such values, and employing them in a critique of society. Value-freedom does not rule out the possibility of a rational normative critique, but only that this can be conducted on the basis of scientifically establishable claims. Further, it is mistakenly assumed in this passage that the practice of empirical science involves commitment to scientism, and that both of these entail rejection of the possibility of normative critique.

We find a similar set of confusions in the following passages from one of Habermas's contributions to *The Positivist Dispute in German Sociology*:

> The dualism of facts and decisions necessitates a reduction of permissible knowledge to strict empirical sciences and thereby a complete elimination of questions of life-practice from the horizon of science.[26]

And describing the implications of this dualism, he claims that it means that:

> decisions relevant in practical life, whether they consist in the acceptance of principles, in the choice of a life-historical outline or in the choice of an enemy, can never be replaced or even rationalized through scientific calculation. If, however, the practical questions which have been eliminated from empirical-scientifically restricted knowledge must be utterly dismissed in this manner from the scope of rational discussions; if decisions in questions of practical life must be absolved from every instance in some way committed to rationality, then the last attempt [to provide some basis for practical decisions] is not surprising: to secure institutionally, through a return to the closed world of mythical images and powers, a socially binding precedent for practical questions (Walter Bröcker).[27]

In the first passage, we see the mistaken claim that value-freedom entails scientism, together with the challengeable assumption that scientism rules out the possibility of political issues being scientifically resolvable − clearly not the view of many advocates of a scientific politics. In the second, Habermas's argument depends on assuming that supporters of value-freedom must believe that, just because normative questions are not scientifically establishable, they are beyond 'the scope of rational discussions'. But this is not so, since the doctrine of value-freedom does not imply the non-rationality of normative judgments.

My next example concerns the scientization of politics, and involves some more complex issues. In *Social Theory and Political Practice*, Fay argues there is a conceptual connection between the practice of a positivistically conceived social science (which he defines similarly to the way I have done so) and a particular form of scientific politics, which he terms 'policy science'. He describes this in the following way, as:

> that set of procedures which enables one to determine the technically best course of action to adopt in order to implement a decision or achieve a goal. Here the policy scientist doesn't merely *clarify* the possible outcomes of certain courses of action, he actually *chooses* the most efficient course of action in terms of the available scientific information. [28]

As Fay is careful to point out, this version of a scientific politics is to be distinguished from another, 'stronger' form, according to which *every* aspect of political decisions is thought to be scientifically resolvable. Instead, it is accepted that value-judgements have to be made, non-scientifically, to establish the goals of political action; and policy science is then allotted the task of discovering the best means for achieving these externally determined ends. Thus, the dichotomy between facts and values is mapped on to that between means and ends. He proceeds, without much difficulty, to show what is wrong with this conception of policy science. Any means to a given end is itself open to evaluation by standards other than those which determine that end, for:

> *all* political proposals, no matter how instrumental, will alter and shape the personal relations of at least some members of a society, and will affect the relative welfare of various classes of

people; as such they embody moral notions of what is permissible, just, or right in human affairs. They are a species of moral statement. [29]

So it is impossible to determine the 'technically best course of action to adopt' by this use of a positivist social science.

The crucial move made by Fay in this attempt to criticize positivist social science via the unacceptability of its supposed consequence for politics (namely support for policy science), is the mapping of the means-ends relationship onto that between facts and values. That this is somehow implied by positivism is also claimed by Habermas:

Since Max Weber, what had long been pragmatically clarified in the relationship between natural sciences and technology seems to have been clarified for the realm of social sciences too; namely, that scientific prognoses can be realized in technical recommendations. These recommendations distinguish between a given initial situation, alternative means and hypothetical ends; all so-called value-judgments are simply attached to the third member of this chain, whilst the if-then relations can themselves be investigated in a value-free manner. This translation presupposes, of course, that in societal practice, as in the technical domination of nature, it is always possible to isolate ends-means relations in which the value-neutrality of the means and the value-indifference of the subsidiary consequences are guaranteed; in which, then, a 'value' is only linked with ends so that these ends may not, for their part, be regarded as neutralized means for other ends. In those realms of practical life for which social-scientific analyses are required, none of the three conditions is, however, normally fulfilled. [30]

Conditions which define the situations of action behave like the moments of a totality which canot be dichotomously divided into dead and living, facts and values, into value-free means and value-laden ends without failing to grasp them as such . . . Consequently, practical questions cannot be sufficiently answered with a purposive-rational choice of value-neutral means. [31]

Now I agree with Fay's and Habermas's objections to this mapping manoeuvre, designed to allow the possibility of scientific judgments about 'the best means'. It is true, also, that this move is frequently made by proponents and practitioners of scientific politics, and indeed generates what one might call a 'scientist mystification of political decisions'. But I see no reason for claiming that the use of a positivist, value-free social science, implies this move. (Nor, incidentally, do I think that Weber was guilty of making it.) For, as Fay correctly argues, what the knowledge produced by this kind of science enables one to do is to make conditional predictions of the form 'if certain conditions obtain, certain results will (invariably or usually) follow'. It provides information about what would happen if certain things were done, and about what are possible (and in some cases, necessary) ways of bringing something about.[32] But this is quite different from the idea that, in relation to a given end, the best means can be discovered independently of any further value-judgements. To show what are the possible ways of achieving some goal, and their other consequences, does not enable us to judge which of these is 'scientifically best'; nor does showing that a certain course of action is necessary for achieving some goal whose desirability is already accepted, entail that it is right or rational to perform those actions. And there is no reason why advocates of a positivist social science should not recognize these points. Thus, however misconceived this idea of a policy science may be, its defects cannot be used to criticize the positivist view of social science.

I will continue this discussion of positivist social science and scientific politics by noting their connections with utilitarianism. According to utilitarians, the rightness of an action is determined by its consequences for human happiness; and the best action (and thus also the best society) is that which produces 'the greatest happiness of the greatest number', which maximizes the total amount of happiness. It follows that, once the utilitarian principle is accepted, political and moral decisions can be made on the basis of scientific knowledge alone.

However, even utilitarianism does not involve the direct mapping of the fact-value distinction onto that between means and ends, at least in most cases. For whilst it in effect transforms all normative questions into scientific calculations of the consequences for its sole end, the maximization of happiness, the goals of *particular* courses of action will typically be far more specific and limited than this. Utilitarians may, for instance, assess the desirability of different forms of punishment in relation to the possible goal of deterrence. But this has itself to be justified by reference to the overall end of maximal happiness; and so, too, must these forms of punishment. Thus showing scientifically that a particular form is the 'best' means of achieving the end of deterrence would not establish it as the right action, since this means would also have to be judged in terms of other of its possible consequences for the overall level of well-being.

Although utilitarianism is an apparently attractive view for proponents of a scientific politics, it is not a 'pure' form of this, unless one believes that its basic principle can itself be scientifically established. Some of the more sophisticated utilitarians, such as J. S. Mill, argued that this was not possible: no proof could be given for the principle of utility, let alone a strictly scientific one – though he did believe that strong reasons could be provided in support of it.[33] By contrast Saint-Simon tended to ignore this issue, and contented himself with claims of the following kind:

> It has been recognized that the rulers are only the administrators of society, that they must direct it in conformity with the interests and will of the ruled, and that, in short, the happiness of nations is the sole and exclusive purpose of social organization.[34]

And:

> In the present situation it is acknowledged that the permanent and sole duty of governments is to work for the happiness of society. But how is society's happiness to be achieved?[35]

The answer, for Saint-Simon, lay in the development and application of the 'positive' sciences, both natural and social. In this way, politics (and ethics) could also become positive sciences.[36]

Further, though utilitarians may find a positivist social science well-suited to their need for making predictions about the consequences of possible actions, there is no reason why support for a positivist social science should entail utilitarianism. For the former is compatible with a rejection of scientific politics, including its only partial, utilitarian form. Advocates of a positivist social science may regard politics as requiring decisions that involve normative issues for which utilitarianism provides an inadequate guide: for instance, questions concerning the equitable distribution of social goods, which utilitarianism can deal with only in terms of the consequences for aggregate-maximization. [37]

Finally, it is worth noting one other version of the scientization of politics, associated with the 'end of ideology' thesis about modern capitalist societies. [38] According to this, such societies had developed to the point at which there was a consensus between previously competing groups about the basic goals of political and economic organization. For instance, significant conflicts between the interests and ideologies of different social classes were said to have been overcome. It followed that political questions could become matters of the most effective means to these accepted goals, and could thus be decided by employing the supposed expertise of social scientists, such as economists, sociologists and psychologists. As with utilitarianism, this is not a pure form of scientific politics, since it is accepted that there are distinctively normative questions which are not scientifically resolvable: but 'in practice' normative consensus made politics a scientific domain.

4 THE HISTORIES OF POSITIVISM

I began this chapter by suggesting a certain paradox in critical theorists' critique of positivism: that this involved the association of positivism with the doctrines both of value-freedom and scientific politics, whilst it seemed that advocates of the former, such as Weber, not only rejected the latter, but regarded value-freedom as a position from which the pretensions of a scientific politics could be revealed and criticized. My account of the logical relationships between these and other positivist doctrines has been intended to explain this paradox and in effect to justify Weber's perception of the situation. I will now sketch out some of the historical relationships between these doctrines, and suggest in particular a partial independence between the histories of scientific politics and value-freedom.

Though anticipated in writers such as Hobbes, and perhaps some of the Enlightenment rationalists,[39] it was the early nineteenth-century positivists, especially Saint-Simon, who were the most influential and enthusiastic advocates of the scientization of politics. In the case of Saint-Simon, this ideal was associated with a form of scientism, and expressed a general commitment to the virtues of scientific knowledge, industry and the organization of society on the basis of a 'scientific outlook'. Whether this combination is philosophically coherent, is dubious — for it could be argued that the advocacy of scientific approaches is not compatible with the belief that only science provides genuine knowledge, since the advocacy of such approaches to social and political questions is not itself an item of scientific knowledge.[40] Nonetheless, philosophically more sophisticated thinkers than Saint-Simon have adopted the same combination: for instance, the authors of the Vienna Circle's first 'manifesto',[41] Neurath, Carnap and Hahn, who declared that:

> endeavours toward a new organization of economic and social relations, toward the unification of mankind, toward a reform of school and education, all show an inner link with the scientific world-conception,[42]

and who concluded their document by claiming:

> We witness the spirit of the scientific world-conception penetrating in growing measure the forms of personal and public life, in education, upbringing, architecture, and the shaping of economic and social life according to rational principles. *The scientific world-conception serves life, and life receives it.*[43]

These passages are particularly interesting since they express a political dimension of the Vienna Circle that has not normally been recognized in its reception amongst Anglo-American philosophers, who have focused primarily on the epistemology of logical positivism.[44] This political element is also evidenced in the inclusion, in the manifesto's list of the various philosophers and scientists whose writings were central to the Circle's discussions, of:

Hedonism and positivist sociology: Epicurus, Hume, Bentham, J. S. Mill, Comte, Feuerbach, Marx, Spencer, Müller-Lyer, Popper-Lynkeus, Carl Menger (the elder). [45]

The appearance in this list of several utilitarians gives some support to the suggestion made in the previous section that, for advocates of a scientific politics, utilitarianism may seem an attractive position. But it also raises the problematic issue of the relations between French positivists and British utilitarians in the nineteenth century. In particular, it is well-known that Mill was highly critical of Comtean positivism: partly because he thought that Comte had not provided a necessary element in any account of science, namely the methods of induction; partly because he believed that Comte was 'jumping the gun' in advocating a scientifically organized society in the absence of the requisite development of social scientific knowledge; and partly also because of the markedly illiberal, authoritarian elements in Comte's politics[46] – which were present also in Saint-Simon's, who claimed, for instance, that 'the cultivation of politics will be entrusted exclusively to a special class of scientists who will impose silence on all twaddle'.[47]

I will return shortly to this question of the possible illiberalism of the scientization of politics. But first, a few comments on the philosophical ancestry of the doctrine of value-freedom, especially its articulation in Weber's writings. It is frequently noted that Weber was strongly influenced by the Heidelberg school of neo-Kantians, whose two best-known figures were Windelband and Rickert.[48] Another member was Richard Kroner who, in *Kant's Weltanschauung* provided a characteristic statement of the Heidelberg interpretation of Kant's philosophy. Kroner's overall view of this is presented in the following passage:

> His entire philosophy receives its particular tone from a two-fold insight. On the one hand, along with modern rationalists since Descartes and Galileo, he sees, in the exactitude of mathematical knowledge, the pattern and ideal of all theoretical study of reality; on the other hand, in spite of his full appreciation of scientific truth, he does not accord it any metaphysical significance. Kant is of the opinion that the point of contact

between man and the supersensible sphere is to be discerned in the facts of man's moral life, in his self-determination, and in the laws of his moral will; for it is on these laws that the dignity and freedom of man rest . . . . Only mathematical relations are knowable, and they are the objects which the mechanical and physical sciences can successfully treat. The world in which we as moral beings act and pursue our ends obviously cannot be penetrated by mathematical knowledge; therefore this world cannot be grasped in its reality by any theoretical [i.e. scientific] means. [49]

Kroner goes on to argue that, for Kant, the limitations he places on the scope and character of scientific knowledge are the result of his view that, without these, morality and freedom would not be possible. Thus:

If morality is possible at all, the duality of nature and freedom must exist, and its existence must be a limitation of knowledge. [50]

Further:

Practical reason [guiding the will of the free subject] does not know objects, it does not know nature; it knows rather the purposes of the will, its norms, its goal. The kind of knowledge which is appropriate in the field of the sciences − objective, theoretical, impersonal knowledge − cannot be applied in the fields of willing and acting. [51]

And in a comment which we might reasonably interpret as indicating what would be Kant's attitude to positivist advocates of a scientific politics, Kroner says:

If Kant had attempted to extend this [mathematical-physical] method, which he deemed to be the only legitimate and feasible method for knowing reality, to the world in which we live as active beings (as indeed the disciples of materialism and naturalism would like to do), then he would have been compelled to abandon the respect he had for moral life. Within a nature interpreted mathematically no morality can exist, because there every action loses its meaning: in such a world the will cannot set any purpose for itself, since mathematics alone orders and determines all things in its own inexorable and absolute way. [52]

Clearly, we have here a view of the relations between

science and norms which is very different from the positivist
doctrines of either scientism or the scientization of politics. It
is also a view of ethics that is in most respects at odds with
utilitarianism which, unlike Kant, focuses exclusively upon
the consequences of actions and not upon the will, and denies
the Kantian claim that morality presupposes the autonomy of
a transcendental subject. Its only point of contact with
utilitarianism, at least in the form presented by Mill, is the
acceptance of a logical dichotomy between scientific and
normative judgments. For Mill was a staunch defender of this
dichotomy, but influenced here by his empiricist forefather
Hume, rather than Kant. [53] Because of this, as I noted earlier,
Mill's utilitarianism does not involve a pure form of scientific
politics. But it is perhaps partly due to the apparent congruity
on this point between Mill's empiricism and Weber's neo-
Kantianism that the doctrine of value-freedom has been
mistakenly associated by critical theorists with the ideal of a
scientific politics.

Further, by noting the neo-Kantian influences on Weber,
we can see why value-freedom has been associated by its
critics with the impossibility of a rational normative critique
of social reality, despite the fact that the doctrine by no
means entails such a view. For it is clear that Weber himself
not only advocated the separation of scientific from
normative issues, but also claimed that the latter were not
open to rational, objective resolution. Instead, they involved
personal commitments to ultimate values which could not be
rationally justified. [54] In this respect, Weber's account of
value-freedom departs from the definition I have provided
for it, which remains neutral on this question, and is thus
consistent with a rejection of this element in Weber's
account. And it is perhaps significant that the Heidelberg
interpretation of Kant that influenced Weber seems in this
respect to depart from other interpretations, which instead
emphasize Kant's commitment to the rationality of
normative judgments, especially through the universalizing
requirements of the categorical imperative. By contrast,
Kroner's reading of Kant is much closer in spirit to the
position of existentialist writers such as Sartre, who, whilst
clearly influenced by Kant, in effect emphasize the autonomy

of the will at the expense of the possible rationality or objectivity of values.[55]

Critical theorists' critique of positivism has typically involved claims about the 'repressive' character of its political implications. My attempt to show the logical independence of various positivist doctrines casts considerable doubt on these claims, and suggests that whatever plausibility they have would exist only when directed at the ideal of a scientific politics. But even here the situation is far from straightforward. First, whilst this political critique has often involved the charge that positivism is intrinsically committed to a defence of the existing social order, it is clear that in many respects this was far from true of the early French positivists such as Saint-Simon. He rightly saw himself as an advocate of radical change. He was not, after all, living in an already scientized society; and it may be that this charge of 'conservatism' (in the sense of preserving the *status quo*, whatever that may be) is partly the result of interpreting nineteenth-century theorists through a twentieth-century vision accustomed to the significantly scientized character of advanced industrial societies. Admittedly Marcuse, in *Reason and Revolution*, emphasizes the radical and progressive politics of (some of) the Saint-Simonians, and contrasts them with Comte's advocacy of *order*. But this contrast is highly problematic. For whilst Marcuse wishes to demonstrate a connection between Comtean conservatism and the epistemological claims of positivism, he fails to show any divergence between Comte's and Saint-Simon's epistemologies which could support their different political positions.[56]

Second, in the context of early nineteenth-century Europe, Saint-Simon's 'radicalism' consisted in, amongst other things, attacking the value of political or religious liberties, by associating these with the 'metaphysical' stage of historical development, which was to be replaced by the positive, scientific one. The 'lawyers and metaphysicians', he claimed, were at one time a historically progressive group through their role 'in modifying the feudal and theological system and ensuring that it did not suppress the scientific and industrial system once it began to develop'.[57] But he bemoaned the fact that the French Revolution, in which the leading part should have been taken by 'the industrials and the scientists', was instead taken over by the lawyers and metaphysicians. It would, he said, 'be superfluous to recall the strange wanderings which resulted, and the misfortunes which resulted from these wanderings'. Further:

> The philosophers of the eighteenth century convinced people in general to accept the right of the individual to practice his own religion and to decide which religion his children should be taught. The philosophers of the nineteenth century will convince people that all children should study the same code of terrestrial morality, since the similarity qf positive moral ideas is the only link which can unite men in society, and since ultimately an improvement of the social condition is nothing more than an improvement in the system of positive morality.[58]

The French positivists were not, of course, the only nineteenth-century theorists to display a marked antipathy towards the individual rights so central to liberalism. We find it also in the Marxist tradition (including Marx himself, for instance in his comments on the intrinsically 'bourgeois' character of such rights).[59] It seems that this is one of several connections between positivism and Marxism, especially where the latter takes the form of a supposedly 'scientific' socialism.[60] And the historical links between scientism, scientific politics and socialism emerged again in one of the most influential members of the Vienna Circle, Otto Neurath, who attempted to demonstrate the utilitarian and scientific bases of Marxist socialism. Thus Neurath argued that 'Marxism is, consciously, the philosophy of the socialist proletariat and promises it happiness'; that Marx 'teaches the decline of the bourgeois order and the coming of the socialist order'; and that 'it is precisely the proletariat that is the bearer of science without metaphysics'.[61]

As mentioned earlier, it was the illiberalism of Comtean positivism and scientific politics that provided one of the main reasons for Mill's opposition to them. This may seem surprising, given the partial links between utilitarianism and the scientization of politics. Yet, as is often noted, there is a definite tension between the utilitarian and liberal-democratic elements in Mill's political philosophy. This emerges, for instance, in his problematic distinction between 'higher' and 'lower' pleasures, and in his equally problematic attempt to define happiness so as to include the interests of 'man as a progressive being'. Both of these revisions of earlier, Benthamite utilitarianism were perhaps necessary if a utilitarian rationale were to be provided for the value of individual liberties and democratic participation. But it is also important to note the legitimacy Mill ascribed to a certain form of authority belonging to those with the scientific and intellectual expertise for making the utilitarian calculations involved in rational political decisions.[62] Thus there may be a connection here between Mill's utilitarian version of the scientization of politics, and the somewhat elitist character of his political position.

5 THE CRITIQUE OF POSITIVISM: A PRELIMINARY ASSESSMENT

I have mainly been concerned in this chapter to identify a number of distinct doctrines that have been called 'positivist', and to examine their logical and historical relationships, and I have said little if anything about their intrinsic merits or defects. But it may be helpful, at least in understanding why the various lines of argument in the following chapters are the ones pursued, to now indicate my view of these positivist doctrines.

Scientism is, I believe, mistaken because not all human knowledge and rational enquiry can be interpreted on the model of scientific knowledge, however this is conceived. In particular philosophy itself, including epistemology, cannot be thus understood, and nor can the normative realms of politics and ethics. So I also reject the possibility of a scientific politics. As for the character of scientific knowledge, theoretical realism is, I believe, to be preferred to positivism. But, more generally, I support realism as against instrumentalism, and empiricism as against rationalism; and in terms of both these dichotomies, theoretical realism is closer to positivism than to non-realist, non-empiricist alternatives.

However, I also believe that in the *social* sciences no form of empiricism provides an adequate epistemology, since the distinctive character of social reality requires the use of hermeneutic, interpretive modes of analysis. So this is an additional reason, for me, for rejecting the positivist view of social science. But I do accept one element of that view, the doctrine of value-freedom. Further, at least consistently with my opposition to scientism, I support the possibility of rational argument about normative issues, and certainly do not regard them as non-rational just because they are not scientifically resolvable.

I will not try to justify these claims here. Some I have argued for elsewhere (such as the place of interpretation in social theory, and the merits of theoretical realism as an account of science).[63] Others, such as value-freedom, will be defended in later chapters. But I will conclude this chapter by outlining my view of critical theorists' critique of positivism. First, this has generally failed to understand the distinct nature of various positivist doctrines, and the logical relations between them. There has too often been a frontal assault on a loosely defined, undifferentiated target called 'positivism', or at least an assumption that, by successfully criticizing one positivist doctrine, the others are thereby shown to fail also. For instance, criticism of the scientization of politics has been taken to entail rejection of scientism, the positivist view of science and value-freedom. But this does not follow, and neither does the converse. Defence of value-freedom is compatible with rejection of a scientific politics; defence of positivist social science with rejection of scientism; and so on.

Second, I believe these mistakes have to a considerable extent misled critical theorists in their attempts to construct an acceptable alternative to positivism, a critical social theory. It seems that their central concern has been to develop a conception of social theory that can be critical of certain features of social reality, including its organization on the basis of a scientific politics, and that is linked to forms of social practice that will succeed in transforming societies that display such features. But whilst I support these general aims, I do not believe that critical theorists are right in thinking that, in order to achieve them, it is necessary to specify the criteria of validity of a critical social theory in such a way that they are logically tied to acceptance of this normative standpoint, and indeed to the successful outcome of practices guided by this kind of theory. In particular, critical theorists are wrong to reject the doctrine of value-freedom. And I think they are partly led to do this by mistakenly believing that it either entails, or is entailed by, the ideal of a scientific politics and scientism. However, I need now to examine the doctrine of value freedom in more detail than I have so far.

2 Value-Freedom and Socialist Theory

In the previous chapter I defined the doctrine of value-freedom in terms of two main elements. First, the criteria of validity for scientific theories are logically independent of the acceptance or rejection of normative commitments of a moral or political kind. Second, it is not possible to establish such normative positions solely by reference to scientific knowledge. My main aim in this chapter is to elaborate these claims, defend them against various objections, and show that certain consequences often thought to follow from them in fact do not. In doing so, I will also be trying to demonstrate the possibility of social theory that is constructed from a critical, socialist standpoint, but which is nonetheless 'value-free'. Hopefully, the apparent inplausibility of such a position will be removed in what follows.

The first two sections deal with the two elements in the doctrine of value-freedom noted above. In section 3, I discuss the concept of 'significance' in social theory, and show how this can be used to identify the distinctive character of a socialist social theory. In the final section, I defend my account of the relations between science and values from the objection that it entails unacceptable forms of political practice.

1 THE LOGICAL INDEPENDENCE OF SCIENTIFIC CRITERIA OF VALIDITY FROM NORMATIVE JUDGMENTS

It is an obvious feature of the vocabulary used to describe social phenomena that much of it has definite normative implications. This is true both of ordinary language, and of many of the central theoretical terms in the social sciences – such as 'alienation' and 'anomie' in the writings of Marx and Durkheim, respectively. It seems that we typically characterize features of social reality – from individual actions to the general structures of social relationships – in ways that at least implicitly indicate our political or ethical attitudes.

Many advocates of 'value-freedom' have believed that these normative elements must be expunged from the concepts of social science, in order that its criteria of validity may be properly scientific. But this, I think, is a mistake. It is possible to maintain that these criteria are independent of normative commitments, without insisting upon the use of a value-free vocabulary; and there is no reason, therefore, why the political or ethical standpoints of social scientists should not be expressed through the concepts they employ, as well as through more explicit normative judgments contained in their work. What matters instead is that, whether or not the concepts used in making descriptive or explanatory claims express such attitudes, it is possible to assess these claims by reference to scientific criteria of validity that are logically independent of any specific moral or political commitments.

Some examples may help to illustrate the view I am proposing here. Consider the claim that a change in the political system of a particular society resulted from the injustice of its economic structure. Now the concept of social justice is clearly a disputed one, in that there are a number of different and mutually incompatible accounts of what justice consists in. Each of these typically involves advocacy of certain principles that should govern the distribution of social goods such as property, income, rights, power and so on. Amongst such principles are equality; level of contribution; needs; or the operation of legal transactions in a market economy.[1] I shall not try to indicate the kinds of arguments that can be used in supporting these principles, but I believe it can be shown that they do not turn exclusively on scientifically establishable claims, whilst not lacking a genuine degree of rationality.

If the concept of justice is to be used in the kind of explanatory claim mentioned above, two requirements must be satisfied. First, which of these competing principles is meant must be specified. Second, it must be possible to determine whether a particular distribution of social goods actually conforms to this principle independently of one's acceptance of this as providing the normatively preferable conception of justice. If these requirements are met (and I see no reason why they cannot be), the explanatory claim involving this concept of justice can be assessed in a value-free manner.

A similar analysis could be provided for many other central political concepts and their place in social theories, such as domination, freedom and exploitation. The last of these, for instance, has a well-defined meaning within Marx's political economy, in terms of the labour theory of value, and appears in a number of theorems concerning the relations between the rate of exploitation and the ratio of constant to variable capital, and so on. At the same time, its employment by Marx has definite normative implications. But acceptance of these is logically irrelevant to the truth or falsity of the explanations of social phenomena that make use of it.

My position here is very similar to Ernest Nagel's, in his defence of the possibility of value-free social science.[2] Nagel introduces a distinction between 'characterizing' and 'appraising' value-judgments. He illustrates this initially by reference to the use of the concept of anaemia in physiology. Nagel argues that considered as a characterizing judgment, whether an organism is anaemic depends upon determining the number of red blood cells that are present; and various different standards may be chosen, involving different definitions of anaemia. However, for any specific definition the degree of anaemia present in the organism is scientifically determinable. At the same time, though, the judgment that an organism is anaemic may also be an appraising one, indicating that this is to be seen as an undesirable or pathological condition, on the grounds that an anaemic organism will be unable to perform certain functions that are themselves necessary or desirable in relation to the norms of survival, reproductive fitness and so on. But acceptance of this appraising judgment is not presupposed by the truth of the characterizing judgment that the organism is anaemic.

Nagel then goes on to argue that the same analysis can be given for many concepts employed in the social sciences: for instance, the judgments that certain attitudes or actions are mercenary, deceitful, cruel and such like.

However, although Nagel's distinction between characterizing and appraising judgments is a useful one, it is important to recognize that in practice, the use of concepts such as justice, exploitation, freedom, will typically be understood to imply that both kinds of judgment are being made. Thus even if the explanatory claim that, say, a certain historical phenomenon was due to the injustice of an economic system is correct, those who reject the normative appraisal implicit in this will quite reasonably tend to indicate this disagreement in the way they express their acceptance of the explanation. They will wish, in effect, to make some normative disclaimer. This can be done in a variety of ways, such as the use of scare-quotes, or of some different term altogether which lacks the normative implications from which they want to dissociate themselves. So, for instance, defenders of market capitalism may employ the term 'exploitation' only in scare-quotes whilst commenting upon the adequacy as an explanatory theory of Marx's political economy. But this does not mean that its adequacy depends upon whether the normative implications of this concept are accepted by those who assess the theory. Equally, there is no reason why those who accept these implications should, in order to display their commitment to a value-free social theory, avoid using the concept of exploitation without such disclaimers. For the requirement that social theories can be assessed by value-independent criteria of validity does not entail the absence of normative concepts in the presentation of such theories.

In this respect, then, my view of the place of values in social theory departs from Weber's. For he seems to have believed that the requirement of 'objectivity' could be met only by purging the social sciences of all normatively loaded concepts. He also argued that it was wrong for social scientists to 'add' to their work any explicit value-judgments, even when these were made quite separately from its strictly scientific elements. But he was at pains to point out that this prohibition was itself a value-judgment, which could not be supported solely by epistemological or methodological arguments. There are, I think, good reasons for rejecting this judgment; but in doing so, as Weber recognized, one is not rejecting his epistemological claims.[3] Weber also believed that political and ethical values could not be rationally justified. But it must be emphasized that this view is in no way entailed by the conception of value-freedom I am supporting here.[4] Nor should the question of their rationality be thought to depend on whether they can be established on the basis of scientific knowledge: to believe this would involve acceptance of scientism, as I argued in the previous chapter.

Having now elaborated this view of the logical independence of scientific criteria of validity from normative commitments, I will consider an objection to it, which raises some highly problematic issues. It might be argued that the view must be mistaken, since it implies something that is impossible: namely the existence of a descriptive vocabulary that is 'value-neutral', free from any normative elements whatsoever. For if it is possible to assess the claims of a social theory by value-independent criteria, despite the fact that they employ concepts that are not value-neutral, it must also be possible to re-state these claims with concepts that have had these normative elements removed. Yet, the objection continues, such a value-neutral reconstruction of the claims of a social theory cannot be achieved.

Whilst this argument has considerable force, I think it can be met in a way that, without providing a completely adequate reply, goes far enough to disarm it. I suggest that, for any concept that appears to express or presuppose a particular normative attitude, it is always possible to replace it by one that does not do this. In other words, in any situation where the statements of a social theory seem objectionable on normative grounds, from a particular moral or political standpoint, it is possible to reconstruct them in a way that removes the normatively problematic element, and thus enables their truth or falsity to be assessed by non-normatively dependent criteria of validity.[5]

By calling this a 'suggestion', I mean that I cannot offer

any proof that this is so. Rather, I am claiming that wherever I have tried to do this, I have produced a reconstruction that seems to me satisfactory. It may of course be that I am too easily satisfied; or that I have not considered the kinds of cases that would be impossible to deal with in this way. But consider the following example. Suppose that someone claims that there is a relationship between the degree of 'industrial unrest' and the 'alienating' character of the work involved in a certain kind of society. Some people might object to the phrase 'industrial unrest' on the grounds that it indicates a standpoint which values order and discipline, and is thus implicitly critical of the activities to which it refers. To meet this I would propose replacing 'degree of industrial unrest' by something like 'the number of strikes and level of absenteeism'; and if the latter part of this new description were found objectionable, for rather similar reasons, it might be replaced by 'the number of days un-worked but not due to illness or injury' – and so on. Others might object to the term 'alienating' because it expresses a negative judgment based on an unacceptable ideal of human labour. In which case, I would propose an alternative such as 'the lack of control exercised by workers over economic production', and so on. By these kinds of reconstruction of the initial statement, I suggest, it is possible to make its scientific assessment independent of potentially challengeable normative claims. And if this is so, the force of this objection is considerably weakened. So I turn now to the second main element in my account of value-freedom: that political and moral judgments cannot be justified solely on the basis of scientifically establishable claims.

2 CAN NORMATIVE JUDGMENTS BE DERIVED FROM SOCIAL THEORIES?

I shall discuss this issue mainly by examining some objections that have been made to the claim that normative judgments cannot be derived from social theories. But first it must be noted that it does not follow from this claim that the truth or falsity of scientific statements is (always) *irrelevant* to accepting or rejecting such judgments. Scientific statements can be, and often are logically relevant to, without actually entailing, normative judgments.

This relevance can take at least three forms. First, many of these judgments depend upon the truth of various singular statements of a scientific kind. For instance, the judgment that someone has acted honestly, requires the truth of the psychological claim that he or she did not, in acting, profess beliefs that he or she regarded as false. Similarly, the judgment that one class exploits another requires the truth of various sociological claims about, amongst other things, the character of the economic relationships between the two, such as the distribution of control over the means of production. Nonetheless, the concepts of honesty and exploitation also have normative elements, such that the truth of these descriptive statements, whilst necessary for acceptance of the normative judgments involving them, are not sufficient. So whilst the falsity of these descriptive statements would entail the rejection of the normative judgments, the truth of the former would not entail the acceptance of the latter (at least if these are understood as appraising, rather than purely characterizing, judgments).

Second, any general theory of the basis of normative judgments that takes account of the consequences of actions will assign an important role to scientific claims. The most obvious example here is utilitarianism, according to which the right action is to be determined by calculating its likely consequences, and comparing these with the likely consequences of others. Here one must be able to make conditional predictions about the consequences of various course of actions; and such predictions normally require knowledge of at least limitedly universal relationships or laws. However, utilitarianism does not assert a direct entailment between predictions of consequences and normative judgments: all such judgments depend also upon acceptance of the principle of utility itself. But the truth or falsity of scientific statements is nonetheless relevant to these judgments; and for anyone who accepts the principle, they will indeed be the only relevant statements for assessing particular judgments.

Third, there is a widely accepted principle that normative judgments should be restricted to actions or situations that are *possible*: that 'ought implies can'. If this is accepted, then it follows that a special kind of conditional prediction will often be important in assessing normative judgments: namely, that there are no possible circumstances in which a certain otherwise desirable state of affairs could be realized.

Two points should be noted about this principle. First, according to one view about the character of scientific laws (adopted by many theoretical realists),[6] these are to be regarded as statements of what is possible or impossible (e.g. 'nothing can travel faster than the speed of light'). If this view is correct then, if there were any genuine laws in the social sciences, they would be highly relevant to normative arguments. Second, one must distinguish between statements of 'absolute' and 'relative' impossibility. In the former, it is claimed that there is *no* set of circumstances in which the specified state of affairs could obtain; whereas, in statements of relative possibility, it is claimed that this is impossible *given* certain conditions (that is, taking these as fixed). Clearly, it is only statements of absolute impossibility that could directly refute normative judgments. At the same time, statements of relative possibility are often highly significant in that they may be sufficient to 'practically' refute some such judgments, by showing that the realization of the advocated state of affairs would require changes of conditions that may, for a variety of reasons, be regarded as impractical or undesirable. For instance it may be a reasonable requirement of a critical social theory that its analyses are guided by values that are actually realizable in a particular historical situation. This requirement is exemplified in the way Marxist theorists have tried to show what it is within the capitalist mode of production that makes possible its transformation towards socialism, and have been opposed to 'Utopian' critiques that are not grounded in this way.

However, claims about what is or is not possible (either absolutely or relatively) need to be treated with considerable caution. For they may often involve concealed normative judgments rather than being, as they are presented to be, scientific 'permitters' or 'disqualifiers' of such judgments.

Consider for example the claim that a socialist organization of society is impossible since one cannot prevent individuals from accumulating income and using it for profitable purposes involving payments to others for their labour. An obvious reply to this might be that 'cannot' in effect means 'can only be achieved by certain (supposedly) undesirable means', such as controls over the employment of wage-labour;[7] and the judgment that such control would be unacceptable, itself involves challengeable normative assumptions. Indeed, it seems that the attempt to conceal such assumptions under the guise of purely scientific statements of impossibility, is one of the most frequent ways in which what can be called a 'scientistic mystification of normative standpoints' is practiced; and many claims about 'human nature' involve versions of this.[8]

With these general comments in mind, I will now examine some objections to the claim that normative judgments cannot be derived from scientific theories. The first is designed to show that social science is necessarily potentially critical of its 'objects', and that it is a mistake to distinguish 'theory' and 'practice' in a way that assigns science to the former and normative judgments to the latter, with no logical connections between them.[9]

The argument for this is as follows. The objects of a social theory include the practices of human agents, which are based in various ways upon their beliefs; and it may often be possible to discover the social determinants of these. But scientific theories are intended to consist of true beliefs; and in the social sciences, many of these will be about the same things as are the beliefs held by those who are the objects of scientific enquiry. It is therefore possible that there will be incompatibilities between these two sets of beliefs: that is, scientific and 'lay' beliefs may conflict. Now, if one regards a certain statement as true, one must also regard it as 'wrong' to hold a belief that is incompatible with it. Therefore, scientific theories are necessarily potentially critical of social reality, to the extent that the latter involves beliefs that can be shown scientifically to be false, internally inconsistent, and so on. In addition, if these defective beliefs can be explained by reference to other features of social reality, these too are to be criticized; and activity aimed at the removal of these features, and thus also of defective beliefs and activities based upon them, is thereby shown to be desirable.

This argument, then, attempts to demonstrate how scientific social theories can and indeed must be potentially critical of their object-domains, in a normative, 'practical', manner. And this in effect gives us a version of the traditional theme in Marxism that social theory involves a 'critique of ideology', a critique that also supports actions aimed at the realization of an ideology-free society. However, I do not believe the argument successfully undermines my view of the relations between social theory and normative judgments; and neither does it show how such a theory is not merely 'critical', but critical in a distinctively socialist manner. I shall take these two points in turn.

I have already argued that it is possible for scientific statements to be logically relevant to the assessment of normative judgments, without the latter being derivable from the former. Much of this objection can be seen as showing how this kind of relevance arises, but without refuting the claim that normative judgments cannot be supported by scientific knowledge alone. For instance, if a course of action or type of practice is justified by social agents on the grounds that this will have certain specific consequences, then clearly it may be possible, scientifically, to show that this belief about consequences is false. But it does not follow from this that the justification of such actions or practices lies exclusively in beliefs whose truth or falsity can be scientifically determined. For example, the practices involved in a capitalist market economy are sometimes supported by the claim that this system maximizes economic growth. And it may be that this claim can be shown to be false. But even were it to be true, there remains an important further kind of possible criticism that focuses upon the belief that growth is a (primary) desirable feature of economic systems; and this belief remains unchallenged by the scientific critique of the claim that growth is indeed maximized by a capitalist market economy. Thus, whilst I accept that scientific statements can be critical in the sense of challenging some kinds of assumptions involved in social practices, this does not undermine my view of the relations between social theory and normative judgments.

However, there is a further feature of this argument for the intrinsically normative character of social theories that is not dealt with by the comments just presented. This is the suggestion that there is a necessary link between the practice of social theory, and the acceptance of a substantive political ideal: namely, that social relationships should be 'ideology-free', and that relationships which require for their existence and reproduction the presence of ideological beliefs are *ipso facto* to be rejected, normatively, and eliminated through an appropriate political practice.

Though I accept this political ideal, I have several reservations both about the justification here provided for it, and about its significance as the basis for a distinctively socialist conception of critical social theory. My scepticism on the former point starts from the following, perhaps naive queries. Is it not possible to adopt as a social ideal the exclusive use of scientific knowledge by an élite that maintains its power by, amongst other means, the production of ideological consciousness? And is it not true that many people seem to think it positively undesirable to 'enquire too deeply' into, or be too 'critical' of, the beliefs which their practices are based upon? The point of both these questions is to suggest that the founding of social practices upon (scientifically) true beliefs expresses a distinct and by no means unchallengeable value, which cannot itself be established by scientific knowledge alone. It is only if such an ideal is already accepted, and justified on some other basis, that the results produced by scientific enquiry will have normative implications.

However, it might be argued that whilst what is discovered through scientific procedures cannot establish the ideal of a society that is free from false beliefs, it is nonetheless the case that to actually engage in the practice of (social) scientific enquiry must involve a commitment to this social ideal. This, I think, is an argument of some significance. But I will leave it aside here, since a particular version of it will be examined much later, in chapter 6, where I discuss Habermas's attempts to provide a rational foundation for normative judgments. Instead, I will consider briefly the adequacy of ideology-freedom as the standpoint of a distinctively socialist form of critical social theory.

Whilst it is true that for socialists societies should be ideology-free in the sense of there at least being no need in them for false beliefs to be disseminated and accepted, it seems that the realization of this ideal is compatible with the absence of several other central socialist principles: for instance, an egalitarian distribution of social goods, and the elimination of private ownership of the means of production. And acceptance of these principles in no way follows from commitment to 'the end of ideological consciousness' (where ideological beliefs are those that can be scientifically refuted). Social practices may be based upon (scientifically) correct beliefs, yet display characteristics that significantly depart from socialist principles. And it follows from this that a socialist critique of non-socialist societies cannot be confined to revealing the falsity of the beliefs upon which they in various ways depend. For it is both logically permissible, and common in practice, for people to accept the ideal of freedom from ideology, yet reject other major socialist principles.

I turn now to examine some claims made by Charles Taylor in an influential attack on the idea of value-freedom in social theory.[10] His main concern is to show that political science can have significant implications for political philosophy, on the grounds that the theoretical frameworks developed in the former typically support or undermine various ideals or values proposed within the latter. Taylor's argument depends on two basic propositions: that such theoretical frameworks have definite consequences as to what kinds of political organization are possible or impossible; and that normative judgments can be established by reference to the extent of satisfaction of human wants or needs. This first premiss, if correct, would not constitute any challenge to the position I am defending. The second involves a modified version of ethical naturalism; and it is, I believe, open to the objection that, like utilitarianism, it cannot deal adequately with political issues than concern the proper *distribution* of want-satisfaction.[11] But I will not pursue this criticism here.

Instead, I want to focus on another major claim made by Taylor which has received little critical attention, but raises important issues about the place of values in social theory.

Taylor argues that if the normative judgments implied by a particular theoretical framework are rejected, then it must follow that the framework itself is also rejected. This, he says, is because theoretical frameworks involve claims about what are the *significant* variables affecting political systems; and, likewise, normative positions also make claims about the significance for humans of the satisfaction of various wants and needs. That is, normative judgments (in this case about the desirability of possible forms of political organization) are interpreted by Taylor as based on claims about the extent to which wants and needs regarded as 'significant' are satisfied. So suppose, for instance, that it follows from a theoretical framework that it is only in a society with a particular form of political organization that certain wants and needs can be satisfied. Then, according to Taylor, we could only deny the desirability of that form of organization if we denied the significance of those wants and needs. But − and this is the part of the argument with which I am concerned − if we deny this, and advocate some alternative set of wants and needs as (more) significant, we must then also deny the adequacy of the initial theoretical framework. For it, like normative standpoints, involves claims about the significance of (amongst other variables) some particular sets of wants and needs. [12]

If Taylor were right about this, it would follow that the first claim in my account of value-free social theory was mistaken: for he would have shown that the criteria of validity for social theories are logically dependent on the acceptance of normative standpoints. I will argue in the next section that his argument rests on a confusion between different kinds of 'significance'. But before doing that I will comment on the relations between this claim and the second one, that normative judgments cannot be derived from social theories. For it might be thought that if the latter is rejected (as it is by Taylor), then the former must also be rejected. That is, if it is accepted that normative judgments can be established by the scientific statements of a social theory, then it may appear to follow that the criteria of validity for the latter cannot be value-independent, since the rejection of a normative judgment would entail rejection of the scientific statements from which it had been derived. But this appearance is misleading. To show this, a partial formalization of the relevant arguments will now be given.

I will refer to the claim that scientific criteria of validity are value-independent as (1); and the claim that normative judgments cannot be derived from scientific statements as (2). Let us represent normative judgments by 'N', and scientific ones by 'S'. Then (2) is represented by $-(S \rightarrow N)$, and its denial, $--(S \rightarrow N)$, by $(S \rightarrow N)$. Now, if $(S \rightarrow N)$ is true, it follows that $(-N \rightarrow -S)$, by contraposition. This means that one could argue from the falsity of a normative judgment to the falsity of the scientific statement which entails that normative judgment. But if this is so, it might seem that if (2) is rejected than (1) must be abandoned, since we have here the denial of a normative judgment leading to the denial of a scientific statement; and this appears to contradict (1), since (1) maintains that the acceptance or rejection of scientific statements can be determined independently of the acceptance or rejection of normative standpoints. Thus it appears that (1) and (2) are logically related, in that the rejection of (2) entails the rejection of (1).

However, this is misleading. For whilst it is undeniable that, from $(S \rightarrow N)$, it follows that $(-N \rightarrow -S)$, it is essential to keep in mind what is the possible basis for the denial of N. According to those who reject (2), this consists in scientific statements. Thus the justification for the denial of N must be the truth of some scientific statement that entails $-N$. Let us call this statement S'. Then the argument for the denial of N must involve the following premises: that $(S' \rightarrow -N)$, and that S' is true. But if $(S' \rightarrow -N)$ is true, and if S' is true; and if our initial scientific statement, S, entails N, then it follows that S must be false. For, if $(S \rightarrow N)$, and $(S' \rightarrow -N)$, then $-(S \& S')$, i.e. S and S' cannot both be true; and if S' is true (and thus N false), then S must be false. In other words, what actually shows S to be false is not the falsity of N, but the truth of some further scientific statements S', from which $-N$ follows, and which is incompatible with the truth of S. Thus, even if (2) is false, because normative judgments *can* be derived from scientific statements, it would not follow that (1) is false.

Putting this argument less formally: if normative judgments are entailed by scientific statements, this does not undermine the objectivity of science, but simply gives (scientific) objectivity to norms. So whatever the merits of Taylor's version of ethical naturalism, or of the argument examined earlier on that social theories are intrinsically normative in their implications, the claim that scientific criteria of validity are value-independent is not thereby refuted. However, it remains to examine Taylor's specific objection to this, which does not depend solely on his ethical naturalism, but also on his use of the (problematic) concept of significance.

3 THE CONCEPT OF SIGNIFICANCE IN SOCIAL THEORY

Weber argued that any investigation in the social sciences must involve the adoption of some overall criteria of significance, or value, which serve to define the 'essential' characteristics of the object of enquiry. Thus the significance of various social phenomena cannot be seen purely as an objective, value-independent feature of them, but is instead ascribed to them by the social theorist. And he maintained that such ascriptions must be understood as expressive of normative standpoints that cannot be validated by the scientifically establishable claims of a social theory.[13]

I believe Weber was right about this, and that his position here adds a major element to a proper analysis of the place of values in social theory. However, the concept of significance is potentially confusing, and it is one of the several virtues of Weber's methodological work that it contains a useful clarification of this. Roughly speaking, he distinguished three forms of significance, which I will call 'normative', 'explanatory', and 'epistemic'.[14] The last of these is a somewhat heterogeneous category, including both the significance of items due to their function as evidence that is relevant to the assessment of scientific claims, and that of items which operate as useful illustrations or exemplifications of some type or kind of social phenomenon. Explanatory significance, by contrast, is ascribable to those items which, according to a particular social theory, contribute to the explanation of the objects of enquiry — for instance, to the forces and relations of production in historical materialism. Any such theory must be aimed at explaining specifiable features of social reality; and it was Weber's view, which I support, that the significance of these *explananda*, what it is that makes them important phenomena to explain, must ultimately be decided by reference to normative criteria. I use the term 'ultimately' to take account of the fact that theories may be designed to explain phenomena whose immediate significance is given by their explanatory function in relation to others, and so on — but not *ad infinitum*. There must be a 'stopping-point' at which significance is ascribed by reference not to explanatory (or epistemic) criteria, but to normative ones.

Thus, whilst epistemic and explanatory significance are scientifically determinable, normative significance is not; but it is an ineliminable feature of the construction of any social theory. It may be helpful here to adopt (or adapt) Popper's terminology of 'problems' and 'solutions' and put the point like this: theories are designed to solve problems, and the significance of these problems, which must ultimately be determined by normative criteria, is distinct from the adequacy of their proposed solutions, which in this case consists in providing explanations supported by evidence. Both this and Weber's account have the further merit of directing our attention to the question of what precisely it is that a particular social theory is designed to explain, to what problem it is addressed. For it seems a frequent defect of much theoretical work that this is left insufficiently specified. For instance, in contemporary debates about the adequacy of Marxist theory to explain the nature of the relationhips between men and women in various kinds of society, it is frequently unclear just which characteristics of those relationships are at issue, and why it is that significance is attached to explaining these rather than others. But without such specifications of the *explanandum*, theoretical debates risk the well-known phenomenon of people talking past one another: apparent disagreements about explanatory adequacy may instead reflect divergent characterizations of the object of enquiry, and so involve no direct incompatibility between theories.

Further, such divergences may be concealed by the apparently competing theorists using the same terms to describe the *explanandum*, whilst the specific senses of these terms in fact differ. For example, I think the explanations for the historical emergence of capitalism in Western Europe proposed by Marx and Weber display this feature to some extent. For it is arguable that what they take to be the 'essential' characteristics of 'capitalism' differ in a way that ultimately expresses their differing criteria of normative significance. Thus, whereas for Marx the central characteristic of capitalism was the class relationship between capital and labour, for Weber it was the rational organization of production.[15] And although this divergence may partly be due to scientifically resolvable disagreements about the explanatory significance of these characteristics, I think it could be shown that this would not provide a complete account. Instead, we should look to the distinct normative standpoints expressed, respectively, in their concepts of alienation and disenchantment, to understand their divergent characterizations of the 'essential' features of 'capitalism'. And if this is so, it would follow that their theoretical explanations are not directly comparable, being aimed at partly differing *explananda*.

The above analysis of the concept of significance in social theory enables us to distinguish two quite different reasons for which a particular theory may be rejected: that it fails to explain adequately the phenomena taken as its *explananda*, or that the normative criteria in terms of which these phenomena gain their significance is unacceptable. That is, we can distinguish between claiming that a theory fails to deal with the problems to which it is addressed, and criticizing the normative standpoint which constitutes these as significant problems. And we are now in a position to consider Taylor's argument that a normative rejection of the political implications of a particular theoretical framework must lead to a rejection of that framework. He provides the following example to illustrate this argument, commenting upon S. M. Lipset's professedly 'scientific' analysis of democracy.[16]

> [according to Lipset] stable democracies are judged better than stable oligarchies, since the latter can only exist where the majority is so uneducated and tradition-bound or narrowed that it has not yet learned to demand its rights. But suppose we tried to upset this judgment by holding that under-development is good for men, that they are happier when they are led by some unquestioned norms, don't have to think for themselves, and so on? One would then be reversing the value-judgment. But at the same time one would be changing the framework. For we are introducing a notion of anomie here, *and we cannot suppose this factor to exist without having some important effect on the working of political society.*[17] [My italics]

Let us accept that the kind of possible normative challenge Taylor outlines expresses the ideals of social existence involved in the Durkheimian concept of anomie.[18] But what precisely is meant by the last, italicized sentence in this passage? To claim that anomie 'exists', or that certain social relationships are anomic, is typically both to make a normative judgment from the standpoint of these ideals, and also to assert that these relationships display certain features such as the absence of conventionally reinforced social norms and stable expectations. Anomic relationships, thus understood, may be taken either as explanatory of certain other social phenomena, such as rates of suicide, or as themselves 'significant' objects of explanation: for instance, the question of what kind of economic system tends to increase or reduce the degree of anomie may be explored.

Thus the concept of anomie serves both to express a normative standpoint, and to characterize a form of social relationships that may be taken as an *explanandum*, or be referred to in the explanation of other phenomena. But to judge that a particular political system, in this case 'democracy', displays anomic social relationships does not by itself entail rejection of a social theory such as Lipset's according to which certain conditions are necessary or sufficient for the existence of a democratic system. For it could well be that the explanatory claims made by this theory are correct, despite the fact that democratic political systems display features that are deemed to be anomic.

Thus the normative challenge described by Taylor need not require the 'rejection' of the theoretical framework, in the sense of claiming that it provides incorrect explanations. And whether or not anomic relationships are themselves explanatorily significant is independent of one's acceptance of the ideal of an anomie-free society. However, the theoretical framework might be 'rejected' for the quite different reason that it fails to analyze various features of a political system that are normatively significant from the standpoint of a concern with anomie. In this case, we would have a normative criticism of the problems to which that framework was addressed, as distinct from a scientific criticism of its ability to deal with the problems it was intended to. It seems that Taylor's argument fails to differentiate these two kinds of criticism, and thereby fails to undermine the account I have given of the relations between scientific criteria of validity and normative judgments.

So far, I have said little about how this account can be applied to the place of specifically socialist values in a critical social theory. This is partly because, according to the position I am advocating, there is nothing epistemologically distinctive about this particular case. That is, I am opposed to those critical theorists who claim that the 'critical' character of their social theories requires that value-independent criteria of validity be rejected, and replaced by some alternative conception of the relations between science and values. But I will now give a brief description of what a socialist social theory consistent with my account of value-freedom would be like, before going on in the next section to defend this against the claim that it has certain unacceptable consequences for political practice.

There are, I believe, a number of normative principles which taken together define a distinctively socialist political philosophy. These include ideals such as the elimination of private ownership of the means of production, the equal distribution of social goods, the absence of dominative relations between groups and individuals, and the democratization of decision-making processes. In saying this,

I do not imply the absence of legitimate disputes and disagreements between socialists about the nature of these ideals, about their relative significance, and about their adequacy to define a set of principles that deals with all normatively significant aspects of social existence. For instance, there are important disagreements about the place and character of individual, legally enforceable, rights in a socialist society; about the significance of direct workers' control of production, as against centralized State planning; and about the adequacy of socialist principles for specifying the character of acceptable social relationships between men and women. However, I do not think these issues, and therefore also the precise character of the critique of non-socialist principles and practices, can be resolved or replaced solely by the construction of social theories which operate, as they should, with value-independent criteria of validity. Socialism is not, in this sense, scientific.

It should be a major aim of socialist social theorists to investigate and explain those feature of non-socialist societies that are significant from the standpoint of socialist values. The concepts employed in such theories will be expressive of this specific critical standpoint; nor is there any epistemological barrier against the inclusion within socialist theoretical work of explicit normative critique and argument. And it will be an important concern of such theorists to determine the presence (or absence) within non-socialist societies of existent and developing possibilities for their transformation towards socialism.

For instance, it is a claim of Marx's political economy that these possibilities do develop within the capitalist mode of production and can, under certain circumstances, be realized. At the same time, it is a consequence of my position that whether these possibilities exist, to what they are due, under what circumstances they can be realized, and whether these will obtain, are issues that must be determined independently of the acceptance of socialist values. Pessimism is, unfortunately, a possible outcome of the scientific investigation of capitalism: and only a form of non-scientific teleology concerning the inevitable development of the historical process towards some ideal condition (such as 'the

realization of the human essence') can sustain an *a priori* —
and thoroughly specious — optimism.

4 SOCIALIST PRACTICE AND THE SEPARATION OF SCIENCE AND VALUES

The kind of account I have given of the relations between
social theory and normative commitments has frequently
been criticized within the Marxist tradition on the grounds
that it leads to the adoption of unacceptable forms of
political practice. In particular it has been said to support
'reformism', the non-revolutionary attempt to gradually alter
or transform capitalist societies through existing political
institutions;[19] and also 'moralism', the belief that moral
exhortation and reasoning are the primary means by which
socialism should be achieved. I will argue that neither of these
criticisms is justifiable, concentrating mainly on the former. I
will examine this through some of the issues involved in the
debates between 'orthodox Marxists' (such as Karl Kautsky)
and 'revisionists' (such as Edward Bernstein) in the Second
International.[20]

It is often claimed that Bernstein's revisionism was
influenced by the late nineteenth-century revival of Kantian
philosophy, an important element of this being the separation
of science from values.[21] Bernstein's acceptance of this, it is
then argued, is logically related to the reformist character of
his evolutionary socialism, with its emphasis upon short-term
improvements in the position of the working class, and upon
parliamentary activity as the major way of achieving these.
For instance, Karl Korsch declared that:

> It was not only such overtly anti-Marxist and un-Marxist
> philosophizing socialists as Bernstein and Koigen, but also most
> of the philosophizing Marxists (Kantian, Dietzgenian and
> Machian Marxists) who since then have shown, in word and
> deed, that they have not really passed the standpoint of
> bourgeois society. This applies not only to their philosophy, but
> by necessary extension also to their political theory and practice.
> There is no need to provide examples of the bourgeois-reformist
> character of Kantian Marxism, as it can hardly be doubted.[22]

To assess this kind of claim about Bernstein's revisionism, it is necessary to distinguish several elements in his overall position.[23] First, there was his view that Marx's historical materialism and political economy, considered as scientific theories, were in some important respects defective. He argued that the actual development of capitalism in Germany was inconsistent with predictions derivable from these theories, and regarded this as requiring their modification. I think this argument depended on too simple a view of the relationship between theories and predictions,[24] but this is not relevant here. Second, Bernstein opposed those formulations of Marxist theory which presented the collapse of capitalism and its replacement by socialism as events that would result inevitably from the internal contradictions of capitalist forces and relations of production, and which ascribed no significant role to forms of political activity which were themselves partly influenced by normative commitments. To Bernstein, this was one important reason why the 'scientific socialism' of Kautsky and others was unacceptable. Third, he argued that the circumstances and attitudes of the German workers' movement were such that – taken together with the necessary revisions of Marxist science, and the error of a deterministic scientific socialism – neither revolutionary nor quietistic tactics were appropriate in an effective struggle for socialism.

But Bernstein had a further set of objections to the idea of scientific socialism. He argued that science alone cannot determine what is ethically desirable; that science must itself be free from values; and that socialism must be understood primarily in terms of its normative demands. Socialism, he said, is 'a piece of the beyond . . . . It is something that *ought* to be, or a movement toward something that *ought* to be.'[25] This does not mean, he argued, that science is irrelevant to socialism. For it provides us with knowledge of existing conditions and developments, which can guide political action; and it enables us to avoid forms of Utopianism that are not grounded in real possibilities.

It is interesting to compare some of these elements in Bernstein's revisionism with another, much more recent, attack upon scientific socialism. This time, it is Louis

Althusser's anti-humanist Marxism that is the target,[26] and
E. P. Thompson the critic.[27] Insisting on the significance of
what he calls 'affective and moral consciousness', both as a
partial determinant of past historical developments and as a
necessary element in contemporary political practice,
Thompson declares:

> This is, exactly, *not* to argue that 'morality' is some
> 'autonomous region' of human desire and will, arising
> independently of the historical process. Such a view of morality
> has never been materialist enough, and hence it has often
> reduced that formidable inertia − and sometimes formidable
> revolutionary force − into a wishful idealist fiction. It is to say,
> on the contrary, that every contradiction is a conflict of value as
> well as a conflict of interest; that inside every 'need' there is an
> affect, or 'want', on its way to becoming an 'ought' (and *vice
> versa*); that every class struggle is at the same time a struggle
> other values; and that the project of Socialism is guaranteed *BY
> NOTHING* − certainly not by 'Science' or by Marxism-
> Leninism − but can find its own guarantees only by *reason* and
> through an open *choice of values*.[28]

Thompson is opposed to those Marxists who regard a
distinctively normative critique of capitalism as 'unscientific'
and *ipso facto* to be abandoned, and who wish to replace this
kind of critique with a science that, to the extent that it is
critical, is confined to the criticism of ideological thought and
practices, where 'ideology' is defined by contrast with
genuine scientific knowledge. He asserts that such knowledge
does not exhaust the realm of what is rationally justifiable;
that normative discourse is subject to its own standards of
argumentation and rationality; and that this discourse,
typically interwined with action and experience, is an
essential feature of the historical process. It is part of the task
of socialist historians to explore the complex and changing
relationships between these normatively impregnated forms
of experience and the systemic features of the class relations
of particular 'modes of production'. Such explorations are
not to be guided by an *a priori* belief that human history is
governed by some teleological principle that guarantees the
eventual actualization of a 'human essence'. But they may
reveal, in a manner governed by objective standards of

evidence and argumentation, actual movements towards the (at least partial) realization of a specific normative conception of social existence, of what Thompson calls an 'empirical *potentia*'.[29]

To study history from this standpoint, he argues, undoubtedly involves a choice of values by the historian; and different values would involve a focus upon different possibilities. But the *potentia* defining the primary object of socialist historians remains 'empirical' in the sense that its existence and development are open to investigations governed by objective criteria. For instance, Thompson makes the following comments about the labour movement and the post-war British government:

> It can be seen that the reforms of '1945' embodied a socialist *potentia*, which was not only nourished by ideal influences (the thought of Marx, of Morris, and of socialist utopians: the strategies of British socialist and communist parties) but whose partial realization was fleshed by actually existent socialist values and practices within the working-class community, at variance with those individualist values and practices of the capitalist system within which, in the final analysis, these reforms were contained. Hence this socialist *potentia* may be seen simultaneously as immanent actuality and as aspiration; that is, it is not to be seen only as a theoretical aspiration, expressed in a passage of Marx's writings; it is an aspiration which requires *both* logical *and* historical examination. Moreover, the defeat of this aspiration, its failure to come to its full realization, may be dealt with not only in terms of its theoretical inadequacy (as, indeed, its characteristic 'reformist' or social-democratic theoretical expression was sadly inadequate) but also in terms of the actual contradictions of social life – the cancellation of socialist meanings within a totality whose meaning and logic of process was capitalist.[30]

Thompson's position on these issues is, I think, quite close to the conception of the relationship between science and values that I have been proposing, and also to Bernstein's view of this. It is significant, therefore, that we find Thompson apparently well able to criticize reformist or social-democratic political strategies, partly on the basis of historical investigations of their employment and outcomes;

and this may suggest that there is no inconsistency between such a view of science and values, and the rejection of reformism.

However, proofs or disproofs of logical relationships cannot rest upon the discovery that, in particular writers, certain views are or are not co-present; nor, upon the fact that these writers *believe* that one is supported by another. (Indeed Lichtheim points out that the markedly anti-reformist Karl Liebknecht, 'was philosophically an adherent of the neo-Kantian school: a circumstance deplored by his political friends'.[31] So much for proofs of the links between epistemology and politics based on this kind of 'argument'.) What matters is whether the supposed logical relationships do in fact exist. So let us now explore this question, in the case of Bernstein's revisionism.

It seems to me that Bernstein's support for evolutionary socialism is independent of his view of the relationship between science and values, and that this view is itself consistent with a quite different conception of political practice. The major elements in his arguments for reformist politics derive from his specific claims about the defects of Marxist science, his assessment of the contemporary political and economic circumstances and his normative judgment that, in political activity, the character of the means employed must themselves express the ideals that define the overall goal of bringing about a socialist society, rather than being assessed solely in terms of their likelihood of achieving this. This normative principle is, of course, challengeable, as are the other elements just mentioned; but none of them follow from his epistemological views. Thus I would reject even the highly qualified judgment of the significance of Bernstein's philosophical position for his reformism by Peter Gay:

> Philosophical questions were not as significant for Revisionism as the analysis of economic and political developments. But whatever the impact of philosophy on the movement, its stress was on ethics and the striving for limited, obtainable goals. It strongly supported the other Revisionist arguments against revolution and in favour of parliamentary gradualism.[32]

However, we need to be clear about what precisely is meant by 'philosophy', here — just as, in the earlier quotation from Korsch, we need to be clear what 'Kantian' means. For 'philosophy' may well include advocacy of specific, substantive normative standpoints, which can have significant implications for the character of political practice; and Kant's philosophy is a case in point. My claim that the separation of science and values does not imply political reformism, together with the fact that this separation was itself *one* feature of Kantian philosophy, must not be taken to mean that no other elements in that philosophy have such implications. Kantian ethics involves, for instance, a radical non-consequentialism (and thus anti-utilitarianism) about the assessment of actions; a requirement of 'respect for persons as ends, not means'; a view of ethical norms as universal and eternal; and so on. These clearly have consequences for political practice (though I doubt whether 'the striving for limited, attainable goals' is one of them); but nothing I have said suggests otherwise.

Turning now to the other 'non-revolutionary' form of political practice mentioned earlier, moralism, it can be shown that this too does not follow from the conception of value-freedom I have been defending, despite claims to the contrary.[33] To argue, as I have, that scientific criteria of validity are independent of normative standpoints; that socialist values cannot be established by social theory; and that a distinctively normative critique is a legitimate and desirable component of the practice of socialist theorists, in no way entails that engagement in such a critique should constitute the sole or primary form of socialist politics, that exhortation or argument are the only acceptable, rational, activities. For it is a misconception of 'reason' to believe that the only rational form of practice is reasoning, and to assume that the dichotomy between 'words' (or 'thought') and 'action' mirrors that between rationality and irrationality.[34] (And incidentally the former dichotomy is itself suspect if one analyses communication in terms of a theory of speech-acts, which has the consequence that speaking is a type of social *action*.[35]) The acceptance of socialist values may justify many kind of (rational) action, of which arguing with people is but one. Strikes, 'violence', or the construction of alternative forms of social relationships are others. The justification of these practices must include, I believe, normative claims (together with their rationales), and cannot be supported solely by reference to social theory. Thus the 'critique' of capitalism cannot be exclusively scientific. But equally, attempts to realize in practice a normative critique need not be limited to public argument and persuasion.

Thus, for example, a normative critique of the unjust distribution of social goods in capitalist societies may motivate the construction of a social theory aimed at explaining this. Such a theory might show that it results from the class-distribution of the means of production, and that it cannot be radically altered − though some of its worst effects could be ameliorated − without a transformation of the capitalist mode of production. Further, it might also be shown that some kinds of political practice aimed at achieving this are less likely to succeed than others: in particular, that 'moralism' is by itself an ineffectual strategy. But these theoretical claims can be assessed independently of commitment to the values in terms of which the initial critique was made; and these values are not themselves scientifically establishable. So there is no inconsistency between this separation of science and values and the rejection of a moralistic politics.

Thus neither moralism nor reformism are entailed by my view of the place of values in social theory. But it is important to emphasize that in arguing for this claim I am not thereby accepting that if they were thus entailed, this would constitute a refutation of that epistemological position. This is for two reasons. First, my argument does not *assume* that there is something definitely wrong with these conceptions of political practice: it operates quite independently of this question. (As a matter of fact, I believe there are many situations in which both of these can form at least important components in a legitimate socialist politics.) Second, I am generally sceptical about attempts to reject epistemological positions on the basis of their supposed political consequences. This is partly because I have not yet come across what seems to be a good argument for such a connection. But it is partly also because, if such a connection were established, one might claim that this provided grounds for accepting the form of political practice, rather than for rejecting the epistemology — unless, of course, it could be shown that no independent justifications for epistemological positions can be provided, which I doubt.

I have mainly been concerned in this chapter to elaborate and defend the conception of value-freedom which, in the previous chapter, was identified as one of the various 'positivist' doctrines rejected by critical theorists. I argued there that this was not only distinct from, but in many ways antithetical to, another of these, the scientization of politics, a version of which is itself an important element in the idea of scientific socialism. And I also argued that this view of the relation between social theory and values could be accepted without being thereby committed to either scientism, or a positivist conception of social theory.

However, the arguments advanced in these two chapters make no attempt to deal with the critique of positivism involved in Habermas's theory of knowledge-constitutive interests. For his critique is intended to show the normative presuppositions of philosophical accounts of scientific knowledge itself (such as the positivist view of science), as distinct from the norms presupposed or entailed by particular social theories that may operate with the same general epistemological assumptions. It thus addresses the question of the relations between science and values at a significantly different level of analysis from the one I have so far explored.

3 Knowledge, Objects and Interests

Habermas's theory of knowledge-constitutive interests is intended to challenge what he regards as the 'false objectivism' of positivism's conception of science and the relationship between theory and practice.[1] This objectivism has two related elements. First, there is the belief that the objects of scientific knowledge exist independently of the epistemological framework on the basis of which they are investigated. Second, there is the claim that such knowledge is value-free, in the sense that the validation of its claims is independent of the acceptance of normative standpoints. According to these objectivist principles, scientific theories are seen as related to practice in the following way. Theories enable us to make conditional predictions about the likely outcomes of a possible course of action. But the ends or values guiding such actions are given independently: that is, they are neither entailed nor presupposed by scientific knowledge itself. Thus scientific theories may be used in practice in various ways, guided by different values; and normative critique is relevant only to these uses of knowledge, not to the acceptance or rejection of the theoretical claims of science itself. Against this view, Habermas argues that the object-domains of forms of knowledge, and their appropriate criteria of validity, are constituted by certain interests; and that the possible forms of practical application of scientific knowledge are determined by this interest-constitution. Thus scientific knowledge is not neutral, normatively; and its objects do not belong to an independent reality.

Habermas develops his position in terms of a threefold division between different forms of knowledge, which I outlined in the Introduction. In this chapter I will focus mainly on the first of these, empirical-analytic science with its technical interest, though with occasional references to the second, historical-hermeneutic science with its practical interest. His account of the third form, critical knowledge, will be discussed in chapters 4 to 6. I will argue here that we should entirely reject the interest-constitution theory but not the claim that there are different forms of knowledge — though my account of the relations between them differs from Habermas's.

I begin in the first section by criticizing an argument developed by Brian Fay which is designed to support Habermas's technical interest doctrine by analysis of the implications of the positivist account of scientific explanation. In section 2 I examine Habermas' conception of object-constitution in empirical-analytic science, and show that it does not — as some critics have maintained — depend upon an instrumentalist account of the cognitive status of scientific theories. In the following section I criticize Habermas's object-constitution doctrine by displaying internal inconsistencies in it. In section 4 I present an alternative view, which challenges the dichotomy between nature and human society implicit in Habermas's position. I argue instead for an ontological pluralism, in which a variety of different kinds of existents are recognized, with complex relations of qualitative identity and diversity between them.

1 DEDUCTIVE-NOMOLOGICAL EXPLANATION AND THE TECHNICAL INTEREST

In *Social Theory and Political Practice*, Fay argues both that the kind of knowledge produced by a positivistically conceived science is such that it can (and can only) be used for the purpose of predicting and controlling natural or social processes, and also that this possible use is in fact constitutive of what is regarded as knowledge. [2] It is this second claim that is crucial here, since by itself the first is perfectly compatible with a rejection of the interest-constitution doctrine. For the former claim could be accepted by positivists who regard scientific knowledge as interest-free: they could argue that the possibility of technical use is simply a *consequence* of the fact that scientific theories make statements about the relationships that hold in an independently existing real world, and that knowledge of these relationships, quite unsurprisingly, may provide the basis for prediction and control. I shall argue that Fay does not succeed in establishing anything more than this epistemologically innocuous claim; though, as will be seen, certain complications arise when we take account of the differences between instrumentalist, positivist and theoretical realist views of science. [3]

Fay's main argument for technical interest-constitution is based on a central feature of the positivist view of science, the deductive-nomological (D-N) model of explanation. He tries to show that according to this model the possibility of prediction (and thus of control − I will from now on consider only prediction, for the sake of simplicity) is constitutive of what is to count as explanation. This, he believes, would enable his main claim to be established, given the further (and plausible) premiss that, for positivists, science aims at gaining explanatory knowledge.

According to the D-N model any adequate scientific explanation requires that a statement describing the *explanandum* (the item to be explained) be deducible from a set of premisses, which contains statements of two kinds: those specifying putative universal laws, and those specifying various particular, antecedent conditions. These two sets of statements describe the *explanans* (that which explains); and explanation consists in deriving the *explanandum*-statement from the *explanans*-statements.

Fay points out how defenders of the D-N model − particularly Carl Hempel, its best-known and most sophisticated advocate − maintain that an important feature of this model is its expression of 'the thesis of the structural identity of explanation and prediction'. This thesis, as Hempel has emphasized, consists in two sub-theses: first, that any adequate explanation must be potentially usable as a prediction (either of the event initially explained, before it occurred; or of an event of the same kind, later); and second, the converse of this. [4] Fay accepts Hempel's defence of the first sub-thesis against a number of objections, which need not concern us here. He does not consider the objections that have been put to the second sub-thesis, apparently regarding the first as sufficient for his argument to succeed. This, I think, is a mistake; and indeed, at some points Fay appears implicitly to assume the truth of both. But as I will argue shortly, though there are in any case grounds for doubting the truth of the second sub-thesis, even if it were true Fay's argument would still not work. For the moment, however, I will regard both sub-theses as correct.

Fay argues that the truth of the structural identity thesis shows that for a positivist conception of science, explanation *consists in* predictive power; for what it is that makes D-N arguments 'explanatory' is that 'they allow one to claim that he *could* have predicted the occurrence of the event if he had been able to have all the relevant information at hand'.[5] In other words, it is the possibility of its predictive use that is definitive, or constitutive, of what it is for something to count as an explanation. I believe Fay is wrong in presenting this as an implication of the D-N model. My objection can be presented in the form of a possible reply to Fay by an advocate of the D-N model.

The reply is this. The structural identity thesis is to be seen as a consequence of the D-N model, but it does not specify what it is that defines the nature of an adequate explanation. The D-N model should instead be seen as a formal elaboration of the basic idea that to explain something is to show that it is an instance of a scientifically established law; and statements of laws are to be taken as descriptions of relationships that hold, universally, between certain kinds of independently existent items (events, processes, states of affairs, etc.) To explain something is to show that it conforms to these laws; and to predict something we require knowledge of them. So although it is true that what we need to know in order to predict something is the same as what we need to know to explain something, this is not because explanation *consists* in the possibility of prediction, but because it consists in the knowledge of laws, which can be used for both explanatory and predictive purposes.

In effect, this reply involves the development of a point made at the beginning of this section: that one cannot argue from the fact that, on a positivist view of science, scientific theories provide the basis for prediction and control, to the claim that it is the possibility of this use that is constitutive of scientific knowledge. Thus, when Fay asks the question, 'why is it the case that in science to explain something is to potentially predict it?', and gives as his answer the constitutive interest doctrine,[6] he ignores the possibility of an alternative answer: that this is because science discovers real relationships between phenomena, that enable us both to predict and explain.

However, in order to recognize the possibility of this alternative answer, we have to avoid confusion about the sense of the 'is' in Fay's question. It might be taken to mean, 'is defined by the ability' (to potentially predict); or, 'puts one in a position' (to potentially predict). The former sense automatically gives Fay his preferred answer, whilst the latter leaves open the alternative answer. But acceptance of the D-N model and the structural identity thesis does not entail that the former sense of 'is' is the only appropriate one.

Further, whatever plausibility Fay's argument has requires acceptance of both sub-theses of the structural identity of explanation and prediction, and not merely the first. Thus, his position would be additionally weakened by rejection of the second, that any law-based prediction is potentially an explanation. I believe there are strong reasons for denying this, but I will not present them here — though it is worth noting that Hempel himself has accepted some of these.[7] Instead, I will now go on to suggest that the constitutive interest doctrine could be more persuasively argued if an instrumentalist conception of science were adopted, rather than a positivist — or even more so, a theoretical realist — one. Indeed, I suspect that Fay is partly misled by the fact that there are some ways of articulating the positivist view which make it very similar to instrumentalism.[8]

Instrumentalists regard the truth or falsity of scientific theories as consisting in their predictive (or manipulative) success or failure. That is, they adopt a pragmatist theory of truth, and regard scientific theories as 'true' only in the sense of being useful tools or instruments. On this view, the claim that an interest in technical control is constitutive of what is to count as scientific knowledge clearly has considerable plausibility. And Fay's argument about the D-N model of explanation, appropriately reconstructed to apply to an instrumentalist version of it, would illustrate this definitional link between explanation and the possibility of prediction. For with an instrumentalist conception of science, what positivists regard as true statements expressing laws, from which other statements describing the *explananda* may be deduced, are instead regarded as devices or instruments for making predictions. (One possible instrumentalist version of the D-N model would involve the re-conceptualization of law-statements as inference-rules: for rules, unlike statements, have no truth-values).

I conclude therefore that Fay's argument for interest-constitution fails in the case of positivism and, *a fortiori*, in the case of theoretical realism. It might succeed when directed at instrumentalism. But instrumentalism is not, in my view, a correct account of the cognitive status of scientific theories, though I cannot support this here. In any case, I will argue in the next section that Habermas's version of interest-constitution does not depend upon adopting an instrumentalist view of science, but would apply equally well to positivism, and probably to at least some forms of theoretical realism.

However, it should be noted that Fay's defence of technical interest-constitution does not depend solely upon the argument just examined; and a brief consideration of his second argument will introduce some important issues to be explored in the next two sections. He suggests that there is a conceptual connection between the interest in technical control, and the ontology (in Habermas's terms, the 'object-domain') of a positivist science. Thus he says that for positivists 'reality is comprised of observable objects and events that are related nomologically', and that this ontology is determined by the constitutive interest in prediction and manipulation.[9] That this is so, he argues, can be brought out by recognizing that historically there have been radically different scientific ontologies, reflecting different interests. For instance, he draws our attention to:

the long tradition in Western thought which holds that to explain something is to show its final cause, i.e. to demonstrate its purpose in the scheme of things, [10]

of which the Christian world-view is one example. (Presumably, another would be an Aristotelian cosmology.)

A world-view of this kind, he suggests, involves a different conception of what it is to understand a phenomenon; and (though he does not say this explicitly), its ontology will be essentially related to this, in that 'objects' will be defined in terms of basic properties that are teleological or meaningful, as compared, say, with the basic properties of Galilean or Newtonian science, represented by Locke as the 'primary qualities': size, shape, motion, and so on. Fay implies that these rival ontologies are constituted by different fundamental attitudes or interests, whose adoption is in some sense a matter of convention. Thus:

> It is important to remember . . . that there exist alternative conceptual schemes which give different accounts of what it means to understand something. What the concept 'understand' means depends on human conventions. [11]

Now it seems to me that it would follow from Fay's comments here that there is nothing intrinsically mistaken about the practice of some kind of hermeneutic science of nature: that is, one that conceptualizes 'nature' as a meaningful entity open to an interpretative understanding involving, for instance, teleological concepts. Such a conception of nature would express a different, non-technical, constitutive interest; and it would be mistaken to make any attempt to reject it on the grounds that 'in reality, nature is not like this', since this claim could be made only from the standpoint of a conception of reality (and thus of explanation and understanding), itself constituted by a different interest, whose adoption is a matter of human convention.

I will not criticize this view now, though I am strongly opposed to it for reasons which will emerge in section 3, where I criticize Habermas's interest-constitution doctrine. But first I will give a fuller account of Habermas's doctrine than I have so far, and show why it does not presuppose an instrumentalist view of science.

2   HABERMAS'S INTEREST-CONSTITUTION THEORY AND INSTRUMENTALISM

A recurrent criticism of Habermas's view that the technical interest is constitutive of empirical-analytic science has been that it presupposes a (mistakenly) instrumentalist conception of the cognitive status of scientific theories.[12] Habermas has persistently denied that this is so;[13] and in various papers written after *Knowledge and Human Interests* he has developed a theory of truth as the validation of scientific claims in what he terms 'discourse', which clearly differs from most forms of pragmatism.[14] My view is that there are definitely instrumentalist elements in *Knowledge and Human Interests*, and certain papers written before then,[15] but that those could easily be eliminated without affecting the basic elements in his account of empirical-analytic science. In showing that this is so, I aim also in this section to clarify precisely what his interest-constitution theory involves.

It may be helpful to articulate Habermas's position by noting both what he accepts, and what he rejects, from Kant's epistemology (or, at least, from his interpretation of this).[16] First, he accepts that there is a basic dichotomy between subject and object, regarding it as plausible and necessary to postulate the existence of an independently existing externality, whose 'facticity' exercises objective limitations upon our (human) attempts to satisfy needs in technical activities such as economic production. In this respect, Habermas rejects Hegel's attempt to transcend the subject-object dichotomy by viewing 'nature' as itself an objectification of a supra-human subjectivity, or *geist*. Thus Habermas speaks of 'the autonomy of nature and the remainder of complete otherness that is lodged in its facticity', and says that:

> Its independence manifests itself in our ability to learn to master natural processes only to the extent that we subject ourselves to them. This elementary experience is expressed in the language of natural 'laws' which we must 'obey'. The externality of nature manifests itself in the contingency of its ultimate constants. No matter how far our power of technical control over nature is

extended, nature retains a substantial core that does not reveal itself to us. [17]

Second, Habermas also accepts from Kant that this externality only becomes an 'object' for us — that is, an object of knowledge — when mediated through a specific set of basic categories: these categories, imposed by the subject, are thus constitutive of what he terms 'the objectivity of the possible objects of experience'. [18] So for Habermas the Kantian categories are constitutive of the object-domain of empirical-analytic science, while it is nonetheless true that, at another level of analysis, there is a non-subject-dependent externality.

Habermas's major departure from Kant consists in denying that the object-constituting categories are imposed by a transcendental consciousness, and insisting instead that they are imposed by the human species, expressing its fundamental interest in control, in the success of rational feedback-controlled instrumental action. This interest is rooted in a particular, species-universal and invariant form of activity, namely labour. Habermas claims that Marx recognized this in his epistemological writings, seeing that:

> labor, or work, is not only a fundamental category of human existence but also an epistemological category. The system of objective activities [i.e. object-producing, productive activities] creates the factual conditions of the possible reproduction of social life *and at the same time* the transcendental conditions of the possible objectivity of the objects of experience. The category of man as a tool-making animal signifies a schema both of action *and* of apprehending the world. [19]

Whether this is a defensible exegesis of Marx — which is, I believe somewhat doubtful [20] — is irrelevant here. Nor, in this context, need we consider the way Habermas — in this case rightly, I believe — goes on to criticize Marx for failing to recognize the distinctive character of the other fundamental dimension of 'the possible reproduction of human life', namely language and communicative interaction. What is important is to focus upon Habermas's replacement of Kant's transcendental deduction of the categories by a theory according to which these are instead to be seen as anthropologically determined. Thus:

> the unity of the objectivity of possible objects of experience is formed not in transcendental consciousness but in the behavioural system of instrumental action,[21]

and:

> The conditions of instrumental action arose contingently in the natural evolution of the human species. At the same time, however, with transcendental necessity, they bind our knowledge of nature to the interest of possible control over natural processes. The objectivity of the possible objects of experience is constituted within a conceptual-perceptual scheme rooted in deep-seated structures of human action; this scheme is equally binding on all subjects that keep alive through labor.[22]

In his later 'Postscript' to *Knowledge and Human Interests*, Habermas attempts to clarify his position, with respect both to its anthropological character, and to its consequences for the understanding of scientific concepts. In a somewhat dense passage, he says that scientific theories can only be constructed 'within the *limits* of prior objectivation of experienceable occurrences', and explains this as meaning:

> in a theoretical language whose fundamental predicates are always related to the independently constituted objects of possible experience. The theory languages, which undergo a discontinuous development in the course of scientific progress, can interpret the structures of an object domain not yet penetrated by science. They can also to some extent reformulate them. But as long as we are not angels or animals, these languages cannot transform the structures themselves into conditions of another object domain. It is always the experience of identical objects of our world which is being interpreted differently according to the state of scientific progress we happen to have reached. The identity of experiences in the manifold of the interpretations we produce of them is assured because of the conditions of possible objectivation. The particular view of quantum theory developed at Copenhagen provides considerable support for this position. It is argued there that the 'classical' conceptions needed to describe a measuring apparatus point up the limits of the autonomous

object domain of bodies in motion. The non-classical theories of modern physics can interpret this domain differently but they cannot put a new object domain in its place.[23]

I interpret this passage as making the following two claims. First, that the constituted object-domain of empirical-analytic science is a distinctively *human* one, in the sense that its nature and limits are generated by features of the human species, and that though the object-domain for a different, non-human species might differ from this, we cannot but accept the limits of our species-nature. Second, all theoretical concepts within empirical-analytic science, at least to the extent that they are taken to have a denotative, referring function, must be subject to certain limits determined by the basic categories imposed, via its technical interest, by the human species. These (on the basis of Habermas's comments elsewhere[24]) are the categories of space, time, substance and causality. Thus Habermas's remarks about the Copenhagen interpretation of quantum mechanics amount, I think, to this claim: that no realist interpretation can be provided for those theoretical terms which, were they to be so understood, would involve commitment to the existence of items whose properties are not consistent with this categorial framework.

Now although Habermas's claim here is by no means unchallengeable, it is undoubtedly not an instrumentalist one. It does not involve a pragmatist theory of truth; nor does it involve the kind of operationalist account of the meaning of theoretical terms which many instrumentalists (along with some positivists) have adopted. Habermas is not adopting the instrumentalist-operationalist view that all scientific concepts must be defined in terms of sets of hypothetical statements about the observable outcomes of possible human operations. Nor is he saying that the truth of scientific statements consists in the success of actions based upon them; nor that theories are instruments for making predictions. Instead, he is claiming that the range of properties intelligibly ascribable to 'objects' is subject to the limitations of a categorial framework that is itself generated by the interest of the human species in technical control.

As I noted above, the ontological limitations proposed by

Habermas are not unchallengable. They do not, so far as I can see, involve a restriction of scientific ontology to what is observable (the characteristic positivist restriction[25]) since, for instance, the properties ascribed to atoms or molecules within classical physics meet his requirement. But the restriction might well rule out a realist interpretation of certain concepts employed in sub-atomic physics which depart from what is, in effect, a Newtonian-Kantian framework; and it runs counter to the kind of 'ontological catholicism' advocated by theorists such as David Bohm, who rejects precisely the restriction imposed by Habermas and accepted in the Copenhagen interpretation of quantum mechanics.[26]

Though Habermas does not suggest such a parallel, I will conclude this discussion by comparing his position to Kant's in one further respect: the adoption of 'empirical realism' in combination with 'transcendental idealism'.[27] On the one hand Kant rejects the subjective idealism of, say, Berkeley, according to which the nature of perceptual objects is ideal and not material. On the other hand, the objects of knowledge are constituted by the imposition of the categorial framework of transcendental consciousness upon an unknowable externality. Thus, in effect, a realist view of the meaning of scientific statements is combined with an idealist view of the constitutive categories. Empirical realism for statements about the objects of experience: transcendental idealism for their constitution *as* objects.

Now, as I have already noted, Habermas departs from Kant's transcendental idealism in certain respects: we might term his alternative position 'quasi-transcendental pragmatism'. In other respects, however, his position seems consistent with Kant's empirical realism. But if this is so, it is difficult to understand − or at least to sympathize with − Habermas's persistent opposition to any form of realist or correspondence theory of truth.[28] He does, of course, wish to combat the 'false objectivism' of positivist philosophy of science, with its supposed failure to recognize the interest-constituted character of its scientific object-domain. But once this has been accomplished by his quasi-transcendental pragmatism, I can see no good reason for him to resist a realist theory limited, in this largely Kantian manner, to the realm of possible objects of knowledge. If I am right about this, then Habermas's development of a version of the consensus theory of truth, in opposition both to realism and pragmatism, is quite unnecessary. However, as I will argue in chapter 6, section 2, the way this theory functions in his attempt to provide a rational foundation for various norms, does not in fact depend upon its being accepted as a preferable alternative to realism.

3 CRITICISM OF HABERMAS'S INTEREST-CONSTITUTION DOCTRINE

Having presented what I take Habermas's theory of knowledge-constitutive interests to be, in the case of empirical-analytic science, and shown that it is not open to the objection of instrumentalist presuppositions, I will now present a different objection to it, by arguing that there is a major internal inconsistency in his position. I do not regard this as the only legitimate criticism that can be made of the theory, though. For instance Thomas McCarthy has outlined an important objection based on the following apparently irresolvable difficulty in Habermas's position. On the one hand, Habermas claims that nature is constituted as an object by the human species' technical interest; whilst, on the other hand, he claims that this species has emerged through an evolutionary process. But if this is so, argues McCarthy, it must be possible to conceive of nature as pre-existent in relation to the human species. In other words, the naturalistic basis of Habermas's quasi-transcendental pragmatism is inconsistent with its human interest-constitutive conception of nature as the object-domain of empirical-analytic science.[29]

My own criticism – which is, I think, compatible with McCarthy's – concerns the relationship between the empirical-analytic and historical-hermeneutic forms of knowledge, and their respective interests, technical and practical. It can be briefly stated like this. Habermas is resolutely opposed to a 'hermeneutics of nature', to a science of nature that is interpretative rather than empirical. But he insists that there is this second form of knowledge which, like empirical-analytic science, must be understood in terms of a theory of constitutive interests. In hermeneutic knowledge, though, the interest differs from the technical one; and this other, practical interest constitutes its own distinctive object-domain of 'meaningful' entities. But − and this is the crucial point − if these two object-domains differ solely by virtue of their different constitutive interests (operating, presumably, upon the same uncategorized, homogeneous 'externality'), what grounds can there be for rejecting a 'hermeneutics of nature', for *not* 'choosing' to constitute it via the practical interest? The only grounds for refusing this possibility would involve abandoning altogether the constitutive-interest doctrine. For it would have to be maintained that 'nature' and 'humans' are themselves ontologically distinct, independently of our interest-determined categorial frameworks: distinctly in such a way that the application of hermeneutic categories to 'nature' is objectively mistaken and inappropriate.

Before developing this criticism, I must comment on a terminological difficulty reflected in my use of scare-quotes around the phrase 'hermeneutics of nature'. For it might be said that *of course* such a science is impossible for Habermas since for him 'nature' is the object-domain constituted by the technical interest and thus cannot, logically, have the characteristics of the object-domain of a hermeneutic science, which is constituted by the practical interest. Thus a 'hermeneutics of nature' is logically impossible. However, what I want to explore is Habermas's opposition to what some other theorists have claimed is possible, namely the ascription of the properties of meaning, purpose, and so on to the objects of a 'natural science', as in an Aristotelian cosmology. For such theorists, 'nature' is not defined in the way Habermas defines it. So, when I continue to refer to a 'hermeneutics of nature', I am using the term 'nature' in a non-Habermassian way. Hopefully, this will not create difficulties in understanding the objection I am presenting.

I will begin to elaborate this objection by considering some passages from Habermas which reveal the problematic

features of his position. They are from papers written a few
years after *Knowledge and Human Interests*, but involve no
relevant departures from his views there. The first describes
in summary form how the two interests constitute their
respective object-domains:

> In the functional sphere of instrumental action we encounter
> objects of the type of moving bodies; here we experience things,
> events, and conditions which are, in principle, capable of being
> manipulated. In interactions (or at the level of possible
> intersubjective communication) we encounter objects of the type
> of speaking and acting subjects; here we experience persons,
> utterances, and conditions which in principle are structured and
> to be understood symbolically. The object domains of the
> empirical-analytic and of the hermeneutic sciences *are based on
> these objectifications of reality*, which we undertake daily
> always from the viewpoint either of technical control or of
> intersubjective communication. [My italics] [30]

And Habermas goes on to say this:

> the technical and practical interests of knowledge are not
> regulators of cognition which have to be eliminated for the sake
> of the objectivity of knowledge; instead, they themselves
> *determine the aspects under which reality is objectified*, and can
> thus be made accessible to experience to begin with. They are the
> conditions which are necessary in order that subjects capable of
> speech and action may have experience which can lay a claim to
> objectivity. [My italics] [31]

In the next passage, Habermas presents these two forms of
knowledge as based upon different interpretations of the
same abstract categorial schema of space, time, substance
and causality. Thus:

> The interpretational schema, 'substance', has a different
> meaning for the identity of items which can be clearly
> categorized analytically from that which it has for speaking and
> interacting subjects themselves, whose ego-identity, as has been
> shown, just cannot be grasped by analytically clear-cut
> operations. The interpretational schema of causality, when
> applied to observable events, leads to the concept of 'cause';
> when it is applied to an association of intentional actions it leads
> to the concept of 'motive'. In the same way 'space' and 'time'
> undergo a different schematism when viewed in regard to

physically measurable properties of observable events from that which they undergo when viewed according to experienced interactions. In the first case the categories serve as a system of co-ordinates for observation controlled by the sources of instrumental action: in the latter case the categories serve as a frame of reference for the experience of social space and historical time from a subjective point of view. [32]

In these passages Habermas contrasts the two object-domains of empirical-analytic and historical-hermeneutic science, and claims that they involve two distinct 'objectifications' of the *same* (undifferentiated) 'reality'. The contrasting objectifications are the result of the different interests, which determine two different sets of categories, or, as he puts it in the last passage, two different 'interpretations' of the same categorical schema. Thus 'nature' and 'social reality' are different objectifications of the same externality: there is no distinctiveness *within* that externality which determines the appropriateness of the differing categorial frameworks.

It may be helpful here to represent the position which I am ascribing to Habermas in diagrammatic form (see Figure 1).

Now, as I noted towards the end of section 1, Fay seems to regard the question of which conceptual scheme is to be adopted in constituting different object-domains as in some way a matter of convention; and he would therefore presumably not rule out the possibility of a 'hermeneutics of nature'. Whatever one may think of this, it at least enables him to avoid the contradiction that is generated in Habermas's position. For, having allowed himself no philosophical space for claiming that the ontological differentiation of nature and society is objectively, non-interest-constitutively based, he at the same times denies the possibility of a 'hermeneutics of nature' that is, an objectification of 'nature' (as, say, a teleological or communicative realm) by the practical rather than the technical interest.

For instance, in 'Science, Technology and Ideology' Habermas criticizes Marcuse's view that it is possible to conceive of a new science and technology not based on the 'technological *a priori*' (Marcuse's phrase) of the empirical-

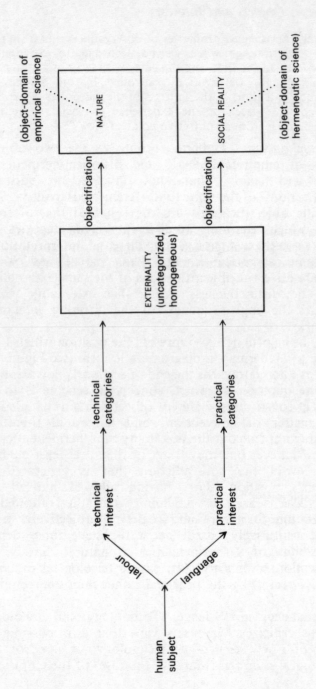

Figure 1

mathematical science that was first fully articulated by Galileo.[33] This new science and technology, according to Marcuse, would not be intrinsically dominative or exploitative in its conception of nature; for it would not (in Habermas's terminology) be constituted by the technical interest. Habermas argues that Marcuse's view is unacceptable, and says that it rests upon an error about the historical specificity of Galilean science. Whilst it is true that this empirical-analytic science is distinctively modern, arising in a particular historical situation, what is modern is only the systematization of a form of knowledge which is not historically specific, but universal to the species, being rooted in an invariant species characteristic, namely labour and rational feedback-guided activity. Thus, in an interview that took place some years after this paper, he had this to say about Marcuse:

> There are two versions of this Marcusean idea of a new science. The first, and stronger version, is that there might be a possibility to develop a type of science which is generically different from what we have now; so that due to its very structure this new science could not be applied in the exploitation of nature. This idea is a very romantic idea. I don't want to be impolite to Marcuse, but I'm convinced that this idea has no real base. The other version is that there might be a change in the relationship between the scientific system and its environment, moreover, its political environment. A change, so that in the future the developments in the science system might be stronger and stronger influenced, and after all guided by political aims and by a discursively formed, politically reasonable will.[34]

It seems that for Habermas the only possible philosophical basis for Marcuse's romanticism would be some version of Hegelian idealism, in which there is an ultimate unity or identity of humans and nature, due to their both being different forms of objectification of the same, supra-human subjectivity. But in *Knowledge and Human Interests*, as elsewhere, he endorses Marx's materialist rejection of Hegel:

> Marx, on the contrary, does not view nature under the category of another subject, but conversely the subject under the category of another nature. Hence, although their unity can only be

brought about by a subject, he does not comprehend it as an absolute unity. The subject is originally a natural being instead of nature being originally an aspect of the subject, as in idealism. Therefore unity, which can only come about through the activity of a subject, remains in some measure imposed on nature by the subject. The resurrection of nature cannot be logically conceived within materialism, no matter how much the early Marx and the speculative minds in the Marxist tradition (Walter Benjamin, Ernest Bloch, Herbert Marcuse, Theodor W. Adorno) find themselves attracted by this heritage of mysticism. Nature does not conform to the categories under which the subject apprehends it in the unresisting way in which a subject can conform to the understanding of another subject on the basis of reciprocal recognition under categories that are binding on both of them.[35]

Now were one to read this passage without knowing of Habermas's interest-constitution theory, it would be quite natural to assume that Habermas here endorses a dichotomy between subject and object − and hence, between a science of the subject and a science of the object − which is 'objective' in the sense that it is not itself solely a product of two divergent objectifications of an uncategorized, homogeneous externality by the human subject. But not only, I suggest, would this be the natural reading: in addition, the assumption just specified is absolutely necessary if Habermas is to be able to reject the possibility of a Marcusean 'resurrection of nature' in the way that he does. But, as I have already argued, it is precisely this assumption that is denied by his theory of knowledge-constitutive interests. Thus the inconsistency at the heart of his position.

There are, of course, two possible ways of resolving this inconsistency: to deny interest-constitution, whilst preserving the doctrine of distinctive object-domains and the rejection of a 'hermeneutics of nature'; or to preserve interest-constitution, and accept this latter possibility. One cannot be sure which option Habermas would choose, but I certainly prefer the former; and in the next section, I shall try to sketch an alternative realist account of the differentiation of scientific object-domains. But before that I will suggest two further problems in Habermas's position, that are related to this central difficulty.

First, when Habermas went on after *Knowledge and Human Interests* to develop the concept of systematically distorted communication prefigured there in his account of Freud, he proposed that we should regard as a significant aspect of such distortion the failure to apply correctly the two interpretations of the categorial schema of space, time, substance and causality. He suggested that a typical manifestation of neurotic or psychotic disorders was the absence of recognition that the social, communicative world consisted not in causal relationships between bodies, but in motivational and intentional relationships between persons. Thus, immediately preceding the passage I quoted above concerning the two interpretations of the categorial schema, Habermas says, in the course of listing a number of features that distinguish normal from distorted communication:

> Finally, normal speech is distinguished by the fact that the sense of substance and causality, of space and time, is differentiated according to whether these categories are applied to the objects within a world or to the linguistically constituted world itself which allows for the neutrality of speaking subjects. [36]

But surely this criterion of distortion presupposes the possibility of a correct and 'objectively' based way of making the differentiation which in pathological conditions is confused? Yet if my previous argument is correct, the theory of interest-constitution does not allow this possibility.

However, this 'mistake' made within distorted communication is not as straightforward as so far indicated. For in the pathological condition one's own actions and communications do *not* appear to be immediately intelligible in terms of conscious motives and meanings. As Habermas argues in his account of Freud in *Knowledge and Human Interests*,[37] distorted action and communication are under the control of unconscious motives and symbolic disguises, and they thus appear, both to the agent and the observer, as belonging to the 'natural' realm of non-intentional causality. This appearance is both revealing, for the reasons just mentioned, but also misleading since, according to Habermas, such actions belong to the realm not of causality, but of quasi-causality (the causality of 'fate' or 'second nature', following Habermas's use of Hegel's and Lukács's terms), from which they can be 'rescued' through a self-reflective therapeutic process guided by a critical social theory.[38] And this is why Habermas claims that:

> In the methodically rigorous sense, 'wrong' behaviour means every *deviation from the model of the language game of communicative action*, in which motives of action and linguistically expressed intentions coincide . . . . This model, however, could be generally applicable only under the conditions of a non-repressive society. Therefore deviations from it are the normal case under all known social conditions.[39]

As is clear from other contexts, Habermas wishes to employ the concept of distorted communication and the conditions for its elimination to features of social relationships that go well beyond the area of individual psychopathology. The Marxist concept of ideology, for instance, is given a similar analysis, and the critique of ideology is seen as methodologically analogous to the therapeutic 'critique' of neurosis.[40] Indeed, consistently I think with Habermas's position here, we might analyse the concept of reification as involving a combination of the 'revealing' and the 'misleading' similar to that presented above. Thus, reified social relationships appear as relations between things. They in fact are not, but equally, neither are they immediately intelligible relationships between autonomous subjects. And this is why a purely hermeneutic social science is inadequate, and must be replaced by a critical social theory which both detects, and aids in overcoming, their quasi-causal character, so ushering in the non-repressive social order of autonomy and intelligibility.

But (and here I introduce the second of my two further points) the possibility of discriminating between causal, quasi-causal, and hermeneutically intelligible relationships surely presupposes that the differentiation of these object-domains is *not* determined by the operation of different constitutive interests. For if it were, there could be no basis for criticizing those forms of social science that depict their 'objects' as either 'fully natural', or 'fully intelligible'; that is, for criticizing the inadequacy of both positivist and hermeneutic social science to deal with object-domains involving distorted communication and action – neurosis, ideology, and so on. It is only if an objectivist, realist alternative to Habermas's quasi-transcendental pragmatism is provided that precisely these aims can (as they should) be achieved by a critical social theory.

In the next section, I sketch the beginnings of such an alternative. But before this there is one more comment to make about interest-constitution. Habermas and several of his commentators have noted that there are various a-symmetries between the functions of, on the one hand, the technical and practical interests, and on the other, the emancipatory interest.[41] I suggest that one a-symmetry is that the latter cannot be constitutive of its object-domain in the way that the two former interests are. For the emancipatory interest does not constitute the object-domain of distorted communication. If anything, it aims at 'constituting' undistorted communication. But here of course the sense of 'constitution' is quite different: critical social theory, guided by the emancipatory interest, aims at the realization of undistorted communication, and at the elimination of the distorted object-domain that it investigates. Thus the emancipatory interest is not ontologically constitutive, in the way that the technical and practical interests are supposed by Habermas to be. However, if my argument in this section is correct, the emancipatory interest cannot have this function if the other interests *are* ontologically constitutive. For if this were so, the objective character of distorted action and communication, and the consequent inappropriateness of either positivist or hermeneutic social science, could not be recognized – just as, if his theory of constitutive interests were accepted, the inappropriateness of a hermeneutic science of nature could not be demonstrated.

4 HUMANS, NATURE AND HUMAN NATURE

I have argued that Habermas cannot consistently maintain both the theory of constitutive interests, and the denial of a hermeneutics of nature. I now wish to challenge the adequacy of his basic contrast between the two object-domains of nature, and human or social reality, with these no longer seen as constituted by different interests, but as interest-independently distinct domains. The dichotomy is, I suggest, mistaken in two ways. First, Habermas's characterization of nature conflates a number of significantly different non-human domains. Second, the contrast is specified in a way that prevents a proper conception of the human species itself, in effect 'de-naturalizing' it. As an alternative to Habermas's ontology I will outline a position that recognizes both a diversity of non-human forms of being, and important continuities between some of these and human being.

Habermas's conception of the object-domain of empirical-analytic science is, I think, appropriate only to inorganic nature, and takes no account of the distinctive features of the (various kinds of) 'objects' of the life-sciences. There is thus a gap in his ontology, between nature as he characterizes it, and the human realm of meanings, communicative activity, etc. What is missing are the various types of organic objects whose properties and appropriate modes of investigation and explanation differ from those of inorganic entities. In other words, the object-domains supposedly constituted by the technical and practical interests are not exhaustive of what there is in the world.[42]

Within the realm of organic objects we can make a number of significant differentiations based upon the presence or absence (either singly or in certain combinations) of the following properties: (1) goal-directedness; (2) experience; (3) purposiveness; and (4) communication. These properties are not the only possible bases upon which such differentiations may be made; and further distinctions may usefully be drawn within each of them. But my account here is intended only as a schematic outline.

First, a few comments about each of these properties. I take goal-directedness as a more extensive concept than purposiveness, though unfortunately there is no established terminology to indicate this in the literature on teleology. Thus, goal-directedness includes all functional concepts within the life-sciences involved in claims such as 'the kidney's function is to aid excretion', or 'the heart's function is to circulate the blood'; and also the homeostatic concepts involved, for instance, in characterizations of the internal temperature-maintenance systems of warm-blooded organisms: here, the concept of negative feedback control is central.[43] I take it that, in all cases of organic goal-directedness, we can normally relate the functions directly performed to the more general functions of life-maintenance and reproductive success, and thus to the fundamental goal-concepts of evolutionary theory. I assume also that a distinction can be drawn between the kinds of teleological concepts so far mentioned, and the concept of purposive activity, of which at least the central cases involve some form of conscious deliberation; but I am not sure whether, for instance, apparently largely innate behavioural patterns such as the nest-building activities of birds, should be classified as fully purposive, or merely non-purposive but goal-directed.[44]

The concepts of experience, and of communication, are perhaps most in need of further internal differentiation. I take the former to include perceptual experience (as distinct from a purely behaviourally defined reactivity to sensory stimuli); bodily sensations or feelings such as pain, nausea, or hunger; and the emotions, such as fear, anger, elation, embarrassment, or jealousy. Both the nature of, and the relations between, these different types of experience are complex; but I will confine myself to just a few comments. First, at least some emotions seem to involve associated bodily sensations – for instance, fear and anger. Second, I assume that species differ in the 'range' of experiences they are able to have: for instance, some may experience bodily sensations such as pain, but not emotions such as elation. Third, there may be important differences between kinds of emotion, especially between those that do, and do not, involve cognitive elements (of varying degrees of sophistication). Thus jealousy, for example, is an emotion associated with quite complex beliefs; whereas fear is not, at least not necessarily. Finally, it seems likely that in species which have the cognitive capacities for emotions such as jealousy, the character of the experiences they 'share' with other species that lack these capacities is thereby altered. Thus primate-fear may differ from bird-fear, just because of the further capacities of primates that enable them, unlike birds, to experience embarrassment.[45]

As for communication, this is also a difficult concept to specify adequately. There are definitions that seem far too extensive, such as 'the transmission and reception of information'. This definition has the consequence of making, for instance, any type of perceptual interaction between environment and perceiver count as 'communication'. Other definitions appear too restrictive, for instance those which require some conscious intention on the part of the 'information-transmitter' (which would probably rule out cases such as bird-calls or bee-dances), or which specify the features which are *peculiar* to human linguistic communication as necessary conditions for *any* kind of communication. I am inclined to follow writers such as Hockett and Thorpe who attempt to identify *all* the characteristics of human linguistic communication, and thus enable comparisons to be drawn between the particular forms of communication in different species, including humans.[46]

The list of properties I have given is intended to be seen as hierarchically ordered, in that each successive property in the list requires, but is not required by, its predecessor. Thus, goal-directedness may exist without communicative capacities, but not vice versa. I am least confident of the ordering of communication and purpose, partly because of the difficulties just noted about their definition. Further, as I pointed out in the case of experience, the presence of a higher-order capacity may typically alter the character of a lower-order capacity. Other examples of this would be the (highly complex) relationship between perceptual and communicative properties (for instance, the role of linguistic concepts in the processing of sensory information); and the effect of conscious-purposive capacities in altering or controlling instinctual goal-directed patterns (such as sexual or reproductive activity).[47] Finally, I assume also that the hierarchical ordering roughly maps onto the historical process of organic evolution, in that 'higher' corresponds typically to (temporally) 'later'. But I do not thereby endorse a corresponding order of normative value, or an 'evolutionary ethics'. Such normative positions must be based on the explicit adoption and justification of anthropocentric values, and cannot be derived solely from evolutionarily defined hierarchies.

In saying that this list of properties enables us to differentiate, objectively, various kinds or levels of organic object-domains, I am denying the legitimacy of certain kinds of reductionism. I do not think it is possible to perform a *conceptual* reduction of these properties to the properties of inorganic entities: that is, to define the former in terms of the latter. But this does not rule out the possibility of an *explanatory* reduction, in which laws or theories at higher levels (involving level-distinctive concepts) are explained by reference to laws or theories of lower levels. That is, one can deny the possibility of inter-level translation or definition of concepts, whilst not denying the existence of a-symmetries between the explanatory power of theories at different levels. Further, I think the kind of conceptual irreducibility that exists, here, is incompatible with an *ontological* reduction, according to which the terms of the higher-level theories are said to in fact refer only to the entities specified in the lower-level theories. Although some cases of conceptual non-translatability are consistent with extensional, and thus ontological, identity (for instance, the much-loved 'The Morning Star is the Evening Star'), I do not think the same extensional identity can exist between the concepts involved in describing, say, perceptual experience or bodily sensations, and those involved in describing neurophysiological states. But this is compatible with regarding neurophysiological states as explanatory with respect to perceptual experience or bodily sensations.[48]

This completes my account of how an ontological plurality of various kinds of organic and inorganic beings should replace Habermas's conception of the object-domain of empirical-analytic science. If this pluralism is accepted, at least in outline, this would strengthen my arguments against his interest-constitution theory. For the theory would then require the identification of a multitude of different interests, one for each object-domain; and there would be no interest-independent basis for 'choosing' one such interest rather than another to perform a constitutive function.

I will now consider how this proposed internal differentiation of the concept of nature into inorganic and (various kinds of) organic object-domains may affect our understanding of the second element in Habermas's dichotomy, the domain of human social reality. Here I think we should adopt an evolutionary perspective which requires recognition both of the *distinctive* characteristics of each species, and also of their *relatedness* to one another through the historical processes of speciation, whose explanation involves focusing upon how the characteristics of different species are adaptively related to their environments. Habermas (along with many other theorists) is, I suggest, inclined to regard 'human nature' as consisting only in those features which *distinguish* this species from others. Instead, we should regard the central features of the human species – as of any other – as including also those that it has in common with others: in particular, with its evolutionary relatives (the species which either are, or share, ancestors). In the evolutionary process there are no complete discontinuities, and one should therefore be suspicious of ontological dichotomies which appear to deny this. Human society is not a gift from God.

For instance, it is probably true that human language is significantly different from all other animal communication systems. But it does not follow that we *are* 'linguistic beings' – that is, no more (or less) than this. Nor does it follow that human communication involves *only* this species distinctive linguistic character; and (despite certain qualifications) studies of human non-verbal communication strongly suggest continuities in this respect with features of non-human primate communication, for example in the facial expression of emotion.[49] Nor, from the fact that learning and conscious-purposive activity have, in humans, species-distinctive features, does it follow that there are no innate components in human ontogeny that are related to this species' evolutionary past. 'Human nature' includes non-human 'nature'.[50]

However, whilst emphasizing that species-nature is not the same as species-distinctive nature, we must not make the mistake of regarding the nature of the human species as a simple combination of distinctive and non-distinctive features. That is, it is not a matter of the conjunction of a number of such characteristics: say, experience + purpose + non-verbal communication + learning + language. For typically, the evolutionary emergence of higher functions affects the character and mode of operation of the lower functions which are continuous with those of evolutionary ancestors. For instance, in humans the evolutionarily 'old' limbic system in the brain, important in emotional activity, is connected in complex ways with evolutionarily 'recent' components.[51] This is why even those emotions which we to some extent share with other species may take a different form in humans. (And that is one important reason why the practice of direct chemotherapeutic or surgical intervention in the human limbic system, for instance in amygdalectomy, is misconceived not only in moral and political terms, but also ontologically.)

This last point raises the question of the relationship between a proper understanding of the nature of human beings and the normative issues involved in practices aimed to change the character of their activities, which will be taken up again much later.[52] But before that we need to examine the claims made for a kind of science which, according to Habermas and other critical theorists, is distinct from both empirical and hermeneutic sciences in its object-domain and criteria of validity. It is a science guided by the emancipatory interest in human autonomy, which is intended to aid its 'objects' in freeing themselves, through a self-reflective process, from patterns of distorted communication and activity. So I turn now to consider Habermas's account of this.

4 Psychoanalysis and Human Emancipation

In the Introduction I noted how Habermas presented psychoanalysis as 'the only tangible example of a science incorporating methodical self-reflection',[1] and thus as a model for the general epistemological features of a critical social theory guided by the emancipatory interest in human autonomy. I will now examine his account in more detail, especially its claims about the relations between autonomy, causality and the unconscious. By doing this I hope to show how certain features of this view of critical social theory can be preserved in a reconstructed form which is basically deterministic, and which builds upon some of my suggestions in the previous chapter about how to characterize the human species by comparison with other 'objects'. Discussion of Habermas's claim about the distinctive criteria of validity for critical theory, which is also developed through his account of psychoanalysis, will be left till the next chapter.

In the first two sections I argue that there are a number of defects in Habermas's account of Freud, considered solely as an exegesis. These mainly concern his interpretation of the concepts of the id and the unconscious, and of the goal of psychoanalytic therapy. By itself this criticism is not, of course, particularly significant. The acceptability of Habermas's view of critical social theory does not depend upon the exegetical accuracy of this account: for he might be wrong in thinking that psychoanalytic theory provides an epistemological model for critical social theory, without this undermining his conception of the latter. Further, we must remember that Habermas asserts that Freud misunderstood, scientistically, the epistemological status of his own theory; and that there are features of the theory which reflect this, and which must therefore be removed if psychoanalysis is to be a 'pure' example of a self-reflective science.[2] However, I shall argue that the exegetical deficiencies in Habermas's account indicate serious problems for the view of critical social theory which he intends psychoanalysis to illustrate. And, in some respects at least, I think Freud's 'self-misunderstanding' is preferable to Habermas's. In particular, I try to defend in the last three sections a deterministic and reductionist position which is generally consistent with Freud's, but which also enables something similar to Habermas's conception of psychoanalysis as an emancipatory process to be preserved.

1 THE ID: ALIENATED EGO OR HOME OF THE INSTINCTS?

The structural model of id, ego and superego, says Habermas, is intrinsically related to the self-reflective character of the therapeutic process in psychoanalysis. In that process the nature and meaning of the distorted communications typical of neurosis are revealed by undoing the work of the unconscious which, through a complex series of defences, has disguised the wishes or desires earlier repressed from consciousness. Thus intelligibility is restored to the 'distorted texts' of neurotic activity, and the patient *recovers* what had been banished from the realm of public communication. I emphasize 'recovers', since this is crucial to Habermas's account: what was lost is found again. The Hegelian theme of reconciliation, of the overcoming of alienation, seems evident here. Thus Habermas says:

> the insight to which analysis is to lead is indeed only this: that the ego of the patient recognize itself in its other, represented by its illness, as in its *own* alienated *self* and identify with it. As in Hegel's dialectic of the moral life, the criminal recognizes in his victim his own annihilated essence; in this self-reflection the abstractly divorced parties recognize the destroyed moral totality as their common basis and thereby return to it.[3]

And, rather less evocatively:

> Analysis has immediate therapeutic results because the critical

overcoming of blocks to consciousness and the penetration of
false objectivations initiates the appropriation of a lost portion
of life-history; it reverses the process of splitting-off. That is
why analytic knowledge is self-reflection.[4]

Now this characterization of the therapeutic process is in
some ways plausible and illuminating — though, as I will
argue in the following section, it is associated with a view of
the goal of psychoanalytic therapy that departs significantly
from Freud's. But what is not so plausible is Habermas's
further claim that the meaning of the concepts 'id' and 'ego'
in Freud's metapsychology can and must be understood by
reference to the therapeutic process characterized in this way.
Habermas's formula here is simple: 'Id = alienated ego', as
we can see in the following passage:

> Freud conceived the defensive process as the reversal of
> reflection, that is, as the process, analogous to flight, through
> which the ego conceals itself from itself. *'Id' is then the name for*
> *the part of the self that is externalized through defense*, while
> 'ego' is the agency that fulfills the task of reality-testing and
> censorship of instinctual impulses. [My italics][5]

This definition of the id is supported by Habermas's
translator, who tells us that:

> *Das Ich* means the I and *das Es* the it. That is, they refer to the
> antithesis between reflexive, personal subjectivity and reified,
> impersonal objectivity.[6]

But this is not how Freud himself conceived of the id; or, at
least, this is only a partial account which excludes what was
equally important for Freud, namely the instincts (or their
psychical representatives, a concept I will discuss shortly).
This view is maintained by Freud throughout what is in this
context a central work, *The Ego and the Id*, where we find
several passages such as this:

> It is easy to see that the ego is that part of the id which has been
> modified by direct influence of the external world through the
> medium of the Pcpt.-Cs [Perceptual-Conscious system]; in a
> sense it is an extension of the surface-differentiation. Moreover,
> the ego seeks to bring the influence of the external world to bear
> upon the id and its tendencies, and endeavours to substitute the

reality principle for the pleasure principle which reigns unrestrictedly in the id. For the ego, perception plays the part which in the id falls to instinct. The ego represents what may be called reason and common sense, in contrast to the id, which contains the passions. [7]

And Freud goes on to say of the ego that:

in its relation to the id it is like a man on horseback, who has to hold in check the superior strength of the horse; with this difference, that the rider tries to do so with his own strength while the ego uses borrowed forces. The analogy may be carried a little further. Often a rider, if he is not to be parted from his horse, is obliged to guide it where it wants to go; so in the same way the ego is in the habit of transforming the id's will into action as if it were its own. [8]

This analogy is pursued later on, in a slightly different form, when Freud presents his well-known picture of the ego as:

a poor creature owing service to three masters and consequently menaced by three dangers: from the external world, from the libido of the id, and from the severity of the superego. [9]

However, whilst Freud's conception of the id departs in this respect from Habermas's, we should note that it does none the less include what Habermas views as the 'alienated ego', namely what has been repressed from consciousness during the kinds of conflictual situations, such as occur during the Oedipal period, which are central to Freud's dynamic theory of psychosexual development and the formation of neuroses. In *The Ego and the Id*, for instance, having described how the ego may be seen as becoming differentiated from the id via its access to the external world through the perceptual-conscious system, Freud comments:

But the repressed merges into the id as well, and is merely a part of it. The repressed is only cut off sharply from the ego by the resistance of repression; it can communicate with the ego through the id. [10]

Thus, briefly, whilst for Habermas 'id = alienated ego (= the repressed)', for Freud 'id = the repressed + the instincts'. More fully, Freud's position is well described by Marie Jahoda in the following terms:

The id is a summary term comprising various functions, such as instinctual drives – hunger, thirst, sexuality – which mobilize the whole person and thus have overt consequences. These consequences are behavioural not just physiological, but the instinctual drives are, of course, 'open to the somatic', in Freud's terminology. There are also other functions subsumed in the id which, similarly, have mobilizing consequences but stem from previous experiences which become repressed; that is, there are memories of ideas, events, actions and feelings excluded from consciousness but activating the person. [11]

Thus whereas for Habermas the apparent objectivity of the id is *only* apparent, since it is really an alienated form of subjectivity which can be restored to consciousness, this is so for Freud only of one component of the id, the repressed, and not for the other, the instincts. In effect, Habermas wishes to understand the id in the same way as, in the previous chapter, I suggested he understood the 'natural-ness' of distorted communication, and the reified character of ideologies: their apparent objectivity is in fact an alienated subjectivity. [12] The id is not then an ineliminable feature of all human activity, as it was (partly) for Freud, but an element in the defective but alterable character of the object-domain of a critical social theory.

It might seem that some support for Habermas's view is given by Freud's well-known dictum, 'Where Id was, there Ego shall be' which Jeremy Shapiro, in one of his translator's notes to *Knowledge and Human Interests*, says should be taken to mean 'Where it-ness was, I-ness shall come into being'. [13] But this ignores the important qualifications in Freud's own work to the meaning of this dictum, which will be explored further in the next section. For Freud, roughly, the id cannot be replaced by the ego, but can only be more effectively and less unhappily controlled or served by it. This is because he views the instincts as ineliminable; and although the specific 'objects' of their driving force may be altered, the pressure of their demands for satisfaction cannot.

However, the contrast between Habermas's and Freud's accounts of the id is more complex than so far presented. This is partly because of the notorious difficulties in conceptualizing Freud's account of the instincts, particularly their biological nature;[14] and partly because Habermas does not simply ignore their place in Freud's theory. Rather, he argues that to the extent that Freud conceived of the instincts in biological terms, he was guilty of a scientific misunderstanding of the epistemological character of his own theory (a misunderstanding evidenced also in his neurologically based energy-model of psychological processes, which I will discuss in the final section of this chapter). So we need now to examine more closely Freud's conception of the instincts.

Freud maintained that the concepts of psychoanalytic theory should be exclusively psychological: they must not be couched directly in physiological or biological terms.[15] In the case of the instincts, this meant they could only be admitted into the theory in the form of what he often called their 'psychical representatives'. His terminology is not always consistent, but I do not think this affects the significant issues here. Sometimes he talked of the instincts *having* psychical representatives; at other times, of their *being* such representatives. The latter usage is involved, for instance, in the following two passages:

> By an 'instinct' is provisionally to be understood the psychical representative of an endosomatic, continuously flowing source of stimulation . . . . The source of an instinct is a process of excitation occurring in an organ and the immediate aim of the instinct lies in the removal of this organic stimulus.[16]

And likewise he defines the 'source' of an instinct as:

> the somatic process which occurs in an organ or part of the body whose stimulus is represented in mental life by an instinct. We do not know whether this process is invariably of a chemical nature or whether it may also correspond to the release of other, e.g. mechanical, forces. The study of the sources of instincts lies outside the scope of psychology.[17]

Elsewhere, however, Freud proposes a distinction between instincts and their ideational representatives, whilst accepting a 'looseness of phraseology' that may blur this. For instance:

> An instinct can never become an object of consciousness − only the idea that represents the instinct can. Even in the

> unconscious, moreover, an instinct cannot be represented otherwise than by an idea . . . . When we nevertheless speak of an unconscious instinctual impulse or of a repressed instinctual impulse, the looseness of phraseology is a harmless one. We can only mean an instinctual impulse the ideational representative of which is unconscious, for nothing else comes into consideration.[18]

In saying that these terminological variations are insignificant, I mean that whichever is used, Freud's basic claim remains the same: that the (instinctual) demands of the id are somatically based. As he says in the *New Introductory Lectures*, in discussing the instincts 'we are studying the psychical accompaniments of biological processes', and he goes on to comment:

> We can distinguish an instinct's source, object, and aim. Its source is a state of excitation in the body, its aim is the removal of that excitation; on its path from its source to its aim the instinct becomes operative psychically.[19]

I do not think Freud ever wavered from this view, despite several (in other contexts very important) changes in his account of *which* instincts humans in fact have, and of their relationships to one another.[20] This view is perfectly compatible with his insistence that the concepts of psychoanalytic theory itself be exclusively psychological. And it is also consistent with three further, and equally strongly held convictions: that all psychological phenomena, and not just the instincts, have a somatic foundation; that psychoanalytic theory must be open, in principle, to a neurological reduction; and that psychological relationships are subject to an overall scientific determinism.[21]

Now Habermas opposes these reductionist and deterministic assumptions in Freud's work, and regards them as important elements in its scientistic misunderstanding. In order to purge psychoanalytic theory of these assumptions, he thinks it necessary, amongst other things, to revise the way that Freud conceived of the instincts. Thus he criticizes Freud for proposing:

> an energy model of instinctual dynamics with an objectivist turn. Thus he sees even the species' process of civilization as

linked to a dynamic of the instincts. The libidinal and aggressive instinctual forces, the prehistorial forces of evolution, permeate the species subject and determine its history. But . . . [t]he conception of the instincts as the prime mover of history and of civilization as the result of their struggle forgets that we have only derived the concept of impulse privatively from language deformation and behavioral pathology. At the human level we never encounter any needs that are not already interpreted linguistically and symbolically affixed to potential actions. [22]

A similar view is expressed in a more recent interview:

> I think that the drives are something real in distorting verbal communication, they have some force in destroying an individual's capacity to act; but I cannot account for this without referring to a communication frame. [23]

In both these passages, two main claims seem to be made. First, that in understanding human action the concept of an instinct is legitimate only if the character of instinctual impulses is specified in an interpretively intelligible form: that is, not biologically, but in terms of linguistic categories referring to possible human desires or actions. Second, that even these (linguistically interpreted) drives are relevant only in the explanation of distorted or pathological activity.

This latter claim involves a major departure from psychoanalytic theory, which I will explore in the next section. But considering now only the former claim, I suggest that it is not altogether inconsistent with Freud's own position. For, as I have noted, Freud himself insists that only the 'psychical representatives' of the instincts (or of their somatic biological sources) are appropriate elements within psychoanalytic theory; and this appears to meet Habermas's requirement of their being interpreted 'linguistically'. For instance, Freud says that instinctual drives are highly variable in the 'objects' to which they are directed at different times, as compared with what he calls their 'aim', which generally remains constant. [24] Presumably, drives specified in terms of their objects at particular times would satisfy Habermas's requirement, since these objects will typically be described in terms of linguistically defined actions, attitudes, desires, and so on. So this requirement would only involve a departure from Freud's position if it were *also* true that 'linguistically interpreted' instinctual impulses are not subject to causal determination, at the level both of psychological relationships, and of their (in Freud's view) biological bases.

It seems that the primary rationale for Habermas's rejection of biologically conceived instincts is his desire to remove the 'objects' of psychoanalytic theory from the domain of an empirical-analytic science which investigates causal relationships between non-meaningful items. But suppose instead, as I think is true, that there can also be causal relationships between meaningful objects. Then the determinism Habermas wishes to avoid by his insistence on a non-biological conception of instinctual impulses, will not thereby be eliminated. Freud, as I have noted, endorsed both a deterministic reductionism, and the use of exclusively psychological concepts in psychoanalytic theory. But Habermas believes that the hermeneutically interpretable realm of communicative activity is non-deterministic: that the category of causality is inapplicable to it. Clearly, this view is incompatible with Freud's deterministic reductionism. But the requirement that there be no biologically defined concepts in psychoanalytic theory does not by itself ensure that this is avoided. For it may be that both determinism and reductionism can be specified in ways that are consistent with this requirement, as I will argue later in this chapter.

To summarize so far, Habermas's mis-interpretation of Freud's concept of the id expresses his wish to purge psychoanalytic theory of deterministic and reductionist assumptions. The missing element in his account of the id is the concept of the instincts. But Habermas does not ignore the instincts: instead, he tries to de-biologize them in a way that is, at first sight, in accordance with Freud's own practice of including within psychoanalytic theory only their 'psychical representatives'. Yet this by itself cannot satisfy Habermas, if it is in fact consistent with what he wants to reject, the deterministic reductionism of Freud's 'scientific misunderstanding' of psychoanalysis. And he thinks this has to be rejected because it is incompatible with the possibility of human autonomy, and with the characterization of psychoanalytic therapy as a self-reflective, emancipatory process. But this I believe is a mistake. Neurophysiological reductionism, properly understood, is compatible with a defensible conception of autonomy, and of psychoanalysis as a means to its realization.

However, we must now examine another of Habermas's departures from Freud, concerning the relationship between unconscious determinants and the goal of the psychoanalytic process. As I have pointed out, Habermas claims that instinctual impulses are relevant only to the explanation of defective activity. This non-Freudian view is related to his equally non-Freudian tendency to regard all unconscious determinants as distorting influences, that are to be eliminated in the self-reflective movement towards autonomy. As with his account of the id, this not only misinterprets Freud but also indicates defects in his conception of critical social theory.

2 THE PSYCHOANALYTIC GOAL: ABOLITION OF THE UNCONSCIOUS OR STRENGTHENING OF THE EGO?

It will be helpful to begin by noting the relationship in Freud's theoretical work between the 'structural' model of id, ego and superego, and the 'topographical' model of the unconscious, preconscious and conscious. Whilst the former was introduced by Freud later on in his development, he did not intend it to directly replace the latter, since the two models were designed to meet different, but compatible, theoretical demands. Roughly speaking, the topographical model is aimed at distinguishing various kinds of psychological processes, and at identifying their distinctive modes of operation. Thus Freud argued that in addition to conscious processes (those of which we are aware at any time), there were not only preconscious ones (such as memories that could be brought to consciousness 'at will', as it were), but also unconscious ones that were far less immediately accessible, and could only be made conscious by overcoming resistances through various therapeutic techniques. [25] He went on to claim that the unconscious, and the conscious and preconscious 'systems' operated in quite different ways, described in his accounts of what he called the 'primary' and 'secondary' processes. [26] By contrast, the structural model is concerned with specifying the three main psychological functions that must be performed within the whole personality; the various sources of conflict between these; and the possible modes of resolution of such conflicts. These functions are assigned, in an at least partly metaphorical way, to the three 'agencies' defined in the model. The difference of aim in constructing these models is reflected in the absence of any simple correspondence between their respective concepts: not even between the conscious (and preconscious) and the ego, since Freud notes that some of the ego's functions are performed unconsciously, particularly the various defence mechanisms, including repression. [27]

Freud initially postulated the existence of unconscious mental processes in order to explain certain features of neurotic behaviour and of his early clinical experience in treating this (such as the use of hypnosis in cases of hysteria), whilst remaining at the level of a specifically *psychological* theory. But he later argued that important evidence of how these processes operated was revealed by the analysis of dreams. Dreams, he argued, were disguised wish-fulfilments – except in the case of (some) infant dreams, in which there was no disguise to be analytically penetrated; and he declared that *'the interpretation of dreams is the royal road to a knowledge of the unconscious activities of the mind.'* [28] In deciphering the manifest content (the dream as reported) the analyst and patient in effect reverse the process of the dream-work, through which its latent content (the unconscious, repressed wish) has been disguised. Freud argued that there were various features of this dream-work that displayed the general mode of operation of the primary processes, such as condensation, displacement, the use of visual imagery and of symbols. The last of these, unlike the first three, involved meanings that were not peculiar to each patient: there was a (possibly universal) language of symbols, especially concerning the male and female genitals, used not only in dreams but in folklore, myth, and so on. [29]

It is important to emphasize that, for Freud, dreams were

not pathological phenomena, and neither were the dreams of neurotic patients essentially different from those of non-neurotic people. This is related to a more general claim: that there is nothing pathological, as such, about the presence and mode of operation of unconscious processes. He says, for instance:

> we must recognize that the psychical mechanism employed by neuroses is not created by the impact of a pathological disturbance upon the mind but is present already in the normal structure of the mental apparatus. [30]

And he suggests that the normal mind's activities are enriched by the fact that both unconscious and conscious (or preconscious) processes are involved:

> For illnesses . . . do not presuppose the disintegration of the apparatus [the mind] or the production of fresh splits in its interior. They are to be explained on a *dynamic* basis − by the strengthening and weakening of the various components in the interplay of forces, so many of whose effects are hidden from view while functions are normal. I hope to be able to show elsewhere how the compounding of the apparatus out of two agencies [the unconscious and the conscious: Freud had not yet introduced his structural model at this time] makes it possible for the normal mind too to function with greater delicacy than would be possible with only one of them. [31]

(I take it that Freud is referring here to the operation of the primary processes in fantasy, art, literature, jokes, and so on.)

Further, Freud says that in calling the processes of the unconscious 'primary' he is claiming that they have a chronological priority in individual development. The secondary processes of the conscious-preconscious emerge 'only during the course of life', and though they may eventually come to achieve control over the unconscious, the latter is never eliminated. Indeed:

> In consequence of the belated appearance of the secondary processes, the core of our being, consisting of unconscious wishful impulses, remains inaccessible to the understanding and inhibition of the preconscious; the part played by the latter is restricted once and for all to directing along the most expedient

paths the wishful impulses that arise from the unconscious. These unconscious wishes exercise a compelling force upon all later mental trends, a force which those trends are obliged to fall in with or which they may perhaps endeavour to divert and direct to higher aims. [32]

More than twenty years later, in *The Ego and the Id*, he expresses a very similar view, but now articulated in the theoretical concepts of the later, structural model. Immediately following the passage I quoted in the first section, concerning the 'three masters' of the ego, [33] he goes on to say:

> As a frontier-creature, the ego tries to mediate between the world and the id, to make the id pliable to the world, and by means of its muscular activity, to make the world fall in with the wishes of the id. In point of fact, it behaves like the physician during an analytic treatment: it offers itself, with the attention it pays to the real world, as a libidinal object to the id, and aims at attracting the id's libido to itself. [I take it that Freud is here referring to the phenomenon of transference.] It is not only a helper to the id; it is also a submissive slave who courts his master's love. [34]

The picture presented here of the ego as the 'submissive slave' of the instinctual id is suggests a parallel to Hume's much-quoted comment that 'reason is the slave of the passions'; [35] and it is associated with a conception of the overall goal of psychoanalysis on Freud's part that differs in several important ways from Habermas's. For Freud, I believe, this goal consists primarily in increasing the extent to which this 'slavery' can be successfully accomplished. The basic ends of human action are determined by the (innate) instinctual impulses of the id, governed by the pleasure principle. The task of the ego, governed by the reality principle, is to maximize the effective satisfaction of these impulses, and to minimize the suffering that results from various forms of their inhibition and repression. In performing this task, the ego is also hindered by the superego; and thus the realization of the goal of psychoanalysis also requires some reduction in the latter's tendency to generate avoidable suffering in the form of 'moral' guilt or anxiety. [36]

Underlying this account is a version of ethical and psychological hedonism, in which the ego is the 'agency' of a prudential, instrumental rationality. This hedonism, however, becomes more complex with the introduction of the death instinct in Freud's later works, where it is argued that the aggressive re-direction of this instinct poses considerable problems for the maintenance of 'civilization' and thus, indirectly, for the amount of pleasure that individuals are able to experience. Freud claimed, amongst other things, that the self-punitive operations of the superego were to some extent necessary to counter the otherwise destructive consequences of these aggressive impulses; though he still believed that the degree of guilt and anxiety produced by the superego in modern societies was excessive, and could be reduced through therapeutic procedures. [37]

Thus Freud's dictum, 'Where Id was there Ego shall be', can only be properly understood as subject to the qualifications implied by the above account. By contrast, Habermas's conception of the goal of psychoanalysis involves a quite different interpretation. Having (mis)-understood the concept of the id as the alienated ego, he presents in effect a literal and unqualified reading of this dictum, so that the abolition of the id is seen as a possible and desirable outcome of the therapeutic process. Likewise the instincts are regarded as the sources only of pathological, neurotic activity; and indeed the same is true of all unconscious determinants. Further, he maintains that in overcoming the power of the unconscious, the patient is thereby removed from the deterministic realm of causality; and on this basis he attempts to distinguish the emancipatory character of psychoanalysis (and thus, more generally, of a critical social theory) from the technical, instrumental character of empirical-analytic science:

> In technical control over nature we get nature to work for us through our knowledge of causal connections. Analytic insight, however, affects the causality of the unconscious as such. Psychoanalytic therapy is not based, like somatic medicine, which is 'causal' in the narrower sense, on making use of known causal connections. Rather, it owes its efficacy to overcoming causal connections themselves. [38]

And in contrasting what he calls the 'depth-hermeneutic understanding' (a concept I will examine in the next section) involved in psychoanalysis with the causal explanation of empirical-analytic science, he says:

> Depth-hermeneutic understanding takes over the function of explanation. It proves its explanatory power in self-reflection, in which an objectivation that is both understood and explained is overcome. This is the critical accomplishment of what Hegel had called comprehending (*Begreifen*). [39]

The reference here to Hegel is worth exploring briefly, for it recalls Habermas's comments on Marx's materialism discussed in section 3 of the previous chapter. Habermas endorses Marx's refusal to accept Hegel's transcendence of the subject-object duality, where nature is the 'object', and humans the 'subject'. Thus, whereas for Hegel all apparent objectivity can be transcended, being regarded as an alienation of *geist*, this is not so for Habermas. It is only so in the case of the apparent objectivity of alienated, reified human subjectivity, of which the id and the unconscious are for him central examples. And it is alienated subjectivity that forms the object-domain of critical social theory, which aims to overcome this domain's alienated character in the movement towards human emancipation. Psychoanalysis then, for Habermas, aims to do just this. It is therefore not to be understood as empirical-analytic science, directed towards technical control through knowledge of causal relationships, but as a critical science directed at the abolition of what only appear to be genuinely causal determinants. Yet, as my account of Freud has been intended to show, this clearly departs from Freud's view, which comes close to specifying the goal of therapy as increasing the 'technical' control exercisable by the ego over both the instinctual impulses and the external world, both being equally 'objective'. There is, as far as I can see, no hint in Freud's position of any opposition to the kind of instrumental conception of reason which Habermas, like other critical theorists, wishes to replace or extend by an alternative view of reason.

Finally, through his association of the de-alienation of the ego with the ending of unconscious determination, Habermas seems to commit himself to the eliminability of all unconscious influences on human activity, and thus of their distinctive mode of operation, the primary processes. We can bring out the possible significance of this by asking: does Habermas then believe that a goal of therapy is the abolition of dreams? For according to Freud dreaming is a non-pathological phenomenon whose character reveals the nature and primacy of the unconscious. Further, it is not only dreams but many other non-pathological activities that display these primary processes which involve, as say in fantasy, the use of condensation, displacement, visual imagery and symbols. So we can ask also: does Habermas regard these, too, as pathological? I do not see how he can avoid this conclusion, without a major revision of his reinterpretation of psychoanalytic theory. [40]

However, as I noted at the outset of this chapter, one cannot directly reject Habermas's conception of critical social theory merely by showing that it does not 'fit' the actual character of the theory he regards as providing an epistemological model for it. And in any case Habermas himself argues that there are elements of a scientistic misunderstanding in Freud's work, which he wishes to remove from it − though, at the very least, it appears that Habermas does not fully recognize the extent to which his preferred (re)interpretation of psychoanalysis differs from Freud. But what matters most is the legitimacy of the assumptions that lead Habermas to make these major revisions; and it is to this issue that the rest of the chapter is addressed. In particular we need to examine his attitude towards determinism and reductionism, and the reasons why he apparently regards these as incompatible with the understanding of psychoanalysis as emancipatory. I shall argue that he is mistaken in thinking this, starting with the question of determinism and human autonomy.

3 AUTONOMY, CAUSALITY AND COMPULSIVENESS

Underlying Habermas's view of the way in which psychoanalysis is to be seen as emancipatory are certain assumptions about the relationship between autonomy and causality. To identify these it will be helpful to review briefly the debates about free-will and determinism, and about the status of purposive explanation, that have taken place within analytical philosophy.

On the former question, the basic disagreement has been between those who regard freedom and determinism (defined as the thesis that all events are fully causally determined) as compatible, and those who do not. Compatibilists have argued that the distinction between free and unfree actions lies not in the respective presence or absence of causal determinants, but in differences in the nature of these causes. By contrast, those who reject compatibilism have opted either to accept determinism and deny the existence of freedom (so-called 'hard determinists'), or conversely to assert the existence of freedom, and deny the truth of determinism (the 'libertarians').[41]

In the partly related debates about the nature of purposive explanation (that is, explanations of human action that make reference to the agent's intentions, aims, motives, and so on), the main issue has been whether this can be regarded as a form of causal explanation. Here, the problem has centred around the generally (though not universally) accepted Humean criterion that, for two items to stand in a causal relationship with one another, there must be a possible identifying description of each that is logically independent of the other. That is, there must be a referential description for each item, such that the truth or falsity of existential claims made using this description, for either item, does not logically entail the truth or falsity of an existential claim about the other. Thus it has been generally agreed that if there is no way of identifying an agent's intentions that is logically independent of his or her performance of the action said to be explained by reference to this intention, then the nature of this explanation cannot be causal. Further, amongst supporters of the causal status of purposive explanation, some have argued that the requisite independent identification of the agent's purpose can be provided within the conceptual framework of purposive language; whilst others have argued that this identification can only be achieved by moving to a neurophysiological level. The latter view has normally been associated with the adoption of an identity-theory concerning the relationship of the 'mental' and the 'physical', according to which the former concepts are taken to in fact refer to physical items.[42]

There is a complex set of relationships between the various positions within each of these debates. I will note only two of these. First, libertarianism (at least, those versions of it which take purposive action as a paradigmatic case of free action) requires rejection of the causal analysis of purposive explanations. Second, both compatibilism and hard determinism are at least consistent with this causal analysis since both accept the possibility of causal explanation for all phenomena, including human actions.

I shall not argue the respective merits of various positions within these debates. But I will assume the causal status of purposive explanation, accepting the analysis of this as involving desires and beliefs as causal determinants of action; and I shall assume also that the logical independence requirement can be met without recourse to neurophysiological identifications.[43] On the question of determinism I shall present a version of compatibilism, and try to show how Habermas's conception of psychoanalysis as emancipatory may be reconstructed from this standpoint, together with the view of purposive explanation just noted. However, it should be noted that I am not thereby committed to the view that compatibilism provides the correct solution to all issues about free-will and determinism. There may be senses or forms of freedom that are incompatible with determinism. My suggestion is only that we can understand the idea of psychoanalysis as an emancipatory process by using a conception of autonomy that accords with a compatibilist standpoint.[44]

Habermas, it appears, maintains a non-causal analysis of purposive explanation, together with a form of libertarianism. But he does not regard all human activity as (already) free: autonomy is an ideal from which much past and present human action falls short. Unfree action is alienated, reified action that remains subject to a specific form of causal determination, which he calls the 'causality of fate', or 'second nature'.[45] And, at least in the case of neurosis, it is the unconscious, or the id (understood in his terms) that provides this freedom-removing causality.

Habermas's denial of the causal status of purposive explanation is displayed in his view of hermeneutic interpretation, and its contrast with what he calls the 'depth hermeneutics' of Freudian theory. He claims that the kind of communicative activity explored in psychoanalysis is not open to successful interpretation by means of normal hermeneutic procedures. The text of the manifest dream content, for instance, does not contain occasional slips or missing items, as might a written text studied by philologists, but what he describes as 'systematic' distortions. Their interpretation requires the employment of a 'depth hermeneutics', which is said to explain these distortions by 'the psychological investigation of causal connections'.[46] By contrast, 'ordinary' hermeneutic interpretation is concerned only with the understanding of meanings; and the identification and understanding of actions by reference to the agent's purpose or intentions are included within this form of interpretation. That is, ordinary hermeneutic interpretation includes the understanding of actions gained through their intentional descriptions.[47] Thus the contrast between this, and depth hermeneutics, is specified at least partly by the presence of causal explanation in the latter, and its absence in the former.

However, for Habermas this is not the only contrast between the two types of hermeneutic interpretation. For in the interpretation of dreams (and thus also, of neuroses), a crucial feature is the discovery of the transformations of the latent content, the unconscious wish, by the mechanisms of the dream-work: condensation, displacement, and so on. The discovery of these transformations enables us to decipher the initially unintelligible text. Whilst remaining within the essentially hermeneutic concern with meanings, normal interpretive procedures are in this way significantly extended.

I now wish to revise Habermas's position on this issue by proposing that the contrast between these two kinds of interpretation be made on the basis of the second contrast alone. That is, what makes depth hermeneutics 'deep' is only the distinctive character of its interpretive procedures, and not (also) its investigation of causal relationships. This would have the virtue (for me) of being consistent with accepting a causal analysis of purposive explanation, whether the purposes are conscious or unconscious. In both cases, I suggest, we are necessarily involved in the interpretation of meanings; but we are also necessarily concerned with questions of causality. We are involved in the former, roughly, because the specification of purposes or intentions involves the identification of beliefs and desires; and the identity of these is given in terms of their propositional content. It is this content that requires interpretive understanding. But whether the agent's beliefs and desires (and, indeed, which of them) are the causal determinants of his or her actions, is a distinct, and not interpretively decidable, matter. On this view, then, any social science must be concerned with both interpretive and causal questions at every level of analysis, whether the ascertained purposes are conscious or unconscious.

This, then, is the first revision of Habermas's position that I propose. The second concerns the analysis of freedom and determinism. Here I suggest a form of compatibilism, which preserves a good deal of the way he wishes to contrast autonomy with its absence, but which is consistent both with determinism, and with the form of reductionism I will present in the next section. There is, of course, an important link between compatibilism and my first revision: to regard purposive explanation as causal requires, other things being equal, that one either rejects the existence of freedom altogether, or regards it as compatible with determinism.

Compatibilists, as I noted earlier, typically distinguish free and unfree actions on the basis of the kinds of causal determinants that are operative. But the criteria for differentiation vary, in different forms of compatibilism. One criterion that has been proposed is the presence or absence of coercion; and a distinction is often drawn between 'external' coercion, for instance threats or sanctions, and 'internal' coercion. It is the latter which is, I think, the more fruitful to pursue, in order to understand how the concepts of autonomy and emancipation, especially in psychoanalysis, may best be analysed. However, I doubt if the concept of coercion is really appropriate here: a better one is 'compulsiveness'.

We can begin to analyse this concept by considering some examples of activities typically regarded as neurotic, such as compulsive hand-washing or theft. In what sense are these compulsive? I propose something along the following lines. In compulsive actions, agents find themselves unable to act in accordance with their beliefs and preferences. For instance, in compulsive hand-washing, the agent typically suffers considerably from the consequences of persistent washing, and sees no benefit accruing from this activity that, in terms of his or her other desires, outweighs this suffering. Yet no amount of attention to the undesired character of these consequences, no amount of effort or determination to disengage from the activity, has any effect. The activity continues, despite constant attempts to end it: the normal degree of control over activity exercised by one's beliefs and desires is absent. A similar situation obtains with kleptomania: despite believing that no desired consequences will follow from theft, the agent is unable to control activity to accord with this attitude.

It should be noted that, on this analysis, there can of course be compulsive *failure* to steal, just as well as compulsive stealing. This would be in line with Freud's view of the operation of the superego as, in effect, a compulsive determinant of 'moral' behaviour. Thus Wilhelm Reich, in his attacks upon 'morality', basically criticized the compulsive character of superego-sustained 'moral' behaviour, and advocated instead the ideal of 'self-regulation'. Freud, by contrast, came to believe that a certain degree of compulsive morality, enforced by the superego, was necessary for the existence of what he termed 'civilization', and thus also for the happiness of individuals. However, the disagreement between Reich and Freud turns largely upon whether Freud was right about the existence of the death instinct, which Reich denied.[48]

But this initial sketch of the concept of compulsiveness needs to be elaborated to meet an important objection: is it not possible for activity to be compulsive, despite the fact that it *does* conform to the agent's beliefs and preferences? For instance, my smoking cigarettes might be compulsive, despite my believing that on balance the pleasure it provides outweighs the risks of suffering involved, and having no other reasons for regarding it as undesirable. To deal with such examples we need to introduce a hypothetical (counterfactual) element into the analysis. Then, smoking would count as compulsive if it were true that, *even if* I came to believe that the risks outweighed the benefits, or indeed that it was a thoroughly undesirable activity that I no longer had any wish to continue, I continued to find myself doing it.

However, the need for another qualification – and one that indicates certain difficulties in specifying an adequate concept of autonomy – is suggested by further consideration of the same example. Perhaps, although it is true that *if* my beliefs and desires changed, the activity would cease, it is none the less compulsive because, in fact, I would display some kind of 'compulsive' resistance to any attempts made to alter these beliefs and desires. For instance, I might stubbornly refuse to take note of medical evidence concerning the risks of smoking; ignore claims made by companions about the discomfort or disgust they experience in my smoke-generating presence; and so on. I display, in some sense, a compulsive impenetrability to relevant information and argument, and remain unmoved by good reasons.

If the analysis of compulsiveness (and thus of autonomy) is to be adjusted to deal with this problem, it seems that we have to talk not just of compulsive actions but also of compulsive, or compulsively held, reasons for actions. In other words, the concept of compulsiveness must include a certain kind of 'resistance to reason'. But this is difficult to define. First, it would seem to require a general specification of what rationality consists in; and this would have to include many different kinds of reason, or reasoning about many different kinds of things – scientific beliefs, moral and political values, the relevance of feelings or emotions to action, and so on. Second, it would be necessary to provide criteria for discriminating between mere disagreement with, and the compulsive rejection of, what is rational (in terms of these standards). I have no suggestions to make here on either of the points. But I think the basic character of this analysis of compulsiveness is correct, and will continue to use it in what follows.

To show how this account can be used to reconstruct Habermas's view of psychoanalysis as emancipatory, we need now to relate the concept of compulsiveness to Freud's theory of the neuroses. This can be done, at least in general outline, by suggesting that the central feature of neurotic activity is its compulsive character; and that this, according to psychoanalytic theory, is due to its control by the repressed elements of the unconscious. The therapeutic process, then, involves the identification and overcoming of those unconscious determinants that render behaviour compulsive. This is what the self-reflective movement from non-freedom to autonomy achieves. It is not though a movement from causality to the absence of causality: autonomous activity is causally determined, but in a non-compulsive manner. Thus the therapeutic process is to be seen as involving the replacement of one kind of causal determination by another. Precisely how this is achieved is a question of the dynamics of the therapeutic situation, in which various techniques are employed by the analyst to enable the transformation to occur.

Further, on the view I am suggesting here, we must also regard the character and outcome of the therapeutic process as causally explicable; though, as will be argued in the next chapter, a theory that explains this process may be only loosely related to a theory that explains the formation of compulsive activity itself. This deterministic view of the therapeutic process does not deny the possible significance, for instance, of self-reflective engagement by the patient as a primary means by which compulsive determinants are removed. But it does require that we see the capacity for self-reflection, its actual operation, and the changes that it can bring about, as causally explicable. In the following sections, I will present a version of neurophysiological reductionism which is, I think, consistent with this standpoint. But before that, some further comments on how this analysis of compulsive activity and the goal of psychoanalytic therapy differs from Habermas's position need to be made.

I argued that Habermas's account of this goal as, in effect, the abolition of the unconscious, involved a depature from Freud in at least two ways: the place of the primary processes, and of the instincts, as ineliminable features of non-pathological activity. In relating the concept of the compulsive to psychoanalysis, I have referred only to the repressed unconscious, thereby excluding the elimination of either of these as a requirement for non-compulsive activity. It seems to me implausible to view phenomena such as dreams or fantasy as compulsive, as undermining autonomy.

As for the (biologically determined) instincts, their relationship to the concept of autonomy is more complex. If there are such instinctual drives then they must be seen at least as placing limits on possible forms of human activity, and thus upon the practical significance of certain possible normative ideals. That is, humans may come to have desires that are not in fact realizable, since the realization would be incompatible with instinctually determined limits. Of course, this issue is extremely problematic because of the difficulties in defining adequately the concept of instinctual drives.[49] (Nor, incidentally, does neurophysiological reductionism entail the existence of such items, as will be seen later.) But if there are such things as instinctual drives (or other such innate elements), it must follow that human autonomy has definite limitations. For it would mean that whatever we wanted or believed, there would be some activities that we would be unable to perform. Whether such inabilities should be described as compulsive, is a somewhat different issue. For one might choose to restrict the application of the concept of the compulsive to those incapacities that are eliminable.

It was Freud's view of the instincts that partly led him, as I argued in the previous section, to regard the rationality of the ego as essentially instrumental, concerned to achieve the most effective satisfaction of their demands. We might wish to modify this picture, for instance by claiming that not all human desires can be understood as derivatives of instinctual impulses.[50] But unless we reject altogether the idea of biologically determined limits upon human activity, we cannot view the ideal of human autonomy in the Promethean way that some of its advocates often seem to, and which is perhaps a consequence of any philosophical position that separates radically the human species from the rest of nature, defining the former only in terms of its species-distinctive features – a view which I criticized in section 4 of the previous chapter.

4 THE REDUCTION OF PSYCHOLOGY TO NEUROPHYSIOLOGY

Having proposed this compatibilist revision of Habermas's view of autonomy as the goal of psychoanalytic theory, I will now try to specify a version of reductionism which is consistent with the proposed concept of autonomy but which preserves an important element in what he regards as Freud's scientistic misunderstanding of psychoanalytic theory, namely the possibility of neurophysiological reduction. As I suggested in the first section, a major reason for Habermas's rejection of Freud's biological instinctualism – and thus for his peculiar understanding of the id – is his general opposition to reductionism, an opposition which is related to his ontological dichotomy between humans and nature. I will argue that reductionism does not entail, though it is consistent with, Freud's instinctualism. Further, the form of reductionism I present does not justify the way that Freud based his conception of psychological processes on a (speculative) neurological model of energy-distribution. Like Habermas, I am sceptical about Freud's use of this model; but for rather different reasons, which I will describe in the final section of the chapter.

The best overall account of scientific reduction has been provided by Ernest Nagel, and I will follow his general approach, though with some modifications.[51] Nagel claims that we should consider reduction as the derivation (and thus explanation, assuming a deductive-nomological model of this[52]) of one scientific theory from another, where each theory is specified in terms of its basic laws. He points out that for such a derivation to be valid, the premisses must include not only statements of the laws of the 'reducing' theory, but also a further set of statements which link the concepts of the 'reduced' to the 'reducing' theory. This requirement reflects the general point that, in deductive arguments, there cannot (non-trivially) be concepts in the conclusion that do not occur in the premises. These additional premises he calls 'bridging statements', an example of which, in the case of the reduction of thermodynamics to statistical mechanics, would be the statement relating temperature to the mean kinetic energy of molecules.

Nagel suggests that different forms of reduction can be analysed in terms of the different character of these bridging statements. Partly now diverging from his account, I suggest there are three possibilities. First, the statements may 'be analytically true, by virtue either of an existing identity of meaning between their respective concepts, or of definitional decisions. Second, they may express claims of contingent identity: that is, the statements' referential terms may be held to identify the same items. In this case, the apparent ontology of the reduced theory is in effect replaced by that of the reducing theory. Third, the bridging statements may specify regular but logically contingent relationships between the items referred to in the basic laws of the theories concerned, these relationships being of a possibly causal nature. I will call the three forms of reduction involving these different kinds of bridging statements, 'conceptual', 'ontological' and 'explanatory', respectively. (It is worth noting that the two best-known recent versions of philosophical materialism as a solution to 'the mind-body problem', namely logical behaviourism and the identity-theory, involve, respectively, conceptual and ontological reductions of mentalistic to physicalistic theories. [53])

It is often thought that any form of reductionism must involve denying the reality of what is 'reduced' to another theoretical level. And this itself is then thought to have undesirable normative implications where what is reduced includes various features of human activity, such as beliefs, desires, feelings, deliberation, and so on, to which considerable significance is normally ascribed in moral and political issues. But although this might be argued with some degree of plausibility in the case of ontological reduction, and perhaps also for conceptual reduction, I do not see how this can be true of explanatory reduction. For here it is not claimed that the items described by the reduced theory are 'really' no different from the items described by the reducing theory. Thus, to propose an explanatory reduction of psychology to neurophysiology does not entail that psychological phenomena are not 'real', and that only neurophysiological events, states, or processes exist. Indeed, quite the opposite seems true: explanatory reduction requires that the theories are about non-identical domains.

However, in saying this I depart from an important feature of Nagel's account. He insists that we should regard reduction as a relationship between (sets of) statements, and not between things or their properties.[54] So, whilst Nagel would in a sense agree that an explanatory reduction does not deny the reality of the reduced items, this is because reduction is concerned only with statements, and not with 'what they are about'. This claim about 'what is reduced' is, I believe, based on Nagel's arguments elsewhere in *The Structure of Science* about the merits of realism as an account of the cognitive status of theories. He says that the difference between realist and non-realist (instrumentalist) views is insignificant: it consists only in a 'conflict over preferred modes of speech'.[55] Now I do not accept this, and I also think that realism is the correct view of the cognitive status of scientific theories. I cannot argue for these claims here; but I will continue to talk in the realist mode, which followers of Nagel can interpret as merely a mode of speech, and which anti-realists will find unpalatable: they will have to provide their own translation.[56]

Where reductionism concerns the relationship between psychology and neurophysiology, the question of realism is of considerable significance (if Nagel is wrong). For explanatory reductionism, from a realist standpoint, involves commitment to something very like the traditional epiphenomenalist solution to the mind-body problem. If psychology is explanatorily reducible to neurophysiology, and both these sciences are about real items, it follows that psychological phenomena such as perceptual experience, bodily sensations, thoughts, feelings, and so on, are the outcome of neurophysiological events, states, or processes. That is, they are epiphenomenal, at least in relation to neurophysiological phenomena, though it would still presumably be possible that they operate as the immediate causes of behaviour, whilst always being effects in relation to neurophysiological items.

Now some people regard this consequence, epiphenomenalism, as showing that either explanatory reductionism or its realist interpretation must be mistaken, for epiphenomenalism has been generally judged as an obviously unacceptable view. But I do not find the usual arguments against it convincing.[57] One is that epiphenomenalism entails the paradoxical consequence that 'the whole of human history would have been just the same even if there had been no psychological phenomena'. Actually, this does not follow. For if psychological phenomena are neurophysiologically determined then, had the former not occurred, then neither would the latter; and 'human history' would indeed have been very different. (This is because the occurrrence of an effect is a necessary condition for the occurrence of its causes, where the latter are sufficient conditions of the former.) Another standard objection comes from an evolutionary perspective: if species-characteristics emerge because of their adaptiveness for the organism why, for instance, should humans experience pain if this has no effects, and cannot therefore be adaptive? But there is a possible answer to this: what is adaptive may be the neurophysiological bases of these sensations, and not the sensations themselves.

The most serious difficulties faced by epiphenomenalism concern the supposed unintelligibility of (even one-way) causal relationships between the ontologically distinct domains of the neurophysiological and the psychological. Perhaps this is an overriding objection. But two points may at least weaken its *prima facie* force. First, of the two traditional rivals to epiphenomenalism, interactionism and materialism, the former shares with epiphenomenalism the supposed unintelligibility of physical-mental causal relations, whilst the latter has its own obvious difficulty, namely its denial of the ontologically distinctive character of phenomena such as thinking and the experiencing of sensations and feelings. Second, I am not convinced that the 'unintelligibility' of neurophysiological-psychological causal relations is any greater than is involved in any form of inter-level explanatory reduction in science. To parody the usual objection to epiphenomenalism: how *could* a change in the chemical composition of the receptor areas in synaptic transmission affect the electrical activity of the neuron?[58]

After this brief excursion into the traditional mind-body problem, let us return to reductionism. Though I cannot argue this here, I believe it is reasonable to accept the possibility of an explanatory reduction of psychology to neurophysiology. At the very least, I think that this kind of reductionism is far more plausible than either of its alternative forms, conceptual or ontological reduction. And I now wish to consider the consequences of explanatory reductionism for the idea of psychoanalysis as an emancipatory process: arguing, in fact, that the two are quite compatible. This will mainly consist in showing that certain supposed consequences of reduction do not follow. Since reductionism has often been opposed on the grounds of its having these consequences, I take it that showing this not to be so provides indirect support for the position.

First, an explanatory neurophysiological reduction of psychology (which I will now call just 'reductionism') does not entail, though it is consistent with, innatism – that is, the view that certain features of the human species are in some sense genetically inherited. The truth or falsity of this latter view would, from a reductionist standpoint, depend upon the actual character of the ontogenetic development of the human neurophysiological system: in particular, upon the relationship between genotypic and environmental determinants. This is a highly complex issue, both conceptually and substantially. It is important, for instance, to recognize that it is conceptually incoherent to think of 'innate' characteristics as those that are determined by genetic factors *alone*, since, from the time of conception, the development of any of an organism's characteristics must result from the relationship *between* genotypic and environmental features. None the less, it may be possible to distinguish between those characteristics that are (relatively) environment-invariant and those that are (relatively) not so: that is, between characteristics which will develop in more or less any of the 'environments' which members of the species normally encounter, and those that are far more sensitive to particular environmental variations. If the concept of innate characteristics is to be used at all, it must be understoood in terms of this kind of contrast.[59] But whether or not there are, for the human species, characteristics that are in this sense 'innate' — and if so, which — is not a question to which reductionism entails a particular substantive answer.

Second, reductionism is compatible with the occurrence of what are often termed 'psychosomatic' phenomena, provided that their usual conceptualization is partly revised. These phenomena range from the relatively straightforward, such as the apparent generation of peptic ulcers by chronic anxiety conditions, to the more esoteric, such as typical somatic forms of hysteria. I will comment briefly on the latter, since the study of hysteria provided an important impetus for Freud's introduction of the concept of unconscious psychological processes. Hysterical symptoms — such as partial paralysis or anaesthesia — often displayed a lack of correspondence between the regions of somatic malfunction, and theoretically intelligible anatomical regions. Thus the malfunction could apparently not be explained by reference to disturbances of normal physiological processes. In other cases, whilst this obvious difficulty for orthodox medical explanation was absent, Freud none the less believed that a psychological explanation was appropriate. For instance, in the clinical histories presented in *Studies On Hysteria*, he and Breuer discuss the case of Frau Cäcilie M., who suffered from:

> a violent pain in her right heel — a shooting pain at every step she took, which made walking impossible. Analysis led us in connection with this to a time when the patient had been in a sanatorium abroad. She had spent a week in bed and was going to be taken down to the common dining-room for the first time by the house physician. The pain came on at the moment when

she took his arm to leave the room with him; it disappeared during the reproduction of the scene, when the patient told me she had been afraid at the time that she might not 'find herself on a right footing' with these strangers. [60]

Frau Cäcilie seemed to them a veritable bundle of such afflictions. A penetrating pain between the eyes in her forehead was, according to her analysts, generated by what she had felt as a 'piercing' look from her grandmother; a stabbing sensation in the heart meant 'it stabbed me to the heart'; a pain, as of nails driven into her head, was analysed in relation to thinking 'Something's come into my head'; and an hysterical aura in her throat, occurring after being insulted, was interpreted via the thought of 'I shall have to swallow this'.

I find these psychoanalytic explanations in principle perfectly plausible – which is not to deny difficulties in their validation. Freud believed such phenomena could be understood by the postulation of unconscious mental processes; and his later development of the concept of the primary processes, in the context of his theory of dream-interpretation, enables one to see how somatic symptoms may be meaningfully related to unconscious thoughts and wishes. In the examples given above, we see the predilection of the unconscious for puns and metaphors, generating the appropriate bodily behaviour and sensations. But there is nothing here that is inconsistent with (Freud's own) commitment to neurophysiological reductionism, provided two assumptions are made: that the operation of the unconscious is itself neurophysiologically explicable; and that the relevant neurophysiological processes are causally related to others, involved more directly in the generation of the somatic hysterical symptoms.

Thus, strictly speaking, 'psychosomatic' phenomena are mis-named, in that their explanation must ultimately itself be 'somatic'. But the concept is none the less very useful. For, in terms of existing knowledge about physical processes – such as the sources of muscular malfunction – there may be no possibility of explanations other than in psychological terms, even though if reductionism is correct, these are themselves to be explained by reference to the complex and largely unknown character of the central nervous system. (Incidentally, many psychosomatic phenomena involve malfunctions of the peripheral areas of the so-called autonomic nervous system that have no apparent causes locatable within that system. The causes are thus dubbed 'psychological'. My version of reductionism suggests that these causes may typically lie in the central areas of the so-called voluntary nervous system. This requires interactions between the two systems, which had until relatively recently been regarded as independent of each other. A defect of Reich's otherwise admirable emphasis on the significance of the somatic character of neurosis, was his exclusive concentration on the autonomic nervous system. This partly prevented him from recognizing the importance of the unconscious primary processes, whose neurological bases cannot be located there, in generating the somatic characteristics of neuroses.[61])

To conclude this discussion of psychosomatic phenomena, it is worth noting one more example: that words can hurt. Clearly the acoustic input of, say, quietly spoken personal insults cannot explain the often painful sensations they cause. Nor indeed can the insulting character of the utterance normally to be understood outside the context of the history of the relationship between insulter and insulted. Some highly complex psychological relationships appear to link the utterance to the sensation. Explanatory reductionism requires us to believe that this mediation is neurophysiologically based, and I see no reason why this should not be so.

I turn now to another supposed consequence of reductionism: that if reductionism is true, then psychotherapy is in principle replaceable by 'neuro-therapy', that is, by some kind of physical intervention in the neurophysiological system. This, I think, is so; but the 'in principle' must be understood here in such a way that, 'in practice', this possibility is almost certainly unrealizable. (Were it to be realizable, however, there would still be important normative issues in the choice between psycho- and neuro-therapy.) For the practical difficulties are not in any simple sense due to the relatively undeveloped state of neurophysiological science. The problem is not that little is yet known that would make this kind of replacement of therapeutic techniques possible, so that all that is needed is a lot more knowledge about a uniquely complex entity, the human central nervous system. Rather the problem is that what is *already* known about this system suggests that the kind of detailed reduction that would be necessary is probably unachievable.

I have in mind the following sorts of considerations. First, with some partial exceptions, the neurophysiological bases of different kinds of human activity are not conveniently located in spatially distinct and independently operating parts of the brain. And even in cases where they to some extent are, in normal functioning, the brain generally appears to display a considerable degree of 'equipotentiality': that is, the same function can often be performed by different neuronal structures when the need arises. [62] Second, even in some of the most successful areas of neurophysiological research, such as investigation of the neuronal structures and processing mechanisms involved in visual perception, what has already been discovered suggests that any hope of a neurophysiological account that would be able to explain the particular perceptual experiences of individuals is unfounded. It is not merely that such experiences cannot be understood as simple functions of the visual information input (or of this together with other sensory information). The difficulty is that although human visual processing may involve mechanisms common to the species, the way in which these actually operate, in one individual at a particular time, will be affected by the past experience (both perceptual and non-perceptual) of that person, by his or her linguistic concepts, by present expectations and mood, and so on. [63] And whilst the general principles upon which each of these kinds of determinant operate may be discoverable, the idea of combining knowledge of these with information about the often unique features of each individual, or even groups of similar individuals, so as to predict or explain their perceptual experiences, is quite implausible.

One other example, from a different (and apparently much simpler) area of neurophysiological research, may be helpful: the study of eating and drinking. To some extent it has appeared possible to locate specific areas of the hypothalamus whose activity controls this behaviour, and to discover feedback systems for these which, for instance, may monitor the concentration of glucose in the bloodstream.[64] But there is obviously a vast gap between knowing this, and being in a position to explain or predict actual human eating or drinking. Past experience, cultural values, emotional states, beliefs about diet, and so on, all influence this. Eating and drinking are complex, socially and individually differentiated activities, and the belief (which I accept) that they have a neurophysiological explanation should not lead to any 'practical' optimism about the possibility of a detailed realization of reduction. For most practical purposes, psychological theories will continue to be far more useful.

What I have suggested here is very much in agreement with Margaret Boden's assessment of the prospects for the neurophysiological reduction of psychology:

> the human neurophysiologist may never be able to offer more than the general principles of brain function. These may perhaps include some differential features of the cerebral mechanisms involved in broadly different types of purposive activity, such as the various instincts and other features marked by the key concepts in a personality theory. But the physiologist may never be able to specify sufficient causal conditions of all those classes of human behaviour that are interesting enough to cry out for explanation and prediction. One could not then explain a man's threat to commit suicide, in any language, nor predict his wife's behaviour should he do so, merely by specifying their physiologically identified brain-states. One would have to rely − as now − on intensional expressions referring to their hopes, beliefs, desires, self-image, and general world-view.[65]

And she concludes:

> Psychology may be empirically reducible to physiology, in principle, even though contingent facts (such as cerebral equipotentiality, as well as the differences between natural languages and between social institutions and conventions) make it extremely unlikely that the reduction will be effected in any thing but a highly schematic form. In other words, psychology may sensibly be said to be 'empirically reducible' to physiology in a weak sense that implies the total dependence of

teleological phenomena on physical causal mechanisms, the absolute necessity of the mechanistic embodiment of the mind, but which does not imply that bridging statements will actually be found to correlate every psychological statement with a specific neurophysiological statement. [66]

I introduced this discussion of what, in practice, were the prospects for reductionism in response to the objection that such a view would involve commitment to the replacement of psycho- by neuro-therapy. I turn now to consider the implications of what I have said for Habermas's objections to Freud's reductionism, which was at times associated with a belief in the possibility of this kind of therapeutic replacement.

5 FREUD'S NEUROLOGICAL ENERGY MODEL

As Habermas notes, Freud viewed psychoanalytic theory as a strictly empirical science, and believed that it would eventually be reducible to neurophysiology. [67] Further, he sometimes claimed that it might one day prove possible to replace psychoanalytic therapy by neurophysiological techniques. For instance in his last work he said:

> The future may teach us to exercise a direct influence, by means of particular chemical substances, on the amounts of energy and their distribution in the mental apparatus . . . . But for the moment we have nothing better at our disposal than the techniques of psychoanalysis. [68]

And twenty years earlier, in the *Introductory Lectures*, discussing whether psycho-analysis was 'a causal therapy' (one that operated upon the causes, rather than the symptoms, of neurosis) he had written:

> In so far as analytic therapy does not make it its first task to remove the symptoms, it is behaving like a causal therapy. In another respect, you may say, it is not. For we long ago traced the causal chain back through the repressions to the instinctual dispositions, their relative intensities in the constitution and the deviations in the course of their development. Supposing, now, that it was possible, by some chemical means, perhaps, to

interfere in this mechanism, to increase or diminish the quantity of libido present at a given time or to strengthen one instinct at the cost of another — this then would be a causal therapy in the true sense of the word, for which our analysis would have carried out the indispensable preliminary work of reconnaissance.[69]

Habermas argues that Freud's reductionism, based on a model of the economics of energy-distribution, is incompatible with his recognition elsewhere of the self-reflective, emancipatory character of psychoanalytic therapy. He notes how Freud tried to define psychological concepts in accordance with this energy-model. Thus, for example, pain and pleasure are conceptualized in terms of the build-up and discharge of energy, and the overall aim of the psychic system is presented as reduction of the tension due to undischarged energy. Habermas claims that this approach led Freud, in his metapsychology, to characterize the function of the ego purely in terms of the economic management of energy. But this, he says, omits just what is revealed in analysis as the major capacity of the ego:

> what does *not* appear among ego functions on the metaphyschological level is the movement of reflection, which transforms one state into another — which transforms the pathological state of compulsion and self-deception into the state of superseded conflict and reconciliation with excommunicated language.[70]

There is something that is correct and important in this criticism of Freud; but it does not require, as Habermas believes, that we reject Freud's general commitment to the possibility of reductionism. That is, I suggest we should be critical of the particular way in which Freud specifies this reduction, and of how this affects his account of psychoanalytic theory, but not thereby of reductionism itself as defined in the previous section. The psychological reality of what Habermas calls 'self-reflective processes' should be recognized; and Freud's energy-model at least conceals their distinctive character. But such recognition is compatible with reductionism though not, probably, with Freud's version of it.

Before developing this response to Habermas, one qualification should be made to his view of Freud's rationale for the use of energy-concepts in characterizing psychological phenomena. It is arguable that Freud was not solely influenced by his early speculations about the energetics of the neurological system, but also by his early clinical experience, and perhaps by the widespread use of energy concepts in commonsense psychological statements. As Jahoda notes, there are:

> a number of clinical observations which cry out for a language of psychic energy: 'the irrepressible nature of the neurotic symptoms (often voiced by the patient in such expressions as "There was something in me that was stronger than me"); the triggering-off of troubles of a neurotic kind following disturbances of sexual discharge . . .' etc. There is a parallel to this in the ineradicable notion of psychic energy in commonsense psychology. We speak of people needing or finding outlets for their energy or concentrating it on one area at the expense of others; when a child seems to have lost his zest we assume that this energy is invested in some secret preoccupation, etc. The need for a systematic approach to the circulation and distribution of psychic energy seems imperative.[71]

However, whilst agreeing with the general direction of these comments, I am sceptical about the implications of her last remark. For it suggests we must conceive of a system of energy-distribution in which, at any one time, there is a determinate total amount of energy quantitatively distributed in various ways (though whether this total is taken to be fixed or variable, and whether an accumulation-discharge model is assumed, is less clearly implied). I am not convinced that either the commonsense or clinical language of psychic energy should be thought to require these kinds of claims about an overall energy-system.[72] None the less, I think it is a defect of Habermas's account of the therapeutic process that these energetic elements are markedly absent. This seems to be due to his almost exclusive concern with the linguistic-communicative features of therapy, and indeed of human activity in general. There is in Habermas's work a strong tendency towards the 'etherealization' of human practice, which leaves little room for its more somatic-experiential character rightly emphasized, for instance, in Reichian therapeutic techniques. [73]

Returning now to the specific nature of Freud's reductionism, I suggest that roughly speaking he worked the wrong way round. That is, he allowed the admittedly speculative neurological energy-model to influence strongly his conceptualization of psychological relationships, instead of first developing theories about these independently, and only then considering the possibility of their reduction to neurophysiology. [74] As Nagel has emphasized, the success of a scientific reduction requires that the reduced theory itself be fully articulated. [75] To try to construct it on the basis of its possible future reduction to an assumed reducing theory – especially when the latter is itself highly speculative – is likely to be extremely misleading. For instance, even if the neurological energy-model were correct, it would not follow that the bridging-statements between its central principles and those of psychoanalytic theory must specify a simple correspondence between the concepts of energy in the two theories. This, whilst possibly attractive on the grounds of elegance or economy, may have little else to recommend it as a plausible theoretical strategy.

For this and other reasons (such as the difficulties Freud encountered concerning the quantitative basis for qualitatively distinct drives, and the implausibility of the tension-reduction goal assumption), [76] I support Habermas's view that psychoanalytic theory should be conceptualized independently of Freud's particular form of reductionism, or at least of some elements of this. And I agree that we should include amongst the functions of the ego the capacity for self-reflective dissolution of the unconscious determinants of compulsive activity. But such a view is compatible with the possibility of a neurophysiological reduction in which, amongst other things, we might hope to discover the bases in the central nervous system for this self-reflective capacity. Nor should we follow Habermas in characterizing the emancipatory process as a movement from causality to its abolition. We, as humans, have the ability to reflect upon our pasts, and to remove from their control over our lives certain unconscious influences. But the process through which this occurs is causally explicable; it involves a capacity that is biologically based and has emerged in the course of the evolutionary history of the species; and we should not assume that because we have this capacity our possible futures are limitless.

5 Theory and Practice in Psychotherapy

In the preceding chapter I examined Habermas's characterization of psychoanalysis as emancipatory. I turn now to the other major element in his view of psychoanalysis as a model for critical social theory, the claim that the criteria of validity for psychoanalytic theory, and of the particular interpretations based upon it, differ significantly from those of both empirical-analytic and historical-hermeneutic sciences. This can be seen as an attempt by Habermas to articulate and justify the general claim made by critical theorists that a distinctive relationship between 'theory' and 'practice' is involved in critical social theories.

Habermas proceeds by examining the relationship between what he calls the 'general interpretations' of psychoanalytic theory, and their employment in the analysis of individual patients in the therapeutic process. These general interpretations are, roughly, the propositions contained in Freud's theories of psychosexual development and the formation of the neuroses. They involve, says Habermas,

> assumptions about interaction patterns of the child and his primary reference persons, about corresponding conflicts and forms of conflict mastery, and about the personality structures that result at the end of the process of early childhood socialization, with their potential for subsequent life history. [1]

Further:

> The learning mechanisms described by Freud (object choice, identification with an ideal, introjection of abandoned love objects) make understandable the dynamics of the genesis of ego structures at the level of symbolic interaction. The defense mechanisms intervene in this process when and where social norms, incorporated in the expectations of primary reference

persons, confront the infantile ego with an unbearable force, requiring it to take flight and objectivate itself in the id. The child's development is defined by problems whose solution determines whether and to what extent further socialization is burdened with the weight of unsolved conflicts and restricted ego functions, creating the predisposition to an accumulation of disillusionments, compulsions, and denials (as well as failure) — or whether the socialization process makes possible a relative development of ego identity. [2]

Apart from the presence here of Habermas's problematic version of the id, [3] this is an admirable summary of these elements of psychoanalytic theory. But Habermas goes on to argue that general interpretations only partially resemble the general theories of empirical-analytic science in their criteria of validity, as can be shown by examining their application to the life-histories of individual patients in the therapeutic process. Such applications he terms 'constructions' — for instance, suggestions by the analyst about particular occurrences in the patient's past; and Habermas claims that:

> The criterion in virtue of which false constructions fail does not coincide with either controlled observation or communicative experience [i.e. with the criteria involved in either empirical-analytic or interpretive sciences]. The interpretation of a case is corroborated only by the successful *continuation of a self-formative process*, that is by the completion of self-reflection, and not in any unmistakable way by what the patient says or how he *behaves*. [4]

So for Habermas the truth or falsity of these constructions — and thus, derivatively, of the general interpretations upon which they are based — is determined partly by how the patient responds to them: that is, by the success or failure of the therapeutic process, itself conceived as a self-reflective movement towards autonomy.

To assess Habermas's view of the criteria of validity for critical social theories, we need first to consider the place of predictions and practical success or failure in the empirical-analytic sciences. I will argue that Habermas's contrast between such theories and the general interpretations of psychoanalysis involves too simple a view of this issue. It will be convenient to begin by examining Karl Popper's well-known attack on the scientific status of psychoanalytic theory, which reveals a similar form of over-simplification.

1 PSYCHOANALYTIC THEORY AS 'SCIENCE': PROBLEMS OF THEORY-TESTING

In a number of autobiographical passages Popper tells us how his early encounters in Vienna with Freudian psychoanalysis, Marxism and Adlerian psychology, and his comparison of them with Einstein's relativity theory, led him to propose falsifiability as the demarcation criterion between science and non-science.[5] In the course of these reminiscences he claims that Freudian theory fails to meet this criterion: its propositions are not falsifiable, and thus not scientific.

The significance of Popper's view can be brought out by considering its implications for the vast literature devoted to the empirical testing (both clinical and non-clinical) of various propositions of Freudian theory. In these studies we find considerable disagreement as to whether any of these propositions are actually supported or refuted by the relevant evidence. For instance, Paul Kline argues that for at least some of them — such as the relationship between child-rearing procedures and the presence of 'anal' character-traits in adults — there is no disconfirming evidence and some positive support; whilst H. J. Eysenck and Glenn Wilson have claimed an absence of support, or some disconfirming evidence, for all of them so far tested.[6] But it would seem that the intelligibility of these disagreements presupposes that Popper's criticism of Freud is mistaken, since the disputed studies all involve attempts to do what Popper claims is impossible — to assess the degree of support for Freudian theory by deriving testable predictions from it. According to Popper this cannot be done: the theory is untestable, unfalsifiable and hence unscientific.

To examine this claim, we must first explore certain difficulties in the falsifiability criterion itself, and its associated account of theory-testing. Popper argues that because of the logical problem of induction it is not possible to verify scientific theories. Such theories consist in 'strictly universal statements', whose possible falsity is logically consistent with any finite amount of supporting evidence: thus they cannot be conclusively verified by establishing the truth of particular predictions derivable from them. Inductive argument, he claims, is not rationally justifiable. But fortunately science – which is for him a paradigmatically rational form of enquiry – does not require the use of inductive argument. It can proceed through deductive argument alone, which is involved in the testing of theories as two distinct points: in the derivation from the theory of testable predictions; and, if these fail, in the argument from this to the falsity of the theory. Theories which have not in their tests been refuted are not to be seen as thereby positively confirmed or supported. Instead, they are said by Popper to be 'corroborated', meaning that they *so far* have not been refuted. But it is essential to his overall position that corroboration is not regarded as providing positive support for the belief that a theory will pass future tests: this, for Popper, would involve mistakenly accepting the legitimacy of inductive argument. [7]

I shall ignore here the debates about Popper's conception of science generated by the work of Kuhn, Feyerabend and Lakatos [8] (though it would be interesting to examine the history of psychoanalysis in terms of their rival accounts), and focus on just two criticisms of Popper's position. [9] First, it seems very doubtful whether any adequate account of the assessment of scientific theories can, like Popper's, do without the idea that successful predictions give some form of positive support to the theories from which they have been derived. To this extent, the 'logic' of theory-testing must be partly inductive. Second, there are at best very few scientific theories that could satisfy Popper's demarcation principle of falsifiability, since it is generally the case that in order to derive determinate predictions from a theory, assumptions that are additional to the propositions of the theory itself have to be made. I shall now elaborate briefly on each of these points.

The first criticism can be justified in a number of ways. For instance, it can I think be shown that scientific practice depends upon the assumption that, other things being equal, a theory that has 'passed' a particular kind of test will continue to do so in future tests of the same kind. Further, it is difficult to understand how it can be rational to base one's actions on well-tested theories, unless their past success is seen to provide some positive grounds for believing that predictions derived from them will turn out to be correct in the future: that is, in this context, when they are acted upon.

However, in saying that one must therefore regard the logic of theory-testing as at least partly inductive, it is important to emphasize that this does not imply acceptance of certain views often termed 'inductivist'. First, it does not mean accepting that any theory can be conclusively verified by reference to positive evidence. Second, it does not entail the view that the logic of evidential support can be mapped onto the calculus of probability statements and their relations; nor that it can be analysed in terms of a frequency interpretation of that calculus. Third, to claim that successful predictions provide positive support for theories is compatible with accepting an a-symmetry between the significance of confirmatory and dis-confirmatory evidence. That is, it may be recognized that negative evidence is a more power-ful reason for rejecting theories than positive evidence is for accepting them; but without thereby rejecting the significance of the latter altogether, as is proposed by 'pure falsificationists' such as Popper. Finally, it seems that any adequate account of positive evidential support must involve comparisons between alternative possible theories. That is, the extent to which successful tests provide good grounds for accepting (provisionally) a particular theory must be partly determined by the relative plausibilty of alternative theoretical explanations of the same evidence. In this respect, I think that most scientific argumentation is concerned with the question of which theory provides the best, or better, explanation; and I doubt whether what philosophers have said about either deductive or inductive argument is of much help here.[10]

Moving now to the second criticism, concerning falsifiability, the basic difficulty is that one cannot derive determinate predictions from most scientific theories without additional assumptions, usually termed 'auxiliary statements'. So whether a theory is falsifiable (and thus 'scientific') may not be knowable at any particular time, since the appropriate auxiliaries may not be available; and it may not be possible to know that they will never become available. One obvious source of this difficulty is the existence of suitable scientific instruments: without these a theory may remain untestable, but clearly this should not by itself lead us to regard it as unscientific. However, once the appropriate auxiliaries are provided, the logical outcome of theory-testing becomes indeterminate with respect to the possible refutation of the theory. For if predictions derived from the theory together with the auxiliary statements fail, all that follows (deductively) is that at least *one* of the premises in the derivation must be false. But which one is false − in particular, whether it is the theory itself or its auxiliaries − cannot thereby be determined. Thus no conclusive refutation of a theory is possible where statements other than those of the theory being tested are required in the derivation of predictions.

These are the basis difficulties for falsificationism.[22] But it will be helpful to add a few further points concerning the character of auxiliary statements. First, it is worth distinguishing two different kinds of auxiliaries: singular statements and theoretical statements. The former are always necessary if predictions about particular phenomena (as opposed to other universal relations) are to be derived from the tested theory. (A simple example of this would be the need to know the actual values of the independent variables in a theory, in order to predict the values of the dependent variables.) The latter, theoretical auxiliaries, may not always be necessary to derive predictions; but very often they are. For instance, any use of instruments will require the theoretical assumptions upon which they are based to be included in the derivation of test-predictions.

The need for auxiliary assumptions (both singular and theoretical) is especially apparent where the tested theory itself involves forms of idealization or abstraction, as most theories in the advanced sciences do.[12] For instance, a theory that uses the concept of a frictionless surface cannot generate determinate 'real world' predictions without additional assumptions about the actual degrees of friction present in a particular surface (singular auxiliaries), and about the deviations from the idealized theoretical relationship that will result from these (theoretical auxiliaries). Finally, a rough distinction can be drawn between those theoretical auxiliary statements that come from the same general theoretical area to which the tested theory belongs, and those that are taken from relatively independent and unrelated areas of theoretical work. An example of the latter would be the auxiliaries involved in using optical microscopes to test a theory about neuronal cell-structures. Here, the auxiliary theory is drawn from optics, and thus from a theoretical area (relatively) independent from neurophysiology.

With these general points about theory-testing and evidential support in mind, we can now return to Popper's criticism of Freudian theory. Its main elements are indicated in the following passages:

> I found that those of my friends who were admirers of Marx, Freud and Adler, were impressed by a number of points common to these theories, and especially by their apparent *explanatory power*. These theories appeared to be able to explain practically everything that happened within the fields to which they referred. The study of any of them seemed to have the effect of an intellectual conversion or revelation, opening your eyes to a new truth hidden from those not yet initiated. Once your eyes were thus opened you saw confirming instances everywhere: the world was full of verifications of the theory. Whatever happened always confirmed it. [13]

Popper goes on to describe an episode in which Adler had 'found no difficulty' in analysing a particular case without ever seeing the person concerned, and had justified his confidence in doing so by his 'thousandfold experience'. Popper says he came to think that all Adler had done was to show in each instance,

> that a case could be interpreted in the light of the theory. But this meant very little, I reflected, since every conceivable case could be interpreted in the light of Adler's theory, or equally of

Freud's. I may illustrate this by two very different examples of human behaviour: that of a man who pushes a child into the water with the intention of drowning it; and that of a man who sacrifices his life in an attempt to save the child. Each of the two cases can be explained with equal ease in Freudian and in Adlerian terms. According to Freud the first man suffered from repression (say, of some component of his Oedipus complex), while the second man had achieved sublimation . . . . [I omit Popper's Adlerian explanation, since I will not be discussing his 'equal ease' claim] . . . . I could not think of any human behaviour which could not be interpreted in terms of either theory. It was precisely this fact − that they always fitted, that they were always confirmed − which in the eyes of their admirers constituted the strongest argument in favour of these theories. It began to dawn on me that this apparent strength was in fact their weakness.[14]

Most discussions of this criticism have assumed that it is fairly clear what exactly Popper is saying. But I do not think this is so, and will therefore proceed by offering a number of different interpretations. The first is that Popper appears to claim that the fact that everything anybody does can be explained in terms of Freudian theory should not be seen as providing massive confirmation for it, but instead as casting doubt upon its scientific status. Taken at face-value, this is a curious argument. For were a theory designed to explain all human behaviour, why should the fact that it can do so actually count against its scientific status, even if we go along with Popper and accept that passing tests shows only that a theory has not been refuted, and not that it is thereby confirmed? Popper, after all, adopts the deductive-nomological model of explanation. So if Freudian theory *can* 'explain everything', this must mean that statements describing every actual (and possible) item of human behaviour can be derived from the theory (together with, of course, appropriate auxiliary statements). Now Popper maintains that scientific status is determined by falsifiability. Falsifiability involves testability; and tests require the derivation of determinate predictions. But if deductive-nomological explanations can be provided, the theory must be testable, and hence scientific: for the logic of explanation and prediction are the same, on this model of explanation.[15]

So it cannot be the case both that a theory can explain everything, and that it is unfalsifiable.

If any plausibility is to be given to Popper's argument, then, we must find another interpretation of it. One alternative might be this: Freudian theory is unscientific because 'it can explain everything' in the sense that for any particular item of behaviour, both its occurrence and its *non-occurrence* can be derived from the theory. Now if this were so it would indeed be an overwhelming objection to the theory: for it would follow that it was internally inconsistent. For if it is true that from precisely the same set of theoretical statements both the occurrence and non-occurrence of some phenomenon can be derived, there must be logical contradictions within this set of statements. (And from contradictory statements any statements can be derived, including further contradictory ones.)

Although Popper does not explicitly claim that Freudian theory is internally inconsistent — and one might expect that he would, if this were his view — this might seem to be suggested by the comments he makes about the hypothetical example of the two men, one of whom pushes a child into the river, whilst the other jumps in to save a child's life. For he suggests that both actions could equally well be 'explained' on the basis of Freudian theory; and this must mean that statements describing both events could be derived from it. However, this by itself would not show that contradictory statements could be derived, since there is no contradiction between the statement 'X pushed a child into the river', and 'Y rescued a child from the river', unless it is also true that 'X' and 'Y' refer to the same person, the child and the river are the same in both statements, and so on.

In any case, Popper also says about this hypothetical example that the former action could be explained by reference to repression, and the latter by reference to sublimation. But if this is so, then even were 'X' and 'Y' to be identical, etc., no internal inconsistency in the theory would be demonstrated, since it would no longer be the case that contradictory statements were derivable from the *same* set of theoretical statements. For in the former case, statements about repression would be present in the assumptions, whilst in the latter these would be replaced by statements about sublimation. Further, if both *explanandum* statements could be derived in this way — and thus the two phenomena explained — how could this show the theory to be unscientific?

So we must try another interpretation of Popper's criticism. Suppose that on the basis of psychoanalytic theory it had been predicted that a person would push a child into a river. And suppose that this does not in fact happen — indeed, that 'the opposite' happens instead. Perhaps what Popper has in mind is that in this and other such cases Freudian theory can remain unrefuted, by substituting 'sublimation' for 'repression' in the set of statements from which the initial prediction was derived. But, if this is Popper's complaint, why should we take it as showing the unfalsifiability of Freudian theory? For all that would be involved would be the substitution of one singular auxiliary statement for another (concerning the occurrence of sublimation instead of repression) together with their related theoretical auxiliaries. In other words, the failure of the prediction is explained by reference to auxiliary statements, not to the main theoretical statements. But as my earlier discussion of theory-testing suggested, there is nothing unscientific about such a procedure.

However — and here we arrive at what seems the only remotely plausible version of his criticism — Popper might go on to claim that such a procedure is indeed unsatisfactory if no justification can be provided for the adjustment other than the fact that by this means the apparent refutation can be avoided: in other words, that the adjustment is entirely 'ad hoc'. But if this is his objection, it would be incumbent upon him to show that Freudian theory is inherently ad hoc in this way. And this seems very difficult to show, though the accusation does point to certain potentially abusable features of Freud's theory. But before briefly discussing these, it is worth dealing with Popper's criticism in the case of his hypothetical example. To avoid the objection that the procedure is ad hoc, all that is required is the possibility of adducing evidence that sublimation rather than repression had occurred, other than the person's child-rescuing behaviour itself. I can see no difficulty in doing this: psychoanalytic explanations are not normally based upon a single occurrence, and possible independent evidence of sublimation should in principle be available.

However, I think it is true that there is a definite potential for 'ad hoccery' in psychoanalytic theory. Consider, for instance, the following (fairly typical) claim by Freud:

> We can at any rate lay down a formula for the way in which character in its final shape is formed out of the constituent instincts: the permanent character-traits are either unchanged prolongations of the original instincts, or sublimations of those instincts, or reaction-formations against them.[16]

Now were this to be all that Freud had to say about the relationships between 'the original instincts' and adult character formation, one could object that this part of his theory is pretty well untestable, since no indication is given of what it is that leads to one rather than another of these three possible processes taking place. In particular the concept of a reaction-formation (like several other psychoanalytic concepts, such as displacement) is especially problematic since, roughly speaking, its supposed presence will generate precisely the opposite behaviour to what would otherwise have been expected. It is therefore a concept with what might be called a 'high ad hoc potential' in explaining away inconvenient phenomena. But this is only a potential: it need not be actualized. In order to avoid the danger, though, Freud's 'formula' here has to be developed in such a way that the conditions in which a reaction-formation occurs be specified independently of the phenomenon which is said to be explained by reference to it. And not only must this be done at a theoretical level, but the attempt must also be made to specify the kind of evidence that would indicate that such conditions were or had been present in concrete situations.

However, as I noted earlier, the absence at a particular time in the development of a theoretical system of the necessary auxiliary statements does not show that the theory is unfalsifiable, and hence unscientific; and the problems just described seem basically to concern the provision of appropriate auxiliaries. So I conclude that there is no good reason for accepting Popper's judgment that Freudian theory is unscientific. But this discussion has put us in a better position to examine the relationship between theory and therapeutic success in psychoanalysis. Thus I turn now to Habermas's view of this relationship.

2 THE CRITERIA OF VALIDITY FOR GENERAL INTERPRETATIONS

Habermas claims that the criteria of validity for general interpretations differ from those of both empirical-analytic and hermeneutic sciences (nor are they simply a combination of the two). He concentrates mainly on the difference from the former, and I shall follow him in this. One major element of the contrast is presented in this passage:

> general interpretations do not obey the same criteria of refutation as general theories. If a conditional prediction deduced from a lawlike hypothesis and initial conditions is falsified, then the hypothesis may be considered refuted. A general interpretation can be tested analogously if we derive a construction from one of its implications and the communications of the patient. We can give this construction the form of a conditional prediction. If it is correct, the patient will be moved to produce certain memories, reflect on a specific portion of forgotten life history, and overcome disturbances of both communication and behaviour. But here the method of falsification is not the same as for general theories. For if the patient rejects a construction, the interpretation from which it has been derived cannot yet be considered refuted at all. For psychoanalytic assumptions refer to conditions in which the very experience in which they must corroborate themselves is suspended: the experience of reflection is the only criterion for the corroboration or failure of hypotheses. If it does not come about, there is still an alternative: either the interpretation is false (that is, the theory or its application to a given case) or, to the contrary, the resistances, which have been correctly diagnosed, are too strong.[17]

But the contrast stated here depends upon Habermas's failure to recognize the place of auxiliary statements in the derivation of predictions from scientific theories. It is of course true that if a prediction *can* be derived from a single hypothesis (together with initial conditions) and the prediction is false (and the statements specifying the conditions are true), then the hypothesis is refuted. But this is not the usual situation in theory-testing. The indeterminacy of outcome which Habermas presents as peculiar to tests of general interpretations is instead typical in testing scientific theories. In the kind of case he considers, the psychoanalytic prediction that, say, the patient will accept a particular construction, will require as one of its assumptions the absence of resistance in the patient. Thus, when the patient rejects the construction it may be that this assumption is false; or that the construction itself is false; or that one or more of the general interpretations from which, together with various singular statements about the patient's past, this construction has been derived, is false; and so on. There is nothing methodologically peculiar about this. For instance, from Newton's first law — that a body will continue either at rest or in rectilinear motion in the absence of external forces — we can predict the actual motion of a particular body only with further assumptions about what forces are operating upon it, and about what laws they are subject to. Failure of the prediction does not refute the law, unless we know these auxiliary statements are true.

There is another feature of the passage just quoted requiring comment, which will help to indicate the extent of the 'gap' between general interpretations, predictions about the patient's production of memories, reflections upon portions of forgotten life-history, and the overcoming of communicative and behavioural disturbances. Now the last of these involves, in effect, some elements of 'therapeutic success'. So it seems that Habermas is claiming it is possible to derive predictions about the successful outcome of the therapeutic process from general interpretations, and then saying that failure of such predictions does not refute these interpretations in the way that failed predictions refute scientific theories.

In general terms, my response to this is the same as that just given for the patient's rejection of a particular construction. But it is worth exploring further the kinds of auxiliaries required to derive predictions about therapeutic success from general interpretations. For, roughly speaking, these auxiliary statements would have to include *a theory about the therapeutic process itself*; and this may involve propositions that are to some extent independent of the general interpretations. So this might be a situation where auxiliary statements are drawn from a relatively distinct area of theory, as in the example given in the previous section, of the use of optical theories in testing physiological theories. If this were so, failure of therapeutic practice might indicate deficiences in the theory of the therapeutic process, and not in the general interpretations of psychoanalytic theory itself.

The fact that predictions about therapeutic results may require auxiliary statements concerning the nature and outcome of therapeutic processes, in addition to general interpretations, also has important consequences for the question of how much confirmation can be provided for these interpretations by successful therapeutic results. I shall comment on this issue later on. But first, the comments just made about the relations between general interpretations and a theory of therapeutic processes must be somewhat qualified, at least in the case of psychoanalysis. For a comparison with the relations between physiological and optical theories may suggest a greater degree of independence between the two theoretical areas than probably exists here. For instance, psychoanalytic therapy makes considerable use of the phenomenon of 'transference', where the patient's feelings towards others, such as his or her parents, are projected onto the analyst. This provides both an aid for the analyst in interpreting the patient's activities, and a means by which the patient can become aware of the nature of these feelings and 'work through' them. So not only is there a partial mapping of the two sets of relationships, with the same theoretical claims potentially explaining them, but the concept of projection employed to explain the process of transference is itself a central one in psychoanalytic theory. Somewhat similarly, the concept of resistance functions both in the theoretical explanation of the therapeutic process and also, partly through its logical relationship to the concept of repression, in these general interpretations. So there is by no means a complete divorce between psychoanalytic theory and the auxiliary statements concerning the therapeutic process. [18]

None the less the derivation of predictions about therapeutic results requires a good deal more in the way of theoretical assumptions than the theory of psychosexual development that Habermas regards as being 'tested' (in a methodologically peculiar manner) in the therapeutic process. And when we take account of these additional assumptions, I believe this supposed peculiarity disappears, depending as it does upon a contrast with an oversimplified view of the logic of scientific theory-testing. However, this is not the only way in which Habermas tries to show what is distinctive about the criteria of validity for general interpretations. He also offers a more positive account (involving a further contrast) as an alternative to their assimilation to the testing of theories in empirical-analytic science, and I will now examine this.

Habermas says that:

> Whereas in other areas theories contain statements about an object domain to which they remain external *as* statements, the validity of general interpretations depends directly on statements about the object domain being applied by the 'objects', that is the persons concerned, to themselves . . .. [Thus] analytic insights possess validity for the analyst only after they have been accepted as knowledge by the analysand himself. [19]

This contrast between scientific theories and general interpretations is further specified as follows:

> When valid, theories hold for all who can adopt the position of the inquiring subject. When valid, general interpretations hold for the inquiring subject and all who can adopt its position only to the degree that those who are made the object of individual interpretations *know and recognize themselves* in these interpretations. The subject cannot obtain knowledge of the object unless it becomes knowledge for the object — and unless the latter thereby emancipates itself by becoming a subject. [20]

In these passages, Habermas appears to make at least two claims: that it is a necessary condition for the truth of any particular psychoanalytic interpretation (and thus, derivatively, of general interpretations) that the patient accepts it; and that, since this self-recognition itself either constitutes or generates 'emancipation', therapeutic success (defined as emancipation) is also a necessary condition for the truth of such interpretations. I begin by commenting on the former claim.

First, Habermas's insistence upon the patient's acceptance as a necessary condition for true interpretations cannot be due to his regarding psychoanalytic theory as a hermeneutic science, and therefore (on some views of the criteria for correct hermeneutic interpretations) requiring agreement by the 'object' of interpretation. For he wishes to show that the criteria of validity for critical social theories, such as psychoanalysis, are distinct from those of both empirical and hermeneutic sciences. Thus he says that:

> As with other forms of knowledge, the testing of hypotheses in the case of general interpretations can follow only those rules that are appropriate to the test situation. Only they guarantee the rigorous objectivity of validity. Whoever demands, to the contrary, that general interpretations be treated like the philological interpretation of texts or like general theories and subjected to externally imposed standards, whether of a functioning language game or of controlled observation, places himself from the very beginning outside the dimensions of self-reflection, which is the only context in which psychoanalytic statements can have meaning. [21]

Second, despite his claim that the patient's acceptance is required for the truth of psychoanalytic interpretations, Habermas also endorses Freud's view that a patient may reject an interpretation which is in fact correct, or indeed accept one that is not. [22] The former case is explained by Freud in terms of resistance: he argues that it is only in the absence of resistance that a patient will agree to the correct interpretation. The overcoming of resistance is, of course, related to the dissolution of repression. For Freud, correct interpretations will only be accepted by the patient when the therapeutic process has succeeded in achieving this. But if this is so, it must be possible to determine the truth or falsity of an interpretation independently of the patient's agreement to it. When resistance and repression are overcome the patient, as it were, no longer has any interest in rejecting correct interpretations. Thus only when the therapeutic process has achieved its aim will acceptance follow.

However, this is not to deny that there are serious problems about the validation of psychoanalytic interpretations, which basically hinge upon the extent to which patients may be said to have some ultimate epistemic 'authority' about the nature of their own unconscious states; and the following brief comments may serve to indicate some of those problems. In the course of the therapeutic process patients may do all sorts of things which, to the analyst, indicate the presence of unacknowledged, unconscious items. For instance, a patient might respond angrily to a particular suggestion as to his or her unconscious feelings towards one of his or her parents. How is this anger to be understood? It might be a defence against a correct interpretation; it might display frustration at the apparent stupidity of the analyst; it might be due to a recent encounter between the patient and someone else, in which a row took place about the personal character of that parent; and so on. Which of these explanations is correct is enormously difficult to judge. Similar difficulties are common in 'everyday life', as well as therapeutic situations. For instance, it seems we sometimes find someone else's interpretation of our motives or attitudes, which we had previously denied or ignored, 'feels' or 'seems' right. And it may be that this 'first person authority', involving some intuitive sense, is the ultimate criterion for assessing such interpretations. But it seems that we often come to revise the judgments previously made with such authority; and also that, in certain situations, and in relation to certain people, we are highly suggestible. Furthermore, our intuitive sense of what is plausible as an interpretation of our unconscious feelings is itself partly influenced by exposure to various theories about the character of unconscious processes, such as psychoanalysis itself. Thus recourse to the patient's acceptance may give a spurious degree of support to psychoanalytic interpretations just because of the cultural influence of psychoanalytic concepts.

The one point that seems clear is that without some resolution of these kinds of difficulties, Habermas's view that the patient's acceptance and self-recognition is a necessary condition for the truth of psychoanalytic interpretations cannot be accepted. So I turn now to his other claim, about the successful outcome of the therapeutic process as a criterion of validity. To assess this in detail one needs to give a specific meaning to the idea of therapeutic success. I shall discuss this issue in the last section of the chapter. For the moment it will be sufficient to assume a fairly loose definition which follows Habermas's emphasis upon achieving autonomy, itself understood as the absence of compulsiveness (discussed in section 3 of the previous chapter).

If Freudian theory is correct, the sources of compulsive activity lie in certain repressed, unconscious states or processes generated in the course of the patient's life-history; and the theory attempts to specify how in general these arise, through what mechanisms they produce neurotic systems, and so on. It follows that if by suitable therapeutic techniques these determinants of the patient's present behaviour can be removed, the goal of psychoanalytic therapy will be at least partly achieved. But the hypothetical is crucial here; for it cannot be said that psychoanalytic theory by itself guarantees either the effectiveness of any particular set of therapeutic techniques, or indeed that any such effective techniques can be devised. That is, the truth of psychoanalytic explanations of the formation of the neuroses is consistent with the failure of therapeutic practices guided by psychoanalytic theory. For although that theory both indicates what needs to be achieved in the therapeutic process, and also provides some theoretical claims about what kinds of techniques may prove effective (such as the use of transference, free association in the interpretation of dreams, and so on), it is quite possible that additional theoretical knowledge would be required, which is not derivable from psychoanalytic theory, to enable effective therapeutic techniques to be developed. Thus successful results of psychoanalytically guided therapeutic processes cannot be regarded as a necessary condition for the truth of psychoanalytic theory: indeed its truth is compatible with a considerable degree of pessimism about the possibilities for therapeutic success. [23]

The question of pessimism will be further explored in the

next section, where I note how some ways in which the relationship of a critical social theory to successful practice has been defined seem logically to exclude the possibility of a true theory with pessimistic predictions. But before pursuing this, two more comments need to be made about Habermas's account of psychoanalytic theory's criteria of validity. First, not only is therapeutic failure compatible with the truth of general interpretations, but therapeutic success through the use of typical psychoanalytic techniques may not give very strong support to them. For it is possible that the effectiveness of such techniques may be explained by a non-psychoanalytic theory. That is, there may be features of the psychoanalytic process which are responsible for whatever success is achieved through it, and the theory that explains why this is so may neither support, nor be supported by, psychoanalytic theory itself. There may, for instance, be ways of removing the compulsive character of neurotic activity which do occur in the therapeutic process, but whose possible theoretical rationale is either unknown, or clearly divergent from the psychoanalytic rationale. This of course is simply a special case of the general point about theory-confirmation noted in the previous section: positive evidence supports a particular theory only to the extent that other theories are unable to explain it or, if they can, to the extent that they are in other respects less plausible.

Second, Habermas appears to believe there is a close link between the patient's acceptance of a psychoanalytic interpretation, and a successful therapeutic outcome: 'the subject cannot obtain knowledge of the object unless it becomes knowledge for the object − *and unless the latter thereby emancipates himself by becoming a subject*, [my italics]. But it is unclear whether he is claiming here that 'becoming a subject' directly results from self-knowledge, or whether the former is an additional process, for which the latter is only a necessary condition, so that both are necessary but partly independent conditions for the truth of psychoanalytic interpretations. I have argued that neither is a necessary condition. But it is worth adding that there is nothing in Freudian theory to suggest that acceptance by itself guarantees a successful therapeutic outcome, since this would ignore (as Habermas tends to throughout) the affective or emotional processes that must be involved in successful therapy, in addition to the cognitive ones. The sense in which acceptance could be a sufficient condition of therapeutic success, in psychoanalysis, seems to be that only when resistance has been overcome, will the patient in fact accept the interpretation. But this would make acceptance the result rather than a determinant of therapeutic success, as I suggested earlier.

3 THEORY AND PRACTICE: THE PLACE OF SELF-FULFILLING
  PREDICTIONS

So far I have argued that Habermas fails to show through his account of psychoanalysis how the relationship of theory to practice differs from that of empirical-analytic or hermeneutic sciences. This does not of course mean there is nothing valuable in his conception of critical social theory, in particular of how such a theory should be guided by an interest in (practical) emancipation; but this may be accepted without also believing that such a theory has distinctive criteria of validity. So I will now examine Brian Fay's account, in *Social Theory and Political Practice*, of how a critical social theory's criteria of validity are tied in a distinctive way to successful practice. Fay's position is strongly influenced by Habermas's, but it has the virtue of including a more explicit account of the supposedly distinctive criteria. [24] However, this virtue has its costs, since I think it reveals more clearly the difficulties of this position.

Fay argues that critical social theories should be addressed to those already experiencing various frustrations and dissatisfactions in their lives, and be designed to aid them in finding a way out of this situation. Partly, this will involve helping them achieve a better degree of self-understanding; and because of this a critical social theory must include hermeneutic elements. Further, such a theory must help its 'clients' come to recognize how various structural features of their society contribute to their plight, and thus help dispel the ideological concealment of such processes. But also, Fay says, a critical social theory must indicate to its clients 'a means by which they can solve the problems which are facing them'; and the truth of such a theory *is thereby judged partially on the basis of whether the satisfactions which it promises are forthcoming*.[25]

As Fay himself partly acknowledges, it is not clear from these requirements alone how this conception of critical social theory differs from positivist or hermeneutic accounts.[26] For it could be argued that, at least with appropriate auxiliary statements (and I shall exclude this complication here, since it has been sufficiently explored in the previous section), it will often be possible to link scientific theories with 'guides to practice' by deriving predictions about the likely outcomes of possible courses of action. It is of course true that many theories are developed without attempting to specify such practical links; but the demand that these be provided makes no difference to the epistemological status of the theories, even if it may be often be a rather difficult demand to satisfy. What is it then that does make critical social theories' criteria of validity distinctive? Fay's answer is contained in the following two passages, the first of which carries on directly from the quotation above:

> It follows from this that the objects of study of this science —
> the social actors about which it seeks to provide an
> understanding — actually help to determine the truth of this
> science's theories by their reaction to them. According to the
> critical model, one criterion of the truth of social scientific
> claims is the response which these people make to these claims,
> and it is for this reason that the application of its purported
> truths requires a central and determining role for the actors who
> are to be affected by it.[27]

The kind of 'response' Fay has in mind here is presumably indicated by this:

> the theories of such a science will necessarily be composed of,
> among other things, an account of how such theories are
> translatable into action, and this means that the truth or falsity
> of these theories will be partially determined by whether they are
> in fact translated into action.[28]

This seems a strange requirement. Not only must a critical social theory inform its clients what they can do to reduce their dissatisfactions, but its truth is to be determined, not just by whether, if the recommended action is taken, these are reduced, but also by whether in fact this course of action is performed. Thus a critical social theory will be refuted by its practical recommendations being ignored rather than (or in addition to) these activities failing when they are performed. I suggest a number of objections to this claim.

Fay says that this distinctive criterion of truth actually follows from the fact that critical social theories are designed to be 'translatable into action'. I cannot see why this is so. It may be possible to derive predictions about the outcomes of courses of action from a theory; but there is no reason for expecting that from the very same set of statements it would also be possible to derive the prediction that when this recommendation is offered to the clients the advice will be taken. To make this kind of prediction we would normally have to add to the initial set of premisses a further set of statements describing some theory about the effects of the dissemination of (various kinds of) theories upon the activities of (various kinds of) human agents. And it is quite possible that this theory would be largely independent of the theory from which the initial 'advice' was derived. If Fay wishes to propose that such theories about the effects of theory-dissemination be developed, well and good; but this is a different matter from his claim about actual translation into practice as a condition for the truth of action-guiding theories. One might perhaps revise Fay's position by saying that it is *pointless* to produce theories which are or will be ignored by their clients; but this would be a significantly different claim that has no implications for the criteria of validity of critical social theories.

It might further be objected that Fay's position is not only epistemologically mistaken, but could also be politically dangerous. For there are hints in what he says that theories can be validated by the self-fulfilling character of their predictions; and if this were to be accepted it might seem to legitimate certain abuses of social theory which, I am sure, Fay would not wish to encourage. In a footnote to the passage I have been commenting on, he says that one of the reasons he has for saying that translation into action only partially determines the truth or falsity of a critical social theory is that:

a theory might be constructed but then lost before it was disseminated, and one would hardly want to claim that, because it never affected social life, it was therefore false. A critical social theory is one which offers an account of future social developments and how they will occur partially because of the existence of this account itself, and if, as a result of the account's not becoming known, the social order develops along lines other than the theory predicted, then the truth of the theory is indeterminate [i.e. rather than its being refuted].[29]

I think it follows from this that where a social theory *is* disseminated, its predictions about a future social development can be confirmed by the fact that those who take notice of it then act in such a way that this development occurs; and presumably if they act so as to prevent its occurrence this would refute the theory. Now imagine the following situation. Some social theorists adopt as their clients a group which feels frustrated and dissatisfied by the presence of non-white immigrants in Britain. They develop a theory to explain how immigration has resulted from the economic relationships between Britain and various other countries, and predict that racial tensions will result in armed conflict between immigrants and non-immigrants. This prediction causes the existing tensions to increase, their clients join the National Front, and eventually the armed conflict results. The predicted rivers of blood begin to flow; and the theory from which the prediction was derived is thereby confirmed in an epistemologically impeccable manner — if this distinctive criterion of validity for action-guiding critical social theory is accepted.

It is important here to be clear about precisely what sorts of claims are contained in the theory from which this self-fulfilling prediction is derived. For although it is true that any prediction that something will happen is confirmed by the occurrence of what is predicted — that is, the future-tense statement is true if what it says will happen, does happen, *whatever* the reason for this occurring − it does not follow from this that the theory from which the prediction was derived is thereby confirmed. For it may be that this theory does not in fact explain the occurrence of the predicted phenomenon, since what actually caused this to occur (in this case, the dissemination of the theory and/or its prediction) is not included in the premises from which this prediction was derived. To illustrate this general point a different kind of example may be helpful. From a theory about the causes of cancer it may be predicted that someone will die within a certain period of time. The person does die, but from a road accident and not from cancer. Clearly, the truth of this prediction does not confirm the theory about cancer; nor would it be confirmed if the person died from an anxiety-related disease brought on by coming to hear of the prediction derived from the cancer-theory.

If these comments about the confirmatory significance of self-fulfilling predictions are correct, then a critical social theory whose predictions succeed as a result of their dissemination is not thereby confirmed. What might be instead confirmed is a different theory, namely one about the effects of the dissemination of social predictions. Now from the standpoint of this latter theory, all that matters is the consequences for people's actions of their coming to hold certain beliefs − such as the belief that what has been predicted from the original theory will indeed happen. It is irrelevant in this context whether this belief is true or false. That is, the theory about the consequences of prediction-dissemination, which may enable us to predict that if people believe a certain prediction is true they will act in ways that make it come true, is indifferent to the *truth* of that belief, being concerned only with the consequences of its being held. Thus the possibility of explaining why (and predicting that) a disseminated prediction may come true does nothing to justify the theory from which that prediction was initially derived. Indeed, it seems that the reverse is generally the case. For if it turns out that a necessary condition for the predicted event's occurrence is that the prediction be disseminated, and affect people's actions, then the success of this prediction must suggest that its initial derivation was not justified, or that its premisses were not true.

It might be argued against this that it may be possible to develop a critical social theory which itself includes propositions specifying the effects of the dissemination of predictions, and that this would avoid the above objection, which depends upon a strict separation of the two theories. This, I think, has to be accepted. But such a theory would not then be able to be used in the way that Fay advocates for a critical social theory. It could only function successfully in what he would surely (and rightly) regard as a manipulative fashion. For this theory would depend for the success of its predictions on being able to predict the consequences of their dissemination. But it would not at the same time allow for the consequences of people not only being informed of these predictions, but also being informed of the basis upon which these have been made, since this would introduce another possible influence on their behaviour, a further factor which would not have been included in the theoretical premisses from which these predictions had been derived. That is, dissemination of this theory (which includes statements about the consequences of dissemination of predictions) will alter the situation upon the consequences of which the original predictions were partly based. And it can be seen, I think, that any attempt to take account of this additional influence by yet further premisses must fail, if the additionally 'augmented' theory is itself to be disseminated.

Thus any theory which tries to take account of the social consequences of the dissemination of predictions can do so only by a strategy of at least partial concealment, of non-dissemination of (some of) its own assumptions. Yet it is a central feature of Fay's account of a critical social theory that those who develop it operate in a relationship of openness and honesty with their clients. Indeed, he argues that this is one of the crucial differences between critical and positivist social theory: the latter, he believes, implies a form of political practice in which social science is used by an élite of experts to control people's behaviour, in a way that excludes the latter's active participation in the process of change, through an open dialogue with theorists. But if my argument about the use of self-fulfilling predictions to confirm social theories is correct, this confirmatory role can only exist in precisely the kind of theorist-client relationship that Fay wishes to reject. Thus it seems either that self-fulfilling predictions are logically irrelevant to the truth or falsity of a social theory, or that they can only be relevant in theories which require for the success of their predictions a 'manipulative' attitude of concealment on the part of theorists towards their clients.

There is one last point to make about Fay's account of critical social theory, which concerns the possibility of pessimism. He argues, as do many other critical theorists, that such a theory must show its clients a 'way out' of their present condition. It must discover the possibilities of change in the existing social structure, and must guide the activities of those who are frustrated, oppressed, and so on. [30] And it appears that this requirement is to be regarded as at least one element in the criteria of validity for such a theory. This seems to me epistemologically bizarre. For it would entail that a critical social theory cannot both be true and pessimistic in its diagnoses. That is, it would mean that any theory which failed to discover possibilities for change in the desired direction was thereby falsified. Optimism becomes an epistemological precondition of a correct social theory.

But this would rule out the possibility of social theories whose consequences suggest that certain otherwise desirable developments have little or no possibility of realization, at least within the reasonably foreseeable future. One might of course argue that theories which are designed to point the way to a better future, but which fail to indicate that and how this might be achieved, are of little value. But to suggest that just because of this, their analyses of the past or present are to be rejected as incorrect or inadequate, seems absurd and unnecessary. We can adopt views as to the most useful or beneficial aims and directions for theoretical work, without at the same time allowing the criteria of validity for the results of such work to be (partly) determined by the justifiability of these views. (This is related to my discussion of the place of values in social theory, in section 3 of chapter 2, where I argued that the adoption of normative standards of significance to determine the problems to which a social theory is directed should not affect the criteria of validity for assessing the content of that theory.)

Thus the epistemological character of critical social theory must allow the logical possibility of pessimism, the discovery that there are limits in the present or future to social transformations. As I noted in section 2 of the previous chapter, it is a feature of Freud's theory of the id that there are biologically determined, innate limits to human activity. I am not concerned here with whether this is in fact so, or whether his particular claims as to the nature of these limits are correct. Rather, I am saying that we should not adopt an epistemological account of critical social theory which logically excludes the truth of any such claims.

4 THEORY, TECHNIQUE AND THEORY OF TECHNIQUE

At various points in this chapter I have emphasized the logical gaps between psychoanalytic theory and the success or failure of psychoanalytic therapy, so that the failure of therapeutic techniques is compatible with the truth of this theory, whilst the success of those techniques may provide little support for it. I have argued that this is primarily due to the fact that in deriving predictions about therapeutic outcomes from psychoanalytic theory, a number of auxiliary statements must typically be assumed, whose own truth or falsity may display various degrees of independence from the explanatory claims made within this theory. Such auxiliaries may usefully be said to comprise a 'theory of technique': that is, an attempt to specify and explain the effects upon the patient of various elements of the therapeutic process. Thus even in those cases where predicted therapeutic success is achieved, it is possible that neither psychoanalytic theory nor its associated theory of technique are significantly supported, since it may be that this success is better explained by an alternative theory of technique.

I want now to explore some implications of these points for understanding the relations between 'theory' and 'practice' in psychotherapy, an exploration which will be continued in the following chapter. I will no longer confine myself to the discussion of psychoanalysis alone, but will consider other types of therapeutic approach such as behaviour-modification, Reichian body-therapies, various kinds of group-therapy, and so on. My basic suggestion will be that there is a legitimate place for a considerable degree of eclectic pragmatism about therapeutic techniques, which partly divorces the assessment of their effectiveness from questions both about their own theoretical rationales, and about the adequacy of possible explanatory theories of the formation of the 'neuroses'. And I now put this last term in scare-quotes, since I do not wish to imply that the concept of therapy should be limited to what is regarded within psychiatry as 'pathological' human activity. For one of the major developments in the field of psychotherapy in the past couple of decades has been the extension of therapeutic techniques to people whose 'problems' do not fall within the standard psychiatric classifications of either neurotic or psychotic disorders. In, for example, the consciousness-raising activities of women's and men's groups, and in the general phenomenon of the 'growth movement' and 'humanistic psychology', precisely this extension has occurred. Overall I think these have been desirable and fruitful developments, with important implications for traditional conceptions both of political activity and of the distinction between 'normal' and 'pathological' human action. [31]

Consider the following example. A man comes to notice that in his relationships with certain other men he experiences an unusual degree of anxiety which, in various ways, makes him unhappy or dissatisfied in his encounters with them. For instance, he may find that in situations of mutual disagreement he is unable to conduct himself as he would otherwise wish: he becomes angry too quickly, his mind goes blank at the crucial moment when he needs to respond to what has just been said to him, he becomes confused, feels panic-stricken, withdraws resentfully, or suchlike. He is puzzled as to why this happens, does not know how to deal with it, and gains neither insight nor ways of improving such encounters from reflection, conversations with friends, and so on. So he becomes a member of some kind of therapeutic group to explore these difficulties. A lot of different things may then happen, some of which might prove helpful.

He might try 'acting out' a typical past encounter, with another member of the group whom he chooses, and being told to state at various points precisely what he is feeling. It might emerge that he suddenly fears that the other person is going to hit him. He is then asked if he can remember being hit by anyone in the past, and who that was. He remembers a childhood episode in which that occurred, involving his father. This episode is then itself acted out, with perhaps other members of the group taking the parts of his mother and sister. He re-experiences something of the fear he had then felt, and perhaps the resentment at not having been rescued or protected by the others. This resentment may 'feed back' into his feelings about other members of the group, in terms of his present relationships with them. He might then also become aware of further dissatisfactions he feels in his relationships with other adults: perhaps that they do not look after him sufficiently, that he is unsupported, vulnerable and so on.

I present this as a reasonably typical example of the beginnings of a therapeutic process. A certain kind of self-exploratory insight is perhaps achieved, in that present difficulties are related to past experiences, and connections between previously unrelated features of his life are suggested. There is nothing sacrosanct about the particular techniques that enabled this to happen: others might have done equally well, and indeed might have 'revealed' something quite different. For instance, he might instead have focused upon another feeling generated in the initial acting-out, say of humiliation or defiance, and have been instructed to follow through that feeling, aided by a particular breathing-technique, to see what emerged; or to engage in an 'internal dialogue' between the humiliated and defiant 'parts' of himself. In all these kinds of ways, some form of therapeutic insight may result.

However, the question I am most interested in about this example is: what is the relationship between the use of these therapeutic techniques, the explanation of this person's difficulties in relating to other men, and the successful resolution of those difficulties? My answer, roughly, is quite likely very little. More specifically I suggest that both of the following are possible: that as a result of this kind of therapeutic experience these difficulties either fade away or are significantly diminished despite the fact that the apparent source of those problems which emerged in that process does not correctly explain their origins; or, that although their origins were correctly identified, he finds that he is no better off when he takes part again in the previously problematic encounters. In other words, therapeutic experience may prove to be successful despite the explanations it 'reveals' being mistaken; or it may prove unsuccessful despite those explanations being correct. And in the former case, why it is that those techniques were effective may remain quite unknown; or their supposed theoretical rationale may be incorrect. Thus therapeutic success, explanatory theories, and theories of technique, may display a high degree of logical independence from one another.

It will be helpful in pursuing this claim further, to consider the contrary view: that therapeutic success requires that the techniques which produce it are based upon a correct explanation of the origins of the person's problematic experiences. As we shall see, whether this view is accepted depends partly on how the success of therapeutic outcomes is defined; and this, I will argue, is itself partly a normative issue.

One way of defending this contrary view would be to claim that success in changing human activity ultimately depends upon the correct identification of its causal determinants. Although we may occasionally come across an effective technique without an adequate explanatory theory, this will always be a more or less random matter; and to do better than this, to have the best chance of arriving at a reliable technique, we must understand the actual sources of the problematic experiences. Thus, in the example considered, the effectiveness of therapeutic techniques must remain a hit or miss affair unless it is discovered whether, for instance, the pattern of anxiety is rooted in the past relationships of this man to his father, and whether this itself must be understood in terms, say, of Freud's theory of the Oedipal conflict.

Against this I suggest that it is often possible to develop quite reliable 'rule of thumb' techniques for change, which do not depend upon acquiring explanatory knowledge. For instance, suppose that in this example, the person reports a few months later that he is still experiencing precisely the same difficulties as before. It might then be suggested to him that he deals with these by training himself in certain anxiety-reducing techniques, such as meditational or breathing exercises, and that he uses these before or during his problematic encounters; or, that he rehearses different ways of dealing with these episodes by acting out preferable scenarios with other members of the group. He follows one of these suggestions, and finds that his anxiey disappears. The successful use of such techniques requires no explanatory theory, not even a theory as to why the technique works. (This would be similar to the present use of acupuncture in treating physical illnesses.) Furthermore, even if a correct explanation of why such situations provoked anxiety had been provided, such non-explanatorily based techniques might still prove necessary.

Two objections might be offered to this. First, it might be argued that the person's initial difficulties may be shown, for instance through a psychoanalytic explanation, to be only one specific manifestation of an 'underlying problem', so that techniques addressed purely to reducing the anxiety will leave unresolved all the other ways in which, say, the unsatisfactory outcome of the Oedipal conflict are or will be expressed. Otherwise, there may result simply a process of symptom-substitution. Second, it might be said that the 'successful' use of the anxiety-reduction techniques cannot be regarded as a genuinely successful therapeutic outcome: to regard it as such misrepresents the proper goal of therapeutic processes. I will consider these replies in turn.

The first one, I believe, depends not upon any *general* claim that can be made about the relationships between explanatory theories, the success of techniques, and theories of technique, but upon the actual truth or falsity of various substantive explanatory theories, such as psychoanalysis itself. For instance, if it is in fact true that repressed unconscious feelings 'live on' within us, maintain their causal power, and can be re-directed in an indefinitely large number of ways (emerging as different 'symptoms'), then certain kinds of therapeutic technique are very unlikely to succeed. But, of course, if this general prediction can be derived from psychoanalytic theory, we must accept the converse point: namely, that if it in fact turns out that these kinds of techniques are successful, this must cast doubt upon the truth of psychoanalytic theory. So we cannot dismiss the possible success of techniques that are not based upon correct explanatory theories *a priori*. Rather, whether or not they are successful will be relevant (though only indirectly, for the reasons outlined earlier in the chapter) to the substantive truth or falsity of particular such theories. For instance, it might turn out that after a period in which the person in my example used his anxiety-reduction technique as a 'prop', he found that he could increasingly often do without it. The sources of the anxiety had, as it were, atrophied. If this were so, it would count against an explanation in terms of unconscious forces which, according to Freud, do not wither away.

I turn now to the second reply, that such a technique would not produce 'genuine' therapeutic success. This depends upon how such success is to be defined, as can be seen by considering the following possible definition of therapeutic success: that it should reduce the extent to which our activities are determined by influences which we do not recognize, and which reduce our capacity to exercise conscious control over our lives. Although this is only a rough outline of a possible goal of therapeutic processes, it is sufficiently specific to generate an interesting consequence: that, *by definition*, no technique can be successful unless it involves some form of self-understanding about the sources of one's present discontents. In other words, the goal of therapy is defined here in terms of an ideal of self-understanding, so that the sort of technique for dealing with anxiety mentioned above would be logically excluded from counting as 'successful' (though such a technique might still be useful to provide the 'emotional breathing-space' necessary for the process of self-understanding to develop satisfactorily). But it is important to note that this way of showing that technique must be tied to explanatory theories is quite different from another way in which this might be argued: namely, by claiming that *as a matter of fact* it is only possible to achieve therapeutic success (defined this time, say, as 'the removal of the distressful feelings') if the persons concerned come to understand the sources of their difficulties. It is possible that this is so: but only if a particular kind of explanatory theory, and associated theory of technique, are actually true.

It must not be thought that there is anything suspect about the former definition of the goal of therapy as self-understanding. Rather, I want to emphasize the diversity of possible definitions, and that what counts as therapeutic success (and thus also what is acceptable as a therapeutic technique) is partly, and necessarily, determined by goal definitions. If, for instance, we adopt as the therapeutic goal the removal of some form of emotional distress, then what might be an 'effective' technique may differ from, say, techniques that are 'effective' in increasing people's range of choices, or that make them 'better adjusted to the demands of society'. That is, the effectiveness of a technique is determinable only in relation to a definition of therapeutic success. And it seems to me that this latter question is ultimately normative. Distress-reduction, more autonomy, better social adjustment, and so on: these are different and often competing therapeutic goals, and — if my arguments about values and social theory in chapter 2 are correct — they are not themselves scientifically resolvable. Further, it is I think clear that many of the debates about the relative efficacity of different therapeutic techniques — such as psychoanalysis versus behaviour modification — are due partly to concealed normative disagreements about therapeutic goals.

The issues raised by questions about psychotherapeutic goals, and their relations to other political and moral values, will be a central concern of the next chapter. But there is one final point to be made here, to avoid a possible misunderstanding of what I have suggested so far. In talking of the effectiveness of techniques being necessarily judged by reference to a normatively specified therapeutic goal, I am not endorsing the view that the means-ends relationship can be straightforwardly mapped onto the science-values dichotomy.[32] For not only will the norms that specify a particular goal be relevant also in evaluating the legitimacy of the means for achieving it; but *other* norms may also be relevant to this evaluation. In the case of therapeutic technique the same is true. For instance, even if our primary therapeutic goal is the relief of distressful feelings (such as anxiety or depression), it does not follow that the only relevant standard in evaluating techniques is their 'effectiveness' in achieving this. Suppose, say, that the use of electro-convulsive or chemo-therapy could be shown to relieve depression: we might still legitimately reject such techniques on other grounds, such as the absence of self-reflective engagement by the person treated, the power-relations involved in the therapist-patient relationship, and so on. It is entirely mistaken to claim, as some advocates of these techniques seem to, that objections on these grounds merely counterpose 'value-judgements' to effective practice'. For effectiveness cannot be specified independently of values, and the character of a therapeutic technique, as well as the goal to which it is said to contribute, must be subject to normative evaluation.

6 The Complexity of Norms in Practice

A recurrent theme in the normative vocabulary of critical theorists is a series of related contrasts between two kinds of social practice. On the one hand there is domination, manipulation, control, technical rationality and distorted communication. On the other there is emancipation, autonomy, self-reflection, reason and undistorted communication. Critical social theories are said to be concerned with a critique of the former, aimed at the realization of the latter. I have argued that it is a mistake to construct an epistemological account of critical social theory that ties its criteria of validity to the successful realization of emancipatory values. But I now wish to challenge what might be called the 'normative naivety' displayed in the way these values have often been specified and justified. In particular, whilst Habermas's work marks a significant advance over some earlier attempts to do this — especially in his more recently developed theories of truth, the normative presuppositions of communication, and the ideal speech situation, which I will discuss later in the chapter — it nonetheless fails to recognize the complexity of normative issues in social practice. I shall begin by indicating this complexity in the context of a particular form of practice, psychotherapy, through discussion of a number of examples of different therapeutic situations.

1 THE POLITICS OF PSYCHOTHERAPY

We can usefully identify three different dimensions of a therapeutic process, within each of which normatively significant issues arise:

(1)   The nature of the goal, and thus of what counts as a successful therapeutic outcome.

(2)   The kind of technique that is employed.

(3)   The form of relationship between 'therapist' and 'patient'. [1]

Habermas's account of psychoanalysis, which he presents as a model for the general character of practices guided by a critical social theory, can be seen to specify the ideal form of these dimensions as follows:

(1)   The therapeutic goal is emancipation, or *autonomy*, understood as the elimination of compulsive, unconsciously determined patterns, and the achievement of directly intelligible conscious-purposive activity and communication.

(2)   The techniques must involve *self-reflection* by the patient, who comes to understand the sources of his or her distorted communications in a previously repressed life-history.

(3)   The analyst-patient relationship is one of *enlightenment*, in which the analyst uses access to psychoanalytic theory to aid the patient in a self-reflective process. Patients, it is assumed, come to the analyst through their own choice and desire for change.

To this picture of psychoanalysis we can counterpose a type of therapeutic situation which appears to display a quite antithetical character in each dimension: the use of behaviour-modification regimes in, say, an institution for 'emotionally disturbed adolescent offenders' convicted of legal offences. [2] Here, attempts are made to alter behaviour patterns defined as socially undesirable by controlling the contingencies of reinforcement: that is, by determining which activities are to generate 'rewarding' consequences, such as money, privileges, or cigarettes. In terms of the three-dimensional framework, such a therapeutic process would look like this:

(1)   The goal is to eliminate 'maladjusted' behaviour, this being defined by people other than the patients.

(2)   The technique involves no significant element of self-reflection: it consists in controlling the environmental variables influencing behaviour, and at most relies upon

a degree of rational calculation of consequences by the patients.

(3) The analyst relates to the patient through an institutionally supported a-symmetry of power, and makes no use of theoretical knowledge to enlighten the patient.

So here we have a type of therapeutic process which represents the complete antithesis of Habermas's favoured case of psychoanalysis. And there are other examples which would display a similar contrast — for instance, the use of compulsorily administered drugs in the same kind of institutional context. However, without denying the significance of this contrast, we must not be misled by it into accepting an exhaustive and exclusive dichotomy between two sorts of therapeutic process. Rather, we must recognize both that the normative character of each dimension may vary independently of the others; and that within each, there is a complexity of issues that is not captured by critical theorists' normatively dichotomous concepts. Both points will be illustrated by considering a number of therapeutic situations that differ from the two so far presented.

First, consider someone who decides to alter their own behaviour by the use of the same kinds of modification techniques as in the second example. In order to stop smoking, say, this person tries to organize his or her environment so that behaviour incompatible with the activity is reinforced, and the existing reinforcements for smoking are removed. (A similar case would be someone, or some couple, who made use of Masters and Johnson techniques to deal with a problematic pattern of sexual activity.[3]) Here, despite the absence of self-reflection, there is also an absence of any dominative power relationships between analyst and patient. It is a freely chosen, self-administered behaviour modification programme; and any theoretical knowledge involved is directly used by the patient. (In this respect, we might even prefer this to the psychoanalytic situation where, as I will point out later, problematic issues about power and control may well arise.) The therapeutic goal seems not to be autonomy, but simply the elimination of an undesired pattern of behaviour: indeed the patient might be quite happy to substitute a different, equally compulsive pattern (say, chewing gum) for the previous one. Nor is it obvious why this should be regarded as objectionable, or inferior to the goal of autonomy — the patient, in effect, 'autonomously' decides that one compulsive pattern is better replaced by another. Further, it may be that the initial pattern is seen as undesirable partly because it interferes with the patient's successful pursuit of other potentially autonomous activities.

Consider now another type of therapeutic situation. The patient, suffering some standard set of neurotic symptoms, decides to seek help from a therapist who uses techniques and theories derived from Reich's earlier writings.[4] In particular, the therapist believes that childhood episodes of repression leave their mark in both psychic and somatic forms. Thus an important therapeutic technique is the identification of various muscular rigidities and distortions in the patient's body, and the attempt, by physical manipulation, massage and breathing methods, to release some of the unconscious feelings and emotions which are present in the patient's bodily 'armouring'. In this way, repressed elements that are embedded (both literally and metaphoriclly) in the patient are brought to the surface, and their compulsive power eventually overcome, with corresponding changes in musculature and posture.

How is this therapeutic process to be characterized, in the three-dimensional framework? The goal, we may say, is emancipatory; and the therapist makes use of a privileged access to theoretical knowledge in guiding the process. But it would be difficult to claim that the technique was self-reflective, at least in the same way that Habermas presents psychoanalysis as being. A lot of what the therapist does involves direct intervention upon the patient's body. Indeed, in one ordinary sense of the term, this body is 'manipulated' by the therapist, at times quite painfully. And, more generally, the therapist is likely to pay as much attention to what the patient's body reveals — for instance, in tensions, types of facial expression, movement, vocal qualities and so on — as to what the patient actually says. The overcoming of resistance may take a somatic form, with a physical struggle between therapist and patient. (Incidentally, according to

Reich this would not involve a metaphorical use of the term 'resistance'; if anything, its usual psychological sense should be seen as metaphorically derived from this physical form.[5])

To some extent, however, this contrast between Reichian technique and Habermassian self-reflection is too strongly drawn, since elements of the latter may also be manifested in this kind of therapeutic situation. Somatic techniques may be used to identify (and partly to discharge) feelings whose sources in the patient's life-history then become subject to reflective processes — though it remains the case that Habermas's picture of self-reflection is extremely rationalistic and non-experiential by comparison with the Reichian alternative. Further, some of the features of the power-relationship between analyst and patient that can be present in psychoanalysis (and which Habermas's concept of 'enlightenment' perhaps tends to obscure) may also be shared here. My next example is partly designed to focus on this issue.

Consider two people who agree to act as co-counselling partners, with perhaps a fairly vague aim of understanding themselves better. They both attend a course, learning about the theory and technique of co-counselling; or perhaps they read a therapeutic self-help manual.[6] The basic structure of their co-counselling sessions is that each takes it in turn to be 'patient' and 'therapist' respectively, specifying, when patient, what kinds of interventions they wish the therapist to make. This might vary from complete passivity on the part of the therapist to quite active engagement — for instance, suggesting possible connections between things the patient has said, asking him or her to repeat some phrase with apparently powerful emotional undertones, or offering to take part in an acting-out exchange. At the end of the session, each partner comments on how useful or otherwise the other's interventions have been.

I will assume that both the goal and the technique of this process correspond fairly closely to Habermas's account of psychoanalysis. But what of the patient-therapist relationship? It might be argued that one of its advantages, by comparison with the standard psychoanalytic situation, is that various a-symmetries of power are removed or reduced in the co-counselling process. Each may 'enlighten' the other in turn, but not on the basis of any privileged access to theoretical knowledge or supposed expertise. If either one, as patient, becomes suspicious about the motives of the other, as therapist, this can be challenged and dealt with on the basis of a presumed equality; so the risk that therapists may protect themselves from acknowledging how their own feelings toward the patient are affecting the therapeutic exchange is reduced. Similarly, the therapist becomes vulnerable to the patient, by engaging also as a patient in this reciprocal process.

To present this comparison in terms of 'advantage' is, of course, to suggest that there may be important considerations which count against the desirability of what Habermas describes as a relationship of enlightenment. It is worth distinguishing two possible objections to this relationship. One is that the standard psychoanalytic situation is prone to various abuses, such as the therapist's antipathy to the patient being concealed under the guise of impersonal expertise, or the therapist's failure to recognize, say, his or her own projections on to the patient. The other is that even without such abuses, the very structure of the relationship is undesirable since it involves a number of important inequalities, especially those of expertise and emotional vulnerability. These may of course be reduced or outweighed by other features of the psychoanalytic relationship: for instance the requirement that therapists undergo a training analysis, or the 'fact' that the professional analyst does have theoretical and technical knowledge without which the patient cannot achieve self-understanding. The point I wish to make, though, is that these are problematic questions, to which differing normative commitments are relevant, and they cannot be resolved by simply endorsing the psychoanalytic relationship as one of 'enlightenment'.

There is another aspect of this comparison between the therapeutic situations of co-counselling and psychoanalysis that raises a further general issue about the normative character of therapeutic processes. In co-counselling the equality between the partners basically takes the form of reciprocity. The two people exchange roles: but the role-differentiation itself is not removed (unlike, to some extent, my earlier example of imposing upon oneself a behaviour modification programme). There is therefore some sense in which each, as therapist, treats or regards the other as an 'object'. That is, each in turn relates to the other in a way which, whilst difficult to specify precisely, seems to involve elements of what critical theorists might regard as a 'technical' interest or attitude.

What I have in mind is that this therapeutic attitude involves the suspension of many important features of normal personal interactions. The therapist is expected to avoid reacting to what the patient says or does in terms of its personal significance for the therapist. The focus is exclusively upon the patient's life, not the therapist's. The kinds of feelings, emotions and judgments which in 'normal' contexts would be generated in the therapist by the patient's actions and communications are kept in abeyance. The therapist's task is to try to understand what is going on for the patient, and to intervene in ways that will aid the therapeutic process. There is a suspension of what Strawson has usefully described as 'the reactive attitude';[7] and the therapist's own interests, which might otherwise often conflict with the patient's, are regarded as inappropriate bases for his or her responses to the patient.

The character of this therapeutic attitude may be further illustrated by introducing one more example of a therapeutic situation, the encounter group.[8] Here, in effect, the rules are that the reactive attitude should have priority – indeed, in an unusually heightened form since in everyday life this attitude is often suppressed, with varying degrees of awareness that this is being done. Of course, the encounter group situation is a special or artificial one, in that the normal consequences of reactive displays in everyday life are themselves partly suspended: the rules legitimate such responses, and protect people from various sanctions that would in other contexts probably apply to them. Further, the encounter group may have a leader, who practices the therapeutic attitude towards the members of the group. But in other such groups, of a self-help kind, the role of therapist may be permanently or temporarily abandoned; and I shall consider only this special case.

In this situation a therapeutic process may occur, with the goal of autonomy, and with at least partially self-reflective techniques, but with no therapist-patient relationship. Members of the group help one another towards the therapeutic goal; but not by the adoption of what I have described as the therapeutic attitude. Instead, they do this as it were 'unintentionally': at the level of their immediate motives in relating to others, they adopt a reactive and not a therapeutic attitude. At another level, of course, they may be making a mutual commitment to aiding one another in the therapeutic process. They offer to each other, as their contribution to this goal, their own feelings and responses. In this respect, therefore, the leader-less encounter group differs from the other examples by the absence of an 'objective' therapeutic attitude.

This contrast between objective and reactive attitudes suggests that the concepts of manipulation, control and so on, often characterized in terms of the idea of treating or regarding a person as an 'object', are highly complex and problematic. What we have, in effect, are a number of quite different senses of manipulation or control, and their absence, many of which correspond to equally distinct contrasts between 'person' and 'object'. I will now identify some of these, making use of the preceding discussion of different therapeutic situations.

First, manipulation or control may be said to occur where one party to a relationship is invested with various kinds of coercive authority or power, such that the other party's wishes, interests or goals are permitted to determine their actions only when they accord with the former's. My example of the behaviour modification regime in an offenders' institution displays this type of relationship. But it also displays a quite different kind of manipulation, the treating of persons as 'objects' in the sense that their feelings, deliberations, aims and so on are systematically ignored by the exclusive focus upon physically describable behaviour, without reference to any so-called 'mentalistic' features.[9] However, this form of 'viewing people as objects' is not a necessary element in relationships involving the previous sense of manipulation. For that kind of a-symmetry of power may be maintained in a way that takes full account of the 'inner life' of the dominated party – which is why psychological torture is often so effective, in both the cells of the police State, and the recesses of family life. We might put this point by saying that many forms of manipulation actually require that someone is viewed as a 'person', not an 'object'.

But in yet another sense of manipulation, namely direct intervention and control of someone's body, manipulation may occur in situations free from this kind of power relationship, as in the somatic techniques of Reichian therapy. Of course, here the patient's body is not regarded exclusively as a physical object, in that the 'embodied' sensations, feelings and emotions are also crucial elements in this process. None the less, certain other elements of the patient's non-physical being are much of the time accorded little significance, such as the deliberative and rationalizing processes that he or she normally relies upon outside the therapeutic situation. Yet it may be that it is precisely by means of this kind of 'manipulative' process that the ideal of autonomous existence can be achieved. Thus, here, treating the person as an 'object' is the way of realizing an emancipatory goal: though in doing this it may also be discovered that our nature as humans is far more closely tied to our bodily existence than previous recognized.

This last point is related to my discussion in section 4 of chapter 3 of the diversity of forms of being, and the error of defining humans only in terms of their species-distinctive characteristics. For some ways in which the contrast between 'person' and 'object' is drawn fail to recognize these points. (Incidentally, such contrasts between persons and things may tend to legitimate ways of relating to non-human living beings that take no account of their sensations, feelings and so on – such as factory-farming). I argued in that chapter that the properties defining different object-domains should not be seen as constituted by different interests. It can now be added that, in trying to identify the normatively significant features of therapeutic processes (and indeed other kinds of social practice), the distinctions between technical, practical and emancipatory interests are inadequate, since we cannot differentiate the various types of therapeutic situation in these terms alone. For instance, what I have described as the therapeutic attitude, which seems to be endorsed in Habermas's conception of enlightenment, could in one sense be said to display a technical, objectifying interest. Yet at the same time there are other, equally significant forms of control or manipulation in therapeutic situations which require for their conceptualization different senses of 'object', 'control' and so on. Thus, I do not think the typical normative vocabulary of critical theory can deal with the complexity of norms in practice.

Having examined this contrast between emancipatory and objectifying or manipulative attitudes, we are in a position to comment on the claim made by critical theorists that a positivist social science is unacceptable because it must display the latter when used as the basis for social practice. There are several distinct issues here. First, I see no reason why a positivist social science can only be used in situations characterized by the kinds of power a-symmetry discussed above, involving either institutionalized coercion, or relationships based upon the assumption of differential degrees of theoretical expertise. Second, though, it does seem possible to argue that social practices guided by such a science may be unable to recognize many of the characteristics of humans that distinguish them from other 'objects', both inorganic and organic. This is because, as I noted in section 2 of chapter 1, the positivist conception of science typically limits a science's ontology to what is observable; and items such as human emotion or deliberation tend thereby to be excluded as scientific objects. [10]

Thus, for example, I doubt whether psychoanalytic theory can be accepted as genuinely 'scientific' from a positivist standpoint, since so many of its central concepts (such as the unconscious, or resistance) seem not to satisfy positivist requirements for the admission of theoretical terms into science. If psychoanalytic theory is to be used as a basis for therapeutic practice, we would at least have to accept a theoretical realist conception of science in place of positivism. None the less, a social theory that 'recognizes' human capacities such as emotion or deliberation can itself be used in ways that are, in important senses, dominative, manipulative and suchlike. A subtle understanding of human motivation and feelings can provide the 'ideal' means by which individuals or groups maintain their control over others. And conversely, the kind of knowledge produced by a positivistically conceived social science, such as behaviouristic psychology, can be used in situations involving egalitarian social relationships and the uncoerced choice by individuals as to how they wish to change their lives. The ontological adequacy of theories, and the normative acceptability of their employment, are thus in many respects quite independent questions.

There is one final aspect of therapeutic practices that I will mention, which raises several questions about the use of psychotherapy as a model for the relations between critical social theory and political practice. This concerns the specification of the goal of a therapeutic process. So far I have said little about this, except for noting some distinctions between the elimination of compulsiveness, the relief of unwanted or distressful feelings or patterns of behaviour, social adjustment and self-understanding. But clearly there are many further issues that arise in this context, and which have a number of moral and political dimensions. Consider, for instance, the example presented in the last section of the previous chapter, in which a man 'discovers' during a therapeutic session that he feels insufficiently protected or nurtured in his present relationships with women, perhaps due to the character of his childhood familial experiences. What are the possibilities now open to him? He might decide – perhaps on the suggestion of the therapist – that he will try in future to be more demanding in his relationship with his wife. Indeed, he might also discover that he finds it emotionally difficult to make such demands; and he might be aided in this respect by further therapeutic techniques. So off he goes to his home, and proceeds to make precisely the kinds of demands of his wife that, viewed from a certain normative standpoint, exemplify a general pattern of domination of women by men, one feature of which is the ascription of nurturing, emotionally supportive roles to the former.

Alternatively, in this same example, suppose the following happens. The man discovers that his childhood-rooted pattern of anxiety in relation to certain other men is preventing him from achieving some kind of satisfaction·that requires a sense of effectiveness and personal contribution in his working life. Having rid himself of these debilitating anxieties, he goes off deciding to assert himself by, for instance, borrowing some money and setting up as an entrepreneur. Later he finds that his therapeutic experience gives him the necessary confidence to 'stand up for himself' when confronted by trade union negotiators. And all this is encouraged and reinforced by his therapeutic experience.

So this 'successful' therapeutic process produces someone who is better able to contribute to the reproduction of dominative sex-role differentiation, or of capitalism. As I argued at the end of the previous chapter, 'success' can only be defined by reference to moral and political values; and these are relevant not only to the character of the patient-therapist relationship and therapeutic techniques, but also the goals of the process. But this last dimension itself involves issues that go well beyond debates about the relative merits of autonomy, adjustment, or the relief of distressful feelings. For it also involves questions about sexism, socialism, individualism and so on. To ignore these questions is to fail to recognize the normative complexity of the therapeutic process. To think that they can be resolved by specifying the ideal of a critical social theory as 'emancipation' is simply naive.

The fact that the conduct of therapeutic processes involves these kinds of political and moral issues also suggests that one should be sceptical about the possibility of using an account of psychoanalysis as a model for other areas of critical social theory and political practice. Of course, the legitimacy of doing this depends partly on just which features of psychoanalysis are being proposed as a model for what; and I find it difficult to get clear about which are the analogies Habermas intends to draw. For instance, he seems at times to suggest a parallel between the 'critique of ideology' and the psychoanalytic 'critique' of neurosis, partly through his conceptualization of both ideology and neurosis as forms of 'distorted communication', and partly through the suggestion that both involve 'unconscious' processes.[11] But this latter point, at least, is misleading. For on Habermas's reading of Freud, the unconscious is identified with the repressed; and this is one important reason for his claim that a necessary condition for the truth of psychoanalytic interpretations is their acceptance by the patient. For in accepting such interpretations, the patient is recovering something that had been temporarily 'banished' from consciousness.[12] But the same is not true of ideology: the 'victims' of ideology may in some sense be said to be 'unconscious' of certain things, but surely not of things that they had at one time been conscious of, and then repressed. To free oneself from ideology is not to recover a lost element of one's past.

Further, the implausibility of conceptualizing ideology by analogy with the repressed unconscious suggests that one cannot directly use the psychoanalytic concept of autonomy as the overcoming of compulsiveness, in order to specify the goal of a critique of ideology. Instead, we should view this kind of critique as involving the criticism of forms of consciousness and social practice by reference to normative ideals or values, many of which are quite distinct from a conception of emancipation based upon the character of psychoanalysis. For, as my last examples were intended to show, achieving therapeutic autonomy is consistent with the adoption and practice by an 'emancipated' patient of attitudes and values that are by no means unobjectionable. And I do not see how their acceptability or unacceptability can be determined without going well beyond the normative concepts supposedly illustrated by the model of psychoanalysis.

However, in his more recent work Habermas has attempted to develop a theory of the rational foundation of norms which involves many concepts and claims that have not been examined up to this point. So I turn now to consider these.

2 COMMUNICATION, TRUTH AND THE IDEAL SPEECH-SITUATION

For critical theorists, positivism removes the possibility of a rational critique of society. I argued in chapter 1 that whilst this might be so for some positivist doctrines, it is not for others: in particular, the value-freedom of science. And in chapter 2, I presented a conception of value-free social theory that was at least compatible with the rationality of values, which could themselves then function in social theory in a way that preserved the independence of its criteria of validity from normative commitments. In now examining Habermas's attempts to provide a rational foundation for normative claims, this view of the relation between science and values will be assumed. Indeed, it seems that Habermas himself may now have abandoned some of his earlier claims about the distinctive criteria of validity for critical social theory. For instance, McCarthy notes that in *Legitimation Crisis*, 'his analysis does not exhibit the type of theory-practice relationship delineated in his [earlier] method-ological writings.'[13] This, I think, is correct; and though I will not argue the case here, I believe that the theoretical programme articulated in that book, and in other writings since then, could be encompassed within the kind of epistemological reconstruction of critical social theory that I have been advocating.

Two main components can be identified in Habermas's work towards a rational foundation for normative claims.[14] First, there is an argument which links participation in communicative activity with the anticipation of what he calls an 'ideal speech situation', whose existence requires the realization of certain normative ideals such as the absence of ideological distortions and a-symmetries of power. The crucial intermediary steps in this argument involve his consensus theory of truth, and the place of what he calls 'discourse' in the validation of truth-claims. Second, he argues that this ideal speech situation also provides the procedure through which rational decisions about the normative issues involved in the organization of society can be made. I will examine these arguments in this and the following section, respectively. Throughout, there are two basic questions that concern me: how successful is Habermas in establishing the values he intends to; and how adequate would these be, if established, as a basis for resolving the kinds of normative issues that typically arise in moral and political decisions?

Habermas believes it possible to construct a theory of 'communicative competence', a 'universal pragmatics' which identifies the universal rules presupposed in human communication, in addition to thrse involved in syntactical competence.[15] Drawing on Austi ı's and Searle's work in the philosophy of language he argues that all speech acts presuppose four types of 'validity claims', concerning comprehensibility, truth, truthfulness (roughly, the speaker's honesty or sincerity) and rightness (roughly, appropriateness in relation to relevant norms). The goal of any communication is to reach an 'understanding' (*Verständigung* – the precise meaning of this term will be discussed in the following section), which consists in 'the intersubjective mutuality of reciprocal understanding, shared knowledge, mutual trust and accord with one another'.[16] Habermas argues that if in the course of ordinary communicative interaction this goal is not achieved, it will be necessary (at least in the case of truth and rightness claims) for the participants to move to a special form of communication which he terms 'discourse'.

In discourse, every assumption of the disputed claims becomes open to question and critical discussion. For truth claims, we have 'theoretical discourse', and for rightness claims, 'practical discourse'. Both require the existence of an ideal speech-situation, whose basic characteristic is the absence among participants of every motive other than 'the unforced force of the better argument'.[17] But this general requirement can only be met if a number of specific conditions are realized. There must be no barriers to open communication arising from repressed motives or self-deception; there must be no relations of domination or control between the participants; and there must be a genuine equality in the opportunities for each to engage effectively in the discursive argumentation.

This account of the discursive validation of problematic claims is used by Habermas to construct a consensus theory of truth for 'theoretical' statements (roughly, scientific statements), according to which their truth consists in what would eventually be agreed upon as a result of discursive argumentation in an ideal speech situation. For instance, he says that 'the *truth* of a proposition stated in discourse means that everybody can be persuaded by reasons to recognize the truth claim of the statement as being justified';[18] and that 'I may ascribe a predicate to an object if and only if every other person who *could* enter into a dialogue with me *would* ascribe the same predicate to the same object'.[19] He regards this as preferable to both pragmatic and correspondence theories: the latter, in particular, he rejects because of its naive objectivism about the relationship between language and reality.[20] However, the merits of Habermas's position as a theory of truth are not altogether relevant to a concern with its possible use for the rational foundation of norms, as I will now argue.

It will be helpful to distinguish three different elements in a theory of truth. First, there is the definitional question of the meaning of 'truth', 'true', etc.: that is, of specifying what truth consists in, what it is for a statement to be true. Second, there is the question of what standards or methodological rules can be used in assessing the truth or falsity of a theoretical claim. Third, we may also be concerned with what kinds of social institutions or procedures are best suited to the successful, rational application of those standards; and with whether these social requirements can only be fulfilled given the existence of further features of social or political organization external to the immediate context of scientific argumentation.

Now, although it seems that Habermas intends his consensus of theory of truth to provide an answer to the first of these questions, it may be that even if it fails in that respect (as I think it does, for reasons which I will not go into here[21]), it is none the less acceptable as an answer to one of the other questions. In particular, I suggest it should be considered in relation to the third, concerning the social requirements for the optimum application of the standards appropriate for the assessment of truth-claims. There is, though, a slight problem here in interpreting Habermas's view of these standards. From what he says, it is not always clear how specific these are to particular types of discourse. That is, it might be that he adopts only a general account of critical argumentation, applicable to all theoretical and practical discourses; or that he also accepts, for instance, specific criteria governing the assessment of evidential support for theories in empirical-analytic science, which differ from those in hermeneutic-historical science, and from those appropriate to practical discourse. In what follows I shall assume the latter interpretation. [22]

We can now present Habermas's argument for the rational foundation of norms. Engagement in communication requires that certain validity claims are established. Where doubt arises about any of these – in particular about truth claims – recourse must be had to discursive argumentation. The successful operation of the standards applied in theoretical discourse requires the existence of an ideal-speech situation. So this situation, the norms it involves, and whatever further social conditions are necessary for their realization, are in effect entailed by communicative activity. It is not consistent, therefore, both to engage in communication and to reject these values. But humans are necessarily communicative beings, so they are implicitly committed to these values.

There are a number of steps in this argument that may be questioned. First, even if communicative activity does involve the validity claims Habermas specifies, it is not clear that engagement in this activity requires commitment to the possibility of their discursive assessment. As Habermas himself notes, the institutionalization of theoretical discourse is by no means a culturally universal phenomenon. In Western Europe, for instance, he seems inclined to identify its emergence, at least in the case of empirical-analytic knowledge, with the rise of modern science. [23] There are, as it were, many societies which manage without theoretical discourse. However, this by no means disproves this step in the argument: that people fail to recognize what is presupposed or entailed by what they do, is both logically possible and a familiar occurrence.

It may be helpful here to consider the way Apel has defended a position very similar to Habermas's.[24] Like Habermas, he contrasts his own position with Popper's 'critical rationalism', which in many respects parallels both his and Habermas's. Popper, whilst endorsing the claim that rationality consists in the possible subjection of any statement to the process of critical argument, in which every assumption is open to challenge and refutation, argues that one cannot provide a rational justification for engaging in this kind of process in the first place. There must be an initial non-rational commitment, a 'leap of faith'. Apel argues that this is a mistake on Popper's part, and is due to his failure to extend the concept of rationality to the presuppositions of *communication*, as distinct from the more restrictive view that rationality consists only in the deductive validity of relations between *statements*. That is, whilst Apel accepts that no deductive proof of the necessity for critical argumentation can be provided – at least, none with premises that are themselves unchallengeable – he believes it possible to show that, from the intrinsically social-pragmatic standpoint of communication, the unavoidability of commitment to the practice and norms of critical argument can be established.

I shall not pursue this issue any further. Instead, I shall go on to examine the later moves in the overall argument assuming, in effect, that it is addressed to those who do accept the need for discursive validation of truth-claims.[25] The main question I wish to focus upon is whether it is true that the ideal speech-situation is a necessary condition for the optimal application of the relevant standards of critical argumentation in theoretical discourse. To answer this, it will be helpful to make a rough distinction between two sets of features that together define the ideal speech-situation, which I will term 'psychological' and 'political'. The latter consists in requirements such as the absence of a-symmetries of power, and the existence of equal opportunities for participation, which I will discuss shortly. In the case of the former, the guiding principle is that participants should be motivated solely by 'the unforced force of the better argument', or, as Habermas puts it elsewhere, 'all motives except that of the cooperative search for truth are excluded'.[26] It would seem that this is intended to rule out at least the following sorts of motivation: those involving unconscious influences, and those displaying certain forms of self-interest. But it is by no means obvious that either of these requirements is necessary for successful theoretical discourse.

Consider, for instance, the frequent expression of unconscious (or at least unacknowledged) aggression or defensiveness in intellectual arguments. It may well be that this is an undesirable feature of the personal interactions involved in argumentation, but I am doubtful whether what makes it objectionable is that the rationality or truth of the outcome is thereby undermined. Or consider the possibility that there is a connection between engagement in certain forms of intellectual activity, and typical manifestations of the anal character, namely parsimony, orderliness and obstinacy.[27] Is it plausible to maintain that these unconscious psychological influences would necessarily distort the outcome of rational enquiry: might they not instead produce a useful degree of tenacity and determination for the individual's engagement in this activity? To put the question more generally, is the obsessional compulsive intellectual less likely, other things being equal, to make positive contributions to theoretical discourse? Further, if we accept Freud's view (noted in section 2 of chapter 4) that the unconscious is not to be identified solely with the repressed, and that its primary processes may well improve the operation of conscious activities, Habermas's requirement would seem to be potentially counter-productive.

Similar doubts arise for the elimination of personal interests. It might be argued that, say, the pursuit of prestige, or personal hostilities, or religious convictions, can often motivate people to engage successfully in theoretical discourse. For instance, accounts of major episodes in the history of science often seem to reveal that, hidden beneath the official picture of scientific activity as determined by an impersonal pursuit of truth, we find instead just these kinds of personal motives.[28] Yet this need not be seen as undermining the rationality of science. For it could be claimed that the impersonality of the standards for scientific argumentation does not require a corresponding impersonality of individual motives. Instead, the need is for an institutional framework in which any distortions that do arise from such sources can be detected and challenged. But the successful functioning of the framework does not necessitate a particular set of motives or attitudes on the part of individual partipants, however desirable these might be for other reasons.

Turning now to the political dimensons of the ideal speech-situation, I again confine myself to indicating some possible difficulties in Habermas's position. These can be brought about by presenting what are, in effect, three competing models for the social organization of theoretical discourse. Two of these, which I will call 'liberal' and 'conservative', could be seen as represented (very) roughly by the positions of Popper and Kuhn. The third, which I will call 'radical', is intended as a possible interpretation of Habermas's position.

According to the liberal model, the social organization of theoretical discourse should parallel the system of rights typically advocated within the political theory of liberalism. These would include: freedom of speech and thought; the absence of discriminatory practices based on religion, sex, race, property, income, occupation and so on; equal opportunity to hold office; the assessment of proposals or claims on their intrinsic merits and not on the personal or social characteristics of their authors; and the making of decisions by reference to explicitly stated impersonal criteria, whose application to particular cases is open to public discussion and criticism. To borrow Popper's phrase, this organization should display the features of an 'open society'; and it may also be argued that this can only be guaranteed for theoretical discourse if the same features are present in the wider society.

The radical model, by contrast, can be understood by analogy with a particular kind of critique of liberalism. According to this, liberal rights can only be made effective (that is, effectively equal) by removing social and economic inequalities which undermine the ability of certain groups or individuals to actually use their formal rights. For example, the radical argues that the equal right to free speech can only be effectively exercised if everyone has full access to the resources necessary for their views to be widely heard and listened to, such as newspapers and television; and this itself might well require an equalization of income, wealth and education. Further, it will be necessary to eliminate the various a-symmetries of power and authority which prevent people's opinions being genuinely taken account of. To have the right to say what one likes is of little value if the opinions expressed have no chance of affecting the decisions being made. Thus equal rights require also the equalization of material resources, power, authority and so on. So the radical model of the ideal speech-situation for theoretical discourse involves analogues of the conditions necessary for the effective equality of liberal rights in the organization of society; and these conditions may also be argued to require implementation not only within the organization of theoretical discourse, but outside it also.

Whereas the radical model takes liberalism as its starting-point, and then radicalizes it, the conservative model entirely rejects many of the central features of both − indeed, it in effect rejects the ideal of discourse. Its starting-point is that the rationality of decisions cannot be specified in terms of the impersonal application of rules. Instead, the concept of rationality is analysed in terms of the judgments of individuals or groups vested with a certain form of authority, which is not itself justifiable (or challengeable) by reference to abstract standards. What is reasonable is what those with the appropriate authority judge it to be. And although such judgments may later be revised, we are not to accept a view of theoretical discourse according to which all assumptions are open to doubt and criticism at any time, with every member of the relevant intellectual community having an equal right to dispute or reject its basic principles or beliefs. The community itself is hierarchically organized; and those who enter it must undergo a lengthy period of apprenticeship, in which they acquire skills and expertise through their relationships with more authoritative members. Finally it may be argued, as in the case of the liberal and radical models, that for this social organization of theoretical discourse to succeed, similar features must be present in the wider society.

I will not attempt to evaluate these three models, though I believe there are plausible elements in each of them. But I want to emphasize two points. First, if Habermas is to justify his advocacy of the ideal speech-situation, which is I suggest represented roughly by the radical model, he must show that this is in fact preferable to the others. Second, the justification that is offered has to take a specific form: it must be shown that the radical model represents the optimal organization for the effective validation of truth-claims. For his argument is designed to provide a rational foundation for various norms, on the basis of what is required for the validation of the claims presupposed by communicative activity. Thus no appeal can be made to normative considerations whose justification is given independently of this argument. If the acceptance of certain norms is to be based on the requirements of successful communication, one cannot at the same time determine the merits of possible forms for its social organization by reference to other ideals.

The significance of this can be brought out by considering one more view of the organization of theoretical discourse, advocated by Feyerabend.[30] A central feature of his position is that one should not first specify the requirements for scientific rationality, and then read off the normative implications for social or political organization from these. Rather, one should proceed in the reverse direction: what kind of scientific practices we adopt should be determined by ideals of social existence. That is, the social organization of theoretical discourse should be assessed, not by reference to the supposed requirements for achieving truth or rationality, but by its effects upon human beings. The pursuit of truth has no exclusive priority as a human value: freedom, pleasure, self-realization and so on, may be of equal or greater importance. Thus the political argument should not be from science to human values, but from human values to science.

Again, I will not comment on the merits of this position: clearly, if it were accepted it would undermine the primary assumption of this attempt by Habermas to provide a rational foundation for norms. But there is anyway a less extreme view than Feyerabend's, which would also reduce the plausibility of Habermas's arguments. This is that although it may be possible to establish (or at least give some positive support for) certain norms on the basis of what is required for the optimal conduct of theoretical discourse, or indeed any form of communicative activity, these norms do not provide anything like a full account of the basic values relevant to the solution of moral or political issues. That is, whatever the merits of this argument for certain values, there may well be other values, of equal significance, that cannot be justified in this way. Further, such additional values may at times conflict, both with each other, and with those established via the requirements of theoretical discourse.

For instance, suppose it could be shown that to maximize the successful operation of critical argumentation, far-reaching measures would have to be taken to remove inequalities of power or material resources. It might then be objected, from some normative standpoints, that this could only be done at considerable cost in terms of the realization of other important values, such as the maximization of economic production, or the absence of a coercive State apparatus.[31] In other words, there may be a plurality of moral and political values, which are not mutually harmonious.[32] Instead, there are situations in which they conflict, and there may be no 'higher' level of normative analysis at which these conflicts can be correctly resolved. So, in response to Habermas's declaration, in an early version of his argument for the normative implications of communicative competence, that the various symmetries required for successful communication represent 'a linguistic conceptualization of what are traditionally known as the ideas of truth, freedom and justice',[33] the following query could be put: is it possible to realize these values without conflicts between them; and even if so, is their realization compatible with that of other, equally important ideals?

However, to assess the legitimacy of these doubts we must examine the second main element in Habermas's account of the rationality of normative claims, his theory of practical discourse. Here the concept of an ideal speech-situation is

used in a rather different way, to specify directly a procedure
by which such claims can be rationally justified.

3 THE RATIONALITY OF PRACTICAL DISCOURSE

In practical discourse the claims to rightness made in
communicative activity are subjected to critical
argumentation, just as the claims to truth are in theoretical
discourse. So, in parallel with his view that the truth of
theoretical claims consists in what is agreed in an ideal
speech-situation, Habermas proposes that the rightness of
practical normative judgments is established by consensus in
that same situation.[34] Further, corresponding to the
standards or principles of argument appropriate to
theoretical discourse, there is a basic principle for practical
argumentation, namely 'the generalizability of interests'.[35]
This principle, however, does not require independent
justification, for it is in fact presupposed by the ideal
speech-situation, which is itself required for the successful
resolution of problematic communicative claims.[36]

Most of the basic features of Habermas's position here are
presented in the following passage from *Legitimation Crisis*:

> If under these conditions [i.e. an ideal speech-situation] a
> consensus about the recommendation to accept a norm arises
> argumentatively, that is, on the basis of hypothetically
> proposed, alternative justifications, then this consensus
> expresses a 'rational will'. Since all those affected have, in
> principle, at least the chance to participate in the practical
> deliberation, the 'rationality' of the discursively formed will
> consists in the fact that the reciprocal behavioural expectations
> raised to normative status afford validity to a *common* interest
> ascertained *without deception*. The interest is common because
> the constraint-free consensus permits only what *all* can want; it
> is free of deception because even the interpretation of needs in
> which *each individual* must be able to recognize what he wants
> becomes the object of discursive will-formation. The
> discursively formed will may be called 'rational' because the
> formal properties of discourse and of the deliberative situation
> sufficiently guarantee that a consensus can arise only through
> appropriately interpreted, generalizable interests, by which I

mean needs that can be *communicatively shared*. The limits of a decisionistic treatment of practical questions [i.e. one that maintains the non-rationality of ultimate normative commitments] are overcome as soon as argumentation is expected to test the generaliz*ability* of interests, instead of being resigned to an impenetrable pluralism of apparently ultimate value orientations (or belief-acts and attitudes.)[37]

As Habermas has himself noted,[38] this position is in many respects similar to that of John Rawls, in *A Theory of Justice*.[39] By taking up this suggested parallel we will be able to identify a number of difficulties in Habermas's view. Rawls argues that one can provide a rational justification for certain principles of justice – namely, the equality of liberties and opportunities, and the limitation of inequalities in the distribution of other primary goods to those which will improve the absolute level of the worst-off group – by showing that they would be freely chosen by rational, mutually disinterested individuals placed in a (hypothetical) original position, in which they are given the task of determining the basic principles upon which a society that they might belong to will be governed.

Rawl's original position is characterized by the following features. There is an equality of power, information and rationality between its members; there is assumed to be a moderate degree of scarcity of material goods, such that whilst social co-operation is clearly beneficial, there are limits to the satisfaction of possible individual desires; it is accepted that any principles must be universal in their applicability, and publicly recognized; and its participants exist behind what he calls a 'veil of ignorance', in that they know nothing about themselves as individuals that would enable them to predict how they would be affected by any particular distributive principle. They are, however, allowed access to all *general* knowledge, contained in the laws or theories of economics, psychology and so on.

Apart from the similarities between this definition of the original position and Habermas's conception of an ideal speech-situation, there are a number of meta-ethical assumptions that appear to be shared by the two theorists. First, they both adopt what is often termed a 'pure procedural' view of the justification of substantive normative principles. That is, a correct or right principle is defined as whatever would be the outcome of a certain set of procedural rules, which specify the conditions under which the relevant decision is to be taken. No procedure-independent criteria can be applied to judge the acceptability of this outcome. [40] Second, they both insist upon *unanimity* between the participants who engage in this procedure, as compared, say, with a majority-decision. Further, as will be seen shortly, such unanimity must not be achieved through compromise between otherwise conflicting interests. Third, there is a shared antipathy towards 'value-pluralism', the view that normative theories must remain content with specifying or justifying a number of distinct values or ideals which are, in certain circumstances, incompatible, and whose realization may therefore require partial sacrifices of some values when they conflict with others. For Rawls and Habermas there must be no trade-off relations between competing values: or at least, not unless there is some higher level principle which provides a rational and determinate solution to all such trade-off situations. [41]

I will now present a number of problems in Rawls's position which, I believe, indicate related difficulties for Habermas's. I will confine myself mainly to the question of the justificatory status of agreement in the original position, which is distinct from the other major question about Rawls's theory, whether it is true that the principles he specifies are in fact those that would be chosen. We can begin by considering the veil of ignorance assumption in the original position. It is significant that in earlier versions of his theory this feature was absent, and it appears to have been added later because without it, the choice-situation could not be shown to have a determinate outcome satisfying the requirement of unanimity. [42] That is, Rawls recognized that if the members of the original position knew of their individual abilities, motives, values, interests and suchlike, they would be unlikely to agree amongst themselves about the best principles of justice. For they would be able to judge that some principles would benefit or harm some of them more than they would others of them.

I believe that the veil of ignorance in Rawls's theory has the function of ensuring that only what are, in Habermas's terms, generalizable interests can be taken into account in the original position. But there are certain difficulties about this requirement in Rawls's theory. First, it tends to undermine the distinctness, or individuality, of the members of the original position; and in a way that makes the further requirement of unanimity (Habermas's consensus) redundant. For although Rawls continues to present the original position as if it involved debate leading to possible agreement between distinct individuals, it turns out that, in effect, no one of them can contribute anything to the discussion that is different from what any one else could. They are all equally rational, well-informed, influential and so on; and they have no individuating features which could give rise to even an initial level of disagreement. Thus the apparent diversity of individuals in effect conceals a complete impersonality, such that the relevant process of decision could be conducted by a single, though highly abstract, individual.

So there is a crucial tension in Rawls's theory between the requirement of unanimity and the individuality of the participants, which is resolved via the veil of ignorance in favour of the former. I shall return shortly to the relevance of this for Habermas's conception of generalizable interests. But I want first to point to a further difficulty in Rawls's theory, that is related to this tension.

Whilst Rawls wishes to ensure agreement, and thus de-individualizes the members of the original position by placing them behind the veil of ignorance, he sees that it is necessary to provide some motivational force for them in addition to what would otherwise be, in effect, a purely instrumental rationality. Part of his solution to this is the assumption of mutual disinterest: participants are said to be self-interested, but in such a way that they have no interest of either a positive or negative form in the extent to which others' interests are satisfied. But what content is to be given to these interests? For if none is provided, the participants, who are concerned with choosing principles of distribution, will have no idea what it is whose distribution matters to them. Rawls's answer to this is his doctrine of primary goods which are defined, roughly, as those goods which are necessary for the successful practice of any possible rational life-plan; and of which it is true that the more one has of them, the better-off one will be.[43]

I shall not discuss what Rawls says about rational life-plans, since the issues raised by this would take us too far from the main concern here. But the basic idea behind the concept of primary goods seems to be this. Rawls wishes to allow that his individuals may turn out (when they emerge from the veil of ignorance) to have a great variety of particular interests and values. He cannot ascribe an actual diversity of these to the members of the original position, on pain of failure to produce unanimity. So instead he argues that the participants can identify a set of primary goods which, on the basis of their general knowledge, they know are such that whatever the particular life-plans they turn out to have, these are the goods whose amount will matter to them.

But there is a major problem here. The possible diversity of life-plans may be so great that no such list of goods could be determined. Alternatively – and this is the line I will follow – even if such a list could be agreed, it may well be insufficiently inclusive.[44] For although there may be some goods that everyone wants for whatever they choose to do with their lives, there may be other goods which are useful for only *some* such choices, and which might indeed prove to be more important than the universal goods. But if this is so individuals will discover (in their 'real lives') that their society has been organized on the basis of principles which, however acceptably they determine the distribution of these universal goods, fails to guarantee them what they need for their own actual life-plans, based on their particular values and interests.

To avoid this difficulty one would have to make the following assumption: that there is a set of goods which is not only universal in the sense of being advantageous for everyone's life-plans, but also includes *everything* that is important for *anyone's* life-plans. It seems to me extremely implausible that any such set exists, unless one is prepared to regard interests or values that are not shared by everyone as in some way suspect or non-genuine. But this would require adopting a very stringent and debatable substantive normative doctrine about what are to be regarded as genuine or desirable human interests.

Just this kind of assumption, however, appears to be made by Habermas. For he says in the passage quoted earlier that in practical discourse the norms agreed upon will concern interests that are common, 'because the constraint-free consensus permits only what *all* can want'.[45] Now it is presumably true, other things being equal, that if a consensus that does not involve compromise is to be achieved, only interests that are common in this sense will be permissible bases for normative proposals. But if 'in fact' individuals in the ideal speech-situation also have interests that are not common, they may find the agreed proposals are either inadequate, in not dealing with issues that are significant for them, or actually undesirable, since their implementation conflicts with these individual interests. How then does Habermas justify the assumption that only common interests are relevant in practical discourse?

A clue to his answer to this is provided by another comment in the same passage. He says that by common or generalizable interests he means those 'that can be communicatively shared'.[46] I suspect this involves the following assumption: that interests which are genuinely communicable are those which everyone would accept as common interests, in an ideal form of communication. That is, communicability implies sharing in the sense of acceptance: the intersubjectivity of successful communication involves not just understanding, but *agreement*. That this is Habermas's view is indicated by the sense of the term he frequently uses when describing the 'understanding' towards which communicative activity is (necessarily) directed, *Verständigung*. McCarthy says of this, and its cognate terms, that:

> Like their English counterparts, but more so, the German terms referring to understanding can typically be used in stronger and weaker senses, running the gamut from mere intelligibility to complete agreement. Thus we speak of understanding a word, sentence, argument; understanding what someone means with a

given utterance; understanding a person's intentions, feelings, desires; coming to an understanding with someone; having reached an understanding with someone; and so on.[47]

Without claiming that Habermas's view that communicable interests are shared interests founders upon ambiguity between these senses, it does appear to depend on the belief that understanding in the weaker senses must ultimately produce understanding in the stronger sense of agreement.[48] I see no good reason for accepting this. It would seem to imply that the successful use of language requires not merely the existence of shared meanings, intersubjectively maintained rules for the use of terms, but also shared beliefs. But those who deny the possibility of a universal and rationally justifiable set of normative principles will not accept this claim; and I do see how it can be established on the basis of a thesis about the shared character of linguistic meanings. If this is so, Habermas's optimism about the possibility of consensual outcomes of practical discourse is unfounded.

Habermas's view is, I suggest, related to another often manifested in arguments for the essentially shared, generalizable character of human needs or interests. It is sometimes claimed that once we recognize that humans are intrinsically social, or even co-operative, beings, we can show that certain kinds of conflictual relationships (such as those typical of capitalist societies) are not genuinely human: that in these relationships humans are operating as a-social individuals, and thus with distortions in their true nature. And in support of the claim that 'by their nature' humans are social, the centrality of phenomena such as language or economic productive activity are emphasized. (Something like this view is found, for instance, in Marx's *Economic and Philosophical Manuscripts*, in his account of human species-being and its alienation.)

But this type of argument is mistaken: it trades upon an ambiguity between descriptive and normative senses of sociality. In the former sense it is certainly true that, for instance, the intersubjective, rule-governed character of language shows that humans are 'social'; and that some ontological theories about humans and society are therefore wrong, namely those which see society as composed of relationships between pre- or non-social individuals. But it does not follow from this that, say, egotistic behaviour is non-human because it is 'non-social'. Both egotists and altruists are 'social' in the descriptive, ontological sense. The former use language, and engage in social relationships, just as much as the latter. To characterize them as 'non-' or even 'anti-social' involves a different sense of the term, referring to certain norms about desirable forms of human activity; and these cannot be justified by pointing to the (descriptively) social nature of humans.

I have been arguing that, corresponding to the difficulty in Rawls's theory that arises in the specification of primary goods — which is related to the tension between the individuality of people in the original position and the requirement of unanimous agreement — there is a similar difficulty in Habermas's view that only generalizable interests can or will emerge in the ideal speech-situation. I will conclude this discussion of his account of practical discourse by considering his attitude towards compromise. Habermas maintains that ideally consensus should not take this form, since agreements based on compromise arise only in situations where the interests of participants are not fully generalizable.[49] Thus compromises indicate an (in principle) eliminable imperfection in the rationality of normative decisions. But he also argues that, in such imperfect situations, it is still important to distinguish justifiable from non-justifiable compromises. The basis for this distinction is the equality of power between the competing parties: only where this exists is compromise genuine.[50]

It seems that Habermas associates this imperfect situation with a further departure from the ideal form of practical discourse, namely 'the competition for scarce goods', which he describes as involving a type of 'strategic action' that is distinct from the communicative consensus of fully rational discourse.[51] This suggests that by generalizable interests Habermas must mean not merely interests that everyone has, but interests whose satisfaction is compatible with the existing level of resources. But this involves some very problematic issues. It can I think be shown that competition between individuals (or groups) for scarce resources can be overcome only in one or both of the following situations: where individual desires (whose satisfaction requires the use of material resources) have a finite upper limit, and the available resources are sufficient to meet these; or where individual desires are such that each person achieves satisfaction primarily through other people's desires being satisfied. Neither condition appears to me realistically achievable: nor do I see, even if either could be achieved, why this should be thought especially desirable.

I will not try to argue for these claims. Instead, I simply note that were they accepted, we should no longer regard compromise outcomes as a sign of imperfection. Rather, we should attempt to specify appropriate procedures for normative decisions that assume the ineliminability (either in fact, or ideally) of conflicting interests and competition for resources. In this context, Habermas's requirement of equal power for compromise to be legitimate is very important. Indeed, many of the features he specifies for an ideal speech-situation might well be preserved, but without the assumptions that support his advocacy of consensus, which founders in my view upon his belief in the rational harmony of genuine human interests, and in the necessity for uncompromising agreement as the outcome of undistorted communication.

Conclusion

I will conclude by first drawing together the main themes in this book, and then considering a number of possible difficulties in what I have said.

I began by arguing there were certain defects in critical theorists' critique of positivism, and of positivist social science in particular. Whilst it is true that the latter is epistemologically inadequate, since it denies the place of hermeneutic interpretation in social theory, and assumes a partly mistaken view of the natural sciences, it is wrong to claim that it presupposes scientism, and nor does it entail the practice of a scientific politics. Further, I argued that the doctrine of value-freedom, rejected by critical theorists as a central feature of positivism, can instead be seen as an important basis for the criticism of a scientific politics, and can be accepted without commitment to scientism. I then suggested how it was possible to conceive of social theories that are critical of social reality from a distinctively socialist standpoint, consistently with this kind of separation between science and value.

My attitude to these issues partly reflects a more general distrust of the assumption within critical theory that it is necessary to overcome or transcend a number of related dichotomies that find their paradigmatic expression in Kantian philosophy: between 'is' and 'ought', 'science' and 'values', 'theory' and 'practice', and so on. My own position, by contrast, tends to preserve these; whilst also (hopefully) preserving the potentially critical character of social theory. It seems to me that the only philosophical standpoint that succeeds in transcending these Kantian dichotomies is Hegel's. But the idealism of Hegel's philosophy is, I believe, essential to this 'success'. It is only through his rejection of the ultimate reality of the finite, material world, and his conception of the world-historical development of the Idea, manifesting itself in a teleologically ordered succession of objectifications, that this transcendence can be achieved. Only if that which is can be deemed real solely in as much as it expresses that which ought to be (its implicit idea or notion), can the duality be (dialectically) overcome: without Hegel's idealism, no transcendence.[1] But I find little that is philosophically attractive about that idealism; and I do not share what seems in some people to be an antipathy towards any kind of duality as such. Idealist metaphysics is something that a critical social theory would do well to be without; and I think there are residual elements of it in much of the Frankfurt School's work, even that of Habermas.

Habermas's own critique of positivism relies partly, but only partly, on his theory of knowledge-constitutive interests. I have argued against this theory, and tried to show, amongst other things, that it in fact undermines the possibility of criticizing either positivist or hermeneutic social theories' adequacy to deal with the actual character of social reality. Instead, I think it preferable to adopt an objectivist, realist view of the differences between the 'objects' of various sciences; and I have suggested that a single dichotomy between humans and nature, as scientific objects, misrepresents the character of both. This dichotomy is associated with the way Habermas presents the ideal of emancipation as a movement from causality to freedom. But I have argued that this conception of autonomy can be reconstructed within a deterministic, reductionist framework.

Habermas's view that there are distinctive criteria of validity for critical social theory rests partly on the claim that the truth of such a theory is tied to its successful translation into practice. I have criticized this, and proposed instead that there are significant gaps between the truth of explanatory theories, the success of techniques, and the theoretical rationale for such techniques. As with my view of the relations between science and values, there is a more general basis for my attitude to these questions. I am sceptical of the way critical theorists (and several other traditions within Marxism) appear to present us with a single package comprising epistemology, a particular social theory, specific forms of practice, and a normative ideal, all supposedly entailing or presupposing each other.

So, whilst Habermas conceives of critical social theory as involving a distinctive form of knowledge which is, in his terms, '*between* science and philosophy',[2] my own position instead represents such a theory as consisting of both science *and* philosophy. In other words, such a theory makes claims that are assessable as science; but the problems towards which it is directed, the aims which it attempts to achieve and, thus, the relevance or significance of its solutions, must be judged in terms of our answers to the kinds of specifically normative questions which have typically been examined within political philosophy. The critique of social reality must combine the realms of sciences and values, and not try to overcome their separation by employing some supposedly distinct form of knowledge or theory. Thus, to Habermas's early claim that:

> The meaning of the actual historical process is revealed to the extent that we grasp a meaning, derived from 'practical reason', of what should be and what should be otherwise . . . and theoretically examine the presuppositions of its practical realization . . . [and we] must interpret the actual course and the social forces of the present form from the point of view of the realization of that meaning,[3]

my response is: yes, but this requires no 'new' form of social theory with distinctive criteria of validity.

Unlike many of his predecessors in the Frankfurt School, Habermas goes well beyond the incantation of Reason as the foundation of critique. He tries to spell out what is involved in the self-reflective movement towards autonomy; to specify a number of particular values which should be realized in social relationships; and to provide a rational justification for them through the presuppositions of communication. But I have argued that he does not altogether succeed in these tasks. It is questionable whether the mode of justification is tenable; and also whether the proposed values are adequate as a basis for resolving the kinds of normative issues inherent in social relationships. The failure is due partly, I think, to an over-simple contrast between humans and natural objects, and partly also to a misplaced faith in the potential harmony between human needs or interests, which leads to a view of conflict or disagreement as expressing necessarily a state of imperfection. Such apparent optimism is not merely unrealistic. It may mis-direct our attention from constructing forms of social organization which, rather than aiming at consensus between perfectly rational homogeneous beings, attempt to equalize the effective power of differentiated groups and individuals, and to resolve their often incompatible demands without viewing these as signs of imperfection. It is inequality (in all its many forms), rather than individualism, that should be the main target for a socialist critique of capitalism.

Despite having confined myself only to certain areas of Habermas's work, my responses to them have involved adopting particular views on a very wide range of issues. Perhaps inevitably, I have often been content with articulating a position that I favour, making little attempt to defend it against significant objections. But there are certainly a number of problems in what I have said that I am to some extent conscious of, and it may be helpful to identify them now.

I have throughout argued from a realist standpoint, whilst also assuming a central role for hermeneutic interpretation in social theory. But there are several apparent difficulties here. First, my account of the relations between science and values makes no explicit reference to the interpretation of meanings; and it might be argued that this account cannot be applied to this kind of analysis. For, as several writers (such as Gadamer) have emphasized,[4] the interpretation of meanings is necessarily performed from within the conceptual framework of the interpreter's own language. So it is not possible to view the meanings identified through such analyses as 'objects' that exist independently of the interpretive framework employed: rather, they are in some way a product of the interaction between interpreter and interpreted. Further, it is apparently obvious that such frameworks are specific to particular groups, cultures, classes, historical periods and so on; and it is therefore unclear how any criteria for correct interpretations can be provided that are framework-independent. But such frameworks are necessarily expressive of particular norms or values. So there cannot be any value-neutral descriptions of social meanings: such descriptions must presuppose, and implicitly express, the norms of the interpretive framework.

Second, it could be argued that even ignoring these problems for a realist, value-free interpretation of meanings, there are anyway major difficulties facing any form of realism even in the natural sciences. These basically concern the subject-dependence of perception: 'the world as perceived' is necessarily 'the world-as-perceived-by-someone'. Thus realism, if it is to be remotely plausible, must be formulated in such a way that, whilst recognizing the active, subject-determined character of perception, it none the less preserves the possibility of a scientific theory being tested by reference to perceptual evidence whose acceptance is logically independent of the truth of that theory. And it is far from clear whether this can be done.

In response to this I offer the following comments. First, I think it is reasonable to believe that certain elements of human perceptual processing mechanisms are 'innate', in the sense that, because of the character of the species' genetically transmitted information, they will develop in all humans except in highly abnormal 'environmental' circumstances.[5] This means that it must be accepted that 'the world as an object for humans' is in some way a humanly constructed world. There is no reason to believe that it is the same for all actual or possible perceiving beings; and there must be species-determined limits on the possibility of conceiving how that world might be for other types of being. Thus any adequate form of realism must accept at least this degree of subject-dependence of 'reality'.

However, the most difficult issues arise when we consider forms of subject-dependence that are not universal for the human species: those that may vary between groups or individuals. Again, I think it is reasonable to believe such differences exist, and that they result from certain learning experiences, including those that involve active bodily engagement with the environment.[6] But I am doubtful whether, as a matter of fact, there are perceptual differences corresponding to every significant difference or disagreement between competing scientific theories.[7] Further, even if there are such differences, it is important to remember that not all results of past learning are irreversible: that is, it may still be possible to learn to see things differently. The problem remains, of course, of what if any sense can be given to learning to see them 'better'; and it is at this point that some form of pragmatism may seem an attractive alternative to realism.

One last point about realism. An important defect of the way this position has sometimes been presented within the philosophy of science is a lack of attention to the role of abstraction or idealization in the construction of scientific theories. By contrast, rationalist conceptions of science have rightly emphasized this, though in a way that has led to a total rejection of empirical evidence as an independent basis for determining the truth or falsity of theories: what empiricists regard as evidence, rationalists see as (mere) illustration.[8] It seems, historically, that the most successful scientific work has involved, at least initially, a considerable divorce between development of the central theoretical concepts and their inter-relationships, and their referential application to 'concrete phenomena'. Galileo's mechanics is an obvious example. However, I think it is wrong to regard abstraction as incompatible with empirical testability; and, in terms of the logic of theory-testing, the abstract nature of 'pure' theories should be understood as one amongst other important reasons why no such tests are possible without the aid of auxiliary hypotheses.[9]

I turn now to another set of problems, which concern the form of reductionism espoused in chapter 4, and the conceptualization there of the relations between the 'physical' and 'psychic' dimensions of human existence. It might be objected that my position involves an archaic Cartesian dualism, differing from this only in adopting an epiphenomenalist rather than an interactionist view. In using the term 'archaic', I have in mind the commonplace observation that this traditional dualism between the mental and the physical has now been 'replaced' in philosophy by a proper focus upon language, rather than consciousness, as the crucial feature of humans for the epistemology of social theory. An important feature of this philosophical transformation has been the rejection of the Cartesian (private) subject: the starting-point for human ontology is not the individual's logically private inner consciousness, but the public, rule-governed language of social reality. The interpretation of social meanings thus replaces the traditional, psychologistic problem of knowledge of minds.[10] Further, it might be objected that there is an inconsistency in the way I both endorse the significance of hermeneutics, and yet discuss the question of reductionism from this Cartesian standpoint.

As a partial reply to this, I suggest the following. First, I have tried to avoid any straightforward dualism between the physical and the mental. In particular, I have argued that it is necessary at least to make differentiations within both of these traditional categories, so that we can recognize the diversity of forms of organic and inorganic existence, and also their relatedness.[11] Thus, in the case of the human species I proposed that we should emphasize not only its distinctive characteristics — such as language, and the capacity for self-reflection — but also others that are to some extent shared with other species which are themselves distinct both from one another, and from inorganic beings. I suggested also that the existence of language may affect the nature of some of these (otherwise) shared characteristics, such as the emotions, though without any proper elaboration of this view.

Further, I am not convinced that the (quite legitimate) emphasis upon the social character of language should be seen as requiring us to replace or abandon the concept of individual states of consciousness. It still seems to me possible, and even necessary, to maintain a distinction between the 'psychological' facts of individuals' having certain experiences (perceptual, emotional, cognitive and so on), and the 'linguistic' or 'conceptual' elements involved in the identification of their contents. So, whilst it is true that the kinds of experiences available to humans are at least partly a function of the specific, socially determined conceptual frameworks within which they operate, this does not rule out thinking of individual humans as the subjects of such experiences. Without some concept of individual experience, I find it difficult to make sense of myself; and this is one reason why I am unconvinced both by traditional philosophical materialism, and by the more recent forms of 'materialism' (previously called 'idealism') which attempt to 'de-centre the human subject' through a structuralist social ontology.[12]

There are also certain problems in my (compatibilist) account of autonomy as the absence of compulsiveness. It might be argued that this account has little to say about the actual character of the self-reflective process through which autonomy is achieved; and that when this is properly understood, it becomes clear that my compatibilist position is mistaken, since the process cannot be conceptualized within a deterministic framework.

What I have in mind here is this. Any self-reflective process can be characterized from a 'first-person' standpoint: that is, from the perspective of someone who is actually engaged in it. And there is a radical difference between the way human agents can, or perhaps must, view their own activities, and the way these can be viewed by others. From the standpoint of the agent, future actions are open to deliberation, choice and decision; and they are related to the present in the mode of intentionality, as things that one may aim to do. Correspondingly, to the extent that one is aware of various features of one's past and present, these are at least partly conceived in the form of possible reasons for (future) action. This first-person framework is non-deterministic: though reasons for action may be seen as causes by an observer, the agent cannot view them in this way; though one's intentions to act may be taken as the basis for predictions by an observer, they cannot be thus conceived by the agent; and whilst an observer may try to work out what one will do, and why, the process of decision and action cannot be viewed in these terms by the agent whilst engaged in that process. Thus the concept and attitudes of a deterministic standpoint cannot be employed 'in the first-person', but only 'in the third-person'.[13]

Though I am unsure whether this objection shows that determinism is unacceptable, I do think it points to important features of human agency. Further, it might be thought to suggest a way of conceptualizing how, for critical theorists, a social theory should be related to human practice. A critical social theory, it could be said, must be designed to enter into the self-reflective processes of groups or individuals; and this involves a quite different relationship to practice than the making of predictions about the outcomes of possible courses of action, which is all that positivist social theory can offer. Thus a positivist social theory is related to action in a different way from a critical social theory: it does not adopt the standpoint of the self-reflective agents of change, but views everything and everyone from the external, objectifying standpoint of a disengaged observer.

But it seems to me that the relationship of theory to practice advocated here is impossible: one is either an 'observer', or an 'agent', and there is no way of bridging or transcending the gap between these two perspectives. This is not to say that, from the standpoint of agency, 'objectifying' theories are of no use. It is certainly possible to produce theoretical knowledge which is helpful for human agents. But to do this is something different from being actually involved in the processes of deliberation and action. One can construct theories about something, or one can be engaged in deciding whether to do it; but one cannot, as it were, theorize in the mode of agency. Critical social theorists have to decide which it is that, at any particular point in their lives, they are to do; but they cannot have it both ways at once.

There is another, quite different, objection that might be made to my account of autonomy and self-reflection: that it involves a mistakenly 'intellectual', 'cognitivist' view of therapeutic processes and their emancipatory goals. In particular, the proposed analysis of compulsiveness, and thus of autonomy, suggests an ideal of rational self-control according to which any influences upon one's actions that are beyond the power of reasoning and decision are regarded as 'compulsive'.[14] But this would imply that, for instance, all emotions and desires are either inherently compulsive 'intrusions' upon rational, autonomous action, or that they are only not so when themselves 'freely chosen' — and both alternatives are unacceptable.

This objection has considerable force, and I do not see how to reconstruct the concepts of self-reflection and autonomy to take account of it. What seems reasonably clear to me is that, at the very least, one must avoid a purely cognitive model of the therapeutic process as the gaining of self-understanding. This is partly just because such processes are as a matter of fact usually quite ineffectual. The caricature of people who spend their lives on the couch, come to understand themselves profoundly, and change in no other way (the Woody Allen syndrome), is well-founded. Therapeutic processes that change the way one lives are typically, amongst other things, both painful and exciting. And their emancipatory outcomes cannot be characterized adequately in terms of the realization of 'reason', at least if this concept is understood, as it usually is, partly in terms of various contrasts such as that between reason and feeling, emotion and so on.

But even were one to succeed in constructing a conception of (therapeutic) emancipation that avoided this rationalist bias, many of the central normative issues in social philosophy would remain unresolved. As I argued earlier, [15] it is not possible to articulate and justify the distinctive character of a socialist society by reference to a psychoanalytically derived concept of autonomy; and the same is true of attempts to do this by reference to the supposedly presupposed values of communicative activity, or of scientific enquiry. [16] I have made no attempt to offer an alternative form of justification. But the account I have suggested of the epistemology of a critical social theory at least has the virtue, I believe, of not making the criteria of validity of such theories logically dependent upon the acceptance of values which, so far as I can see, have not been adequately specified or substantiated by critical theorists themelves.

Notes

In all quotations in the main text, the square brackets denote comments, explications, etc., added by the present author.

For full publication details see the Bibliography, p.224.

INTRODUCTION

1 See, e.g. Horkheimer, *Critical Theory*; Marcuse, *Negations* and *Reason and Revolution*. A good account of the early period of the School is Jay, *The Dialectical Imagination*.

2 For an excellent critical presentation of the whole range of Habermas's writings, see McCarthy, *The Critical Theory of Jürgen Habermas*. References to particular works by Habermas will be given as they are discussed later.

3 A useful guide to this tradition is Outhwaite, *Understanding Social Life*. On positivist social science, see Keat and Urry, *Social Theory as Science*; Benton, *Philosophical Foundations of the Three Sociologies*; and Keat, 'Positivism and Statistics in Social Science'.

4 See, respectively, Habermas's *Legitimation Crisis* and *Communication and the Evolution of Society*.

5 What follows is strongly influenced by the account of critical social theory in Fay, *Social Theory and Political Practice*.

6 Habermas, *Knowledge and Human Interests*, p.67.

7 *Ibid.*, p.36.

8 Habermas, *Theory and Practice*, p.8.

9 *Ibid.*, p.8.

10 Habermas, *Human Interests*, p.271.

11 *Ibid.*, p.272.

12 *Ibid.*, p.214.

13 See especially Habermas, 'On Systematically Distorted Communication'; 'Towards a Theory of Communicative Competence'; and 'What is Universal Pragmatics?'

14 See McCarthy, *Habermas*, ch. 4. for a discussion of these areas of Habermas's work, and the relevant references.

1: THE CRITIQUE OF POSITIVISM

1 In Horkheimer, *Critical Theory*, pp.132-87.
2 Marcuse, *Reason and Revolution*, Part II, ch. II.
3 Habermas, 'The Analytical Theory of Science and Dialectics', and 'A Positivistically Bisected Rationalism'.
4 See especially the essays in Weber, *The Methodology of the Social Sciences*.
5 Habermas, 'The Classical Doctrine of Politics in relation to Social Philosophy', in his *Theory and Practice*, pp.41-81. McCarthy, in *Habermas*, presents this opposition to a scientific politics as a central theme in much of Habermas's work.
6 See Hayek, *The Counter-Revolution of Science*, for an interesting analysis of nineteenth-century positivism.
7 Saint-Simon, *Selected Writings on Science, Industry and Social Organization*, p.209.
8 In Weber, *Methodology*, pp.1-49.
9 Dahrendorf, *Essays in the Theory of Society*, p.2.
10 Habermas, 'Analytical Theory', p.144.
11 See Popper, 'The Logic of the Social Sciences'; and Albert, 'The Myth of Total Reason', and 'Behind Positivism's Back?'.
12 Habermas, *Human Interests*, p.4.
13 See Kolakowski, *Positivist Philosophy*.
14 Popper, 'Science: Conjectures and Refutations', and 'The Demarcation between Science and Metaphysics', in his *Conjectures and Refutations*, pp.33-65 and 253-93.
15 Habermas, *Human Interests*, p.vii.
16 For a fuller definition of the positivist view of science, see Keat and Urry, *Social Theory as Science*, ch. 1.
17 See Kolakowski, *Positivist Philosophy*; and Popper, 'A Note on Berkeley as Precursor of Mach and Einstein', in *Conjectures and Refutations*, pp.166-74.
18 Fay, *Social Theory and Political Practice*, pp.22-3.
19 An example of this is Duhem, *The Aim and Structure of Physical Theory*.
20 A classic defence of instrumentalism in astronomy is Duhem, *To Save the Phenomena*; an influential criticism, Popper's 'Three Views concerning Human Knowledge', in *Conjectures and Refutations*, pp.97-119.
21 See Keat and Urry, *Social Theory as Science*, pp.63-5.
22 The recent resurgence of theoretical realism in the philosophy of science has been strongly influenced by the work of Rom Harré, e.g. *The Principles of Scientific Thinking*. See also Benton,

Philosophical Foundations; Keat and Urry, *Social Theory as Science*; and Bhaskar, *A Realist Theory of Science*, and *The Possibility of Naturalism*.
23 Many of the issues involved arise in the much disputed analysis of Galileo's conception of scientific knowledge: see Shapere, *Galileo: A Philosophical Study*; McMullin (ed.), *Galileo: Man of Science*, Part IV; Koyré, *Metaphysics and Measurement*; and Feyerabend, *Against Method*, pp.69-145.
24 But see below, ch. 2, sec. 2, for further discussion of the relation between these two elements in the doctrine of value-freedom.
25 Horkheimer, 'The Latest Attack on Metaphysics', in *Critical Theory*, p.164.
26 Habermas, 'Analytical Theory', p.145.
27 *Ibid.*, p.146.
28 Fay, *Social Theory*, p.14.
29 *Ibid.*, p.52.
30 Habermas, 'Analytical Theory', p.159.
31 *Ibid.*, p.160.
32 Fay, *Social Theory*, p.36.
33 See the discussion of this question by Mandelbaum, 'Two Moot Issues in Mill's *Utilitarianism*', pp. 221-33.
34 Saint-Simon, *Selected Writings*, p.207.
35 *Ibid.*, p.208.
36 *Ibid.*, p.113.
37 See Williams, 'A Critique of Utilitarianism', pp. 135-50; and Miller, *Social Justice*, ch.1.
38 See Waxman, *The End of Ideology Debate*.
39 See Hayek, *Counter-Revolution*, p.107.
40 This is argued by Habermas in 'Dogmatism, Reason and Decision', in his *Theory and Practice*, pp.253-82.
41 Significantly entitled 'The Scientific Conception of the World: The Vienna Circle', reprinted in Neurath, *Empiricism and Sociology*, pp.299-318.
42 *Ibid.*, p.305.
43 *Ibid.*, p.318.
44 For instance, Ayer (ed.), *Logical Positivism*; and Passmore, *A Hundred Years of Philosophy*, ch.16.
45 'The Scientific Conception of the World', in Neurath, *Empiricism and Sociology*, pp.303-4.
46 See Mill, *Auguste Comte and Positivism*.
47 Saint-Simon, *Selected Writings*, p.230.
48 See Beck, 'Neo-Kantianism', p.473.

49   Kroner, *Kant's Weltanschauung*, p.2.
50   *Ibid.*, p.62.
51   *Ibid.*, p.63.
52   *Ibid.*, p.50.
53   See the discussion of Mill's view of the dichotomy in Ryan, *J. S. Mill*, pp.101-4.
54   See Weber, 'Politics as a Vocation', and 'Science as a Vocation', in Gerth and Mills (eds.), *From Max Weber: Essays in Sociology*, pp.77-128, 129-56.
55   On this point see Solomon, *From Rationalism to Existentialism*, pp.1-5.
56   Marcuse, *Reason and Revolution*, pp.323-60.
57   Saint-Simon, *Selected Writings*, pp.227-8.
58   *Ibid.*, p.170, note.
59   See, e.g. Marx, *Critique of the Gotha Program*, p.324.
60   According to Hayek, the phrase 'scientific socialism' was first used in 1845, by K. Grün, applied to Saint-Simon's position: see Hayek, *Counter-Revolution*, p.167.
61   Neurath, *Empiricism and Sociology*, pp. 289, 290 and 260.
62   On this issue see Friedman, 'An Introduction to Mill's Theory of Authority'; and Ryan, *J. S. Mill*, chs. 4, 5 and 7.
63   Keat and Urry, *Social Theory as Science.* (See 2nd edn., 1981, for further discussion of theoretical realism's relation to positivism and hermeneutics).

2: VALUE-FREEDOM AND SOCIALIST THEORY

1   See Miller, *Social Justice*, chs. 2-4, for an examination of these and other principles of social justice.
2   Nagel, *The Structure of Science*, pp.491-4.
3   See Keat and Urry, *Social Theory as Science*, pp.196-204, for a fuller discussion of Weber and some of his critics.
4   Nagel, *The Structure of Science*, p.493, footnote 38, makes a similar point about his own position.
5   This reply is partly similar to an argument in Hare, 'Descriptivism', pp.241-7. It is also analogous to the treatment of the problem of theory-neutrality in Keat and Urry, *Social Theory as Science*, pp.50-4.
6   E.g. Bhaskar, *A Realist Theory of Science*; and Sloman, *The Computer Revolution in Philosophy*, ch. 2.
7   See, e.g. Nozick, *Anarchy, State and Utopia*, ch.8.
8   See also ch. 6, sec. 3, below.

9   My account of this objection is based on its presentation in Edgley, 'Reason as Dialectic', and in Bhaskar, 'Scientific Explanation and Human Emancipation'. See also Edgley, 'Dialectic: A Reply to Keat and Dews', and Keat, 'Scientific Socialism – A Positivist Delusion?'.

10   Taylor, 'Neutrality in Political Science'.

11   See, e.g. Lessnoff, *The Structure of Social Science*, pp.136-41. For a criticism of ethical naturalism which is generally consistent with my standpoint in this chapter, see Philips and Mounce, 'On Morality's having a Point'.

12   Taylor, 'Neutrality in Political Science', pp.39-42.

13   Weber, *Methodology*, especially pp.67-85.

14   *Ibid.*, pp.131-63; but my classification is slightly different from Weber's.

15   See, e.g., Giddens, 'Marx, Weber, and the Development of Capitalism'.

16   Lipset, *Political Man*.

17   Taylor, 'Neutrality in Political Science', p.41.

18   See, e.g., Lukes, 'Alienation and Anomie'.

19   The definition of 'reformism' is of course highly problematic: see, e.g., the discussion in Miliband, *Marxism and Politics*, ch. 6.

20   See, e.g. the accounts of these debates in Gay, *The Dilemma of Democratic Socialism*; and Lichtheim, *Marxism: An Historical and Critical Study*, Part Five.

21   Cf. ch. 1, sec. 4, above.

22   Korsch, *Marxism and Philosophy*, p.33, footnote 7.

23   See Bernstein, *Evolutionary Socialism*.

24   See the discussion of this in ch. 5, sec. 1, below.

25   Quoted in Gay, *Democratic Socialism*, p.158.

26   See especially Althusser, *For Marx*.

27   Thompson, 'The Poverty of Theory'.

28   *Ibid.*, p.363.

29   Thompson, 'An Open Letter to Leszek Kolakowski', pp.131-56.

30   *Ibid.*, p.146.

31   Lichtheim, *Marxism*, p.292, footnote 2.

32   Gay, *Democratic Socialism*, p.165.

33   E.g. by Edgley, 'Reason as Dialectic', p.7.

34   Here I follow the excellent analysis in Edgley, 'Reason and Violence'.

35   See, e.g. Searle, *Speech Acts*. The relevance of this to Habermas's theory of truth is discussed in ch. 6, sec. 2, below.

3: KNOWLEDGE, OBJECTS AND INTERESTS

1 Habermas, *Human Interests*, p.307.
2 Fay, *Social Theory*, ch. 2.
3 See ch. 1, sec. 2, above.
4 Hempel, *Aspects of Scientific Explanation*, p.367.
5 Fay, *Social Theory*, p.35.
6 *Ibid.*, p.39.
7 Hempel, *Aspects of Scientific Explanation*, p.374. See also Keat and Urry, *Social Theory as Science*, pp.11-13 and 27-32.
8 See ch. 1, sec. 2, above; and Keat and Urry, *Social Theory as Science*, pp.63-4.
9 Fay, *Social Theory*, p.40.
10 *Ibid.*, p.41.
11 *Ibid.*, p.40, footnote 28.
12 E.g. Albert, 'The Myth of Total Reason', pp.170-1, and 'Behind Positivism's Back?', pp. 240-2; and Lobkowicz, 'Interest and Objectivity', p.204.
13 E.g. Habermas, 'A Positivistically Bisected Rationalism', pp.207-9 and 'A Postscript to *Knowledge and Human Interests*', pp.179-82.
14 I will discuss this theory in ch. 6, sec. 2, below.
15 E.g. in his comments on dispositional properties in Habermas, *Human Interests*, pp.129-32, and 'A Positivistically Bisected Rationalism', p.209, footnote 12.
16 Habermas, *Human Interests*, chs. 1-3.
17 *Ibid.*, p.33: strictly, this is Habermas's account of Marx's view, but he clearly endorses it here.
18 *Ibid.*, p.35.
19 *Ibid.*, p.28.
20 Cf. Cohen, 'Marxism: A Philosophy of Nature?'.
21 Habermas, *Human Interests*, p.34.
22 *Ibid.*, p.35.
23 Habermas, 'Postscript', pp.171-2.
24 Habermas, 'On Systematically Distorted Communication', p.212; see the further discussion of this in sec. 3 below.
25 See ch. 1, sec. 2, above.
26 See Bohm, *Chance and Causality in Modern Physics*, chs. 3-4, and Heisenberg, *Physics and Philosophy: The Revolution in Modern Science*.
27 See, e.g., Strawson, *The Bounds of Sense*, Part Four.
28 See McCarthy, *Habermas*, pp.291-310.
29 *Ibid.*, pp.110-25.

30 Habermas, *Theory and Practice*, p.8.
31 *Ibid.*, p.9.
32 Habermas, 'On Systematically Distorted Communication', p.212.
33 See Marcuse, *One-Dimensional Man*, ch. 6.
34 Frankel, 'Habermas Talking: An Interview', p.46.
35 Habermas, *Human Interests*, pp.32-3. Cf. Colletti's criticisms of Marcuse's Hegelianism, in *Marxism and Hegel*, chs. 4, 5 and 9.
36 Habermas, 'On Systematically Distorted Communication', p.212.
37 Habermas, *Human Interests*, chs. 10 and 11.
38 I borrow the term 'quasi-causality' from Fay, *Social Theory*, pp.84-5, but use it in a somewhat different sense, as a shorthand for Habermas's terminology, the meaning of which will be explored in ch. 4, sec. 2, below.
39 Habermas, *Human Interests*, p.226.
40 E.g. Habermas, *Theory and Practice*, pp.25-32. On the concepts of ideology and reification, see, e.g., Keat and Urry, *Social Theory as Science*, ch. 8.
41 See, e.g., McCarthy, *Habermas*, pp.92-4.
42 However, see Habermas, *Communication*, pp.131-42, for an implicit modification of his earlier dichotomy. On the general differences between the organic and inorganic, see Beckner, *The Biological Way of Thought* chs. 1, 2 and 9; and Thorpe, *Animal Nature and Human Nature*, ch. 1.
43 On the concepts of teleology and function, see Beckner, *The Biological Way of Thought*, chs. 6 and 7; and on negative feedback, see Oatley, *Brain Mechanisms and Mind*, ch. 7.
44 On innate patterns of 'purposive' behaviour in animals, see Barnett, *'Instinct' and 'Intelligence'*, ch. 10; and Thorpe, *Animal Nature and Human Nature*, ch. 4.
45 For discussions of the (numerous) different conceptualizations of emotion, see Arnold (ed.), *Feelings and Emotions*; and Lyons, *Emotion*.
46 See the various contributions in Part A of Hinde (ed.), *Non-Verbal Communication*, where these definitional issues are examined.
47 I return to some of the issues in ch. 4, sec. 4, below.
48 These different kinds of reduction are discussed more fully in ch. 4, secs. 4 and 5, below.
49 See, e.g., Ekman (ed.), *Darwin and Facial Expression*.
50 So in *general* terms I am sympathetic to the approach advocated in Midgley, *Beast and Man*, especially chs. 10-13. But cf.

the comments on innateness in ch. 4, sec. 4, below.
51 See, e.g. Rose, *The Conscious Brain*, chs. 6 and 10.
52 See ch. 6, sec. 1, below.

4: PSYCHOANALYSIS AND HUMAN EMANCIPATION

1   Habermas, *Human Interests*, p.214.
2   *Ibid.*, ch. 11 *passim*.
3   *Ibid.*, pp.235-6. On the centrality of the theme of reconciliation
in Hegel's philosophy, see Plant, *Hegel*.
4   Habermas, *Human Interests*, p.233.
5   *Ibid.*, p.242.
6   *Ibid.*, p.344, translator's note 31.
7   Freud, *The Ego and the Id*, p.25.
8   *Ibid.*, p.25.
9   *Ibid.*, p.56.
10 *Ibid.*, 24.
11 Jahoda, *Freud and the Dilemmas of Psychology*, p.63.
12 See ch. 3, sec. 3, above.
13 See note 6 above. Freud's dictum was enunciated in his *New
Introductory Lectures on Psychoanalysis*, p.112.
14 Helpful guides to this problematic area of Freud's work are
Fletcher, *Instinct in Man*, ch. 5; and Nagera (ed.), *Basic
Psychoanalytic Concepts on the Theory of Instincts*.
15 See, e.g., Freud, *Introductory Lectures*, lecture 1; *The
Interpretation of Dreams*, pp.684-5; and the Editor's Introduction
to this, pp.39-42.
16 Freud, *Three Essays on the Theory of Sexuality*, pp.82-3.
17 Freud, 'Instincts and their Vicissitudes', p.123; cf. the Editor's
Note to this paper, pp.111-13.
18 Freud, 'The Unconscious', p.177.
19 Freud, *New Introductory Lectures*, pp.128-9; and cf. his
comment: 'The concept of instinct is thus one of those lying on the
frontier between the mental and the physical', *Three Essays on the
Theory of Sexuality*, p.82.
20 On these changes see, e.g., Fletcher, *Instinct in Man*,
pp.234-53; and Freud's own account in *New Introductory
Lectures*, lecture 32.
21 On Freud's determinism, see his *Introductory Lectures*,
lectures 2 and 6; and his *New Introductory Lectures*, lecture 35.
22 Habermas, *Human Interests*, p.285.

23 Frankel, 'Habermas Talking', p.53.
24 Freud, 'Instincts and their Vicissitudes'.
25 See, e.g., Freud, 'The Unconscious'.
26 See especially *The Interpretation of Dreams*, pp. 745-69.
27 My account of the topographical model partly conflates several different stages in its development: see Freud, *New Introductory Lectures*, lecture 31, for a fuller account, including the relations between the topographical and structural models.
28 Freud, *The Interpretation of Dreams*, p.769.
29 *Ibid.*, ch. VI; *Introductory Lectures*, lecture 10; and *New Introductory Lectures*, lecture 29.
30 Freud, *The Interpretation of Dreams*, p.768. See also *Introductory Lectures*, p.339.
31 Freud, *The Interpretation of Dreams*, p.769.
32 *Ibid.*, p.763.
33 See p.97 above.
34 Freud, *The Ego and the Id*, p.56.
35 See Fletcher, *Instinct in Man*, p.198, where this parallel is noted.
36 See, e.g., *The Ego and the Id.*, ch.V; *Introductory Lectures*, lecture 28; and *New Introductory Lectures*, lecture 34.
37 See especially *Civilization and its Discontents*. As is often noted, e.g. in Robinson, *The Sexual Radicals*, pp.19-63, Freud's introduction of the death instinct into his theory led to a marked change of attitude towards the social consequences of sexual repression from that expressed in, e.g. his earlier '"Civilized" Sexual Morality and Modern Nervous Illness'. Rejection of the death instinct was a major reason for Reich's disenchantment with Freud: see, e.g. Reich, *The Function of the Orgasm*, ch. 5, and *The Sexual Revolution*, Part I, ch. 1.
38 Habermas, *Human Interests*, p.271.
39 *Ibid.*, p.272.
40 This issue is returned to briefly in ch. 6, sec. 2, below, in discussion Habermas's conception of an 'ideal speech situation'.
41 My classification here roughly follows that given in the Introduction to Berofsky (ed.), *Freewill and Determinism*. See also Honderich, *Punishment: The Supposed Justifications*, ch.4.
42 On this last issue, see Borst (ed.), *The Mind-Brain Identity Theory*, pp.13-33. For a discussion of both this, and the logical status of purposive explanation, see Shaffer, *The Philosophy of Mind*, pp. 39-50 and 77-106.
43 Both points are defended in Keat and Urry, *Social Theory as Science*, pp.151-9.

44 Cf. Fay, 'How People Change Themselves', who adopts a fairly similar strategy in this respect.
45 Habermas, *Human Interests*, p.271.
46 *Ibid.*, pp. 216-17.
47 See Habermas's account of Dilthey, in *Human Interests*, ch.7.
48 See note 37 above. Curiously Marcuse, in *Eros and Civilization*, produced a critical account of the social function of sexual repression quite similar to Reich's, but accepted Freud's death instinct. I am doubtful about the consistency of this position.
49 See, e.g., Boden, *Purposive Explanation in Psychology*, ch.V; and Midgley, *Beast and Man*, ch.3. Cf. also pp.122-3 below, and the references in note 59.
50 For a discussion of this question, see Boden, *Purposive Explanation*, ch. VI.
51 Nagel, *The Structure of Science*, ch. 11. See also Boden, *Purposive Explanation*, pp.52-9; what I go on to call 'explanatory' reduction corresponds to Boden's 'empirical' reduction; and her concept of 'strict' reduction includes what I call 'ontological' and 'conceptual' reduction.
52 See ch. 3, sec. 1, above.
53 For an account of materialist and other 'solutions', see Shaffer, *The Philosophy of Mind*, chs. 3 and 4.
54 Nagel, *The Structure of Science*, pp. 364-6.
55 *Ibid.*, p.152.
56 For a criticism of Nagel's view, in *The Structure of Science*, ch. 6, see Maxwell, 'On the Ontological Status of Theoretical Entities'.
57 See, e.g. Shaffer, *The Philosophy of Mind*, pp.68-71.
58 See Rose, *The Conscious Brain*, pp. 61-94, for a standard account of the neuron.
59 See Rose, *The Conscious Brain*, ch.8; and Barnett, *'Instinct' and 'Intelligence'*, chs. 9 and 10, for useful discussions of these issues; and note 49 above.
60 Freud and Breuer, *Studies in Hysteria*, p.252.
61 See, e.g. Reich, *The Function of the Orgasm*, ch. 7. For a standard account of the autonomic and voluntary nervous systems, see Hilgard et al. *Introduction to Psychology*, ch. 2.
62 See Rose, *The Conscious Brain*, ch.4.
63 See Gregory, *Eye and Brain*, especially chs. 7, 9, 11 and 12.
64 See Rose, *The Conscious Brain*, pp. 280-4.
65 Boden, *Purposive Explanation*, pp.154-5.
66 *Ibid.*, p.155.
67 Habermas, *Human Interests*, p.247.

68 Freud, *An Outline of Psychoanalysis*, p.182.
69 Freud, *Introductory Lectures*, p.487.
70 Habermas, *Human Interests*, p.245.
71 Jahoda, *Freud*, p.101. The quotation early in this passage is from Laplanche and Pontalis, *The Language of Psychoanalysis*, p.247.
72 See, e.g. the critical discussion of energy-discharge models in ethology in Manning, *An Introduction to Animal Behaviour*, ch. 4.
73 See ch. 6, sec. 1, below.
74 For Freud's early formulation of this energy-model, see his *Project for a Scientific Psychology*.
75 Nagel, *The Structure of Science*, p.345.
76 On these issues, see Fletcher, *Instinct in Man*, pp.174-83 and 239-53.

5: THEORY AND PRACTICE IN PSYCHOTHERAPY

1 Habermas, *Human Interests*, p.258.
2 *Ibid.*, p.258.
3 See ch. 4, sec. 1, above.
4 Habermas, *Human Interests*, p.266.
5 E.g. Popper, 'Science: Conjectures and Refutations', pp.33-8.
6 See Kline, *Fact and Fantasy in Freudian Theory*; and Eysenck and Wilson, *The Experimental Study of Freudian Theories*.
7 See Popper, 'Science: Conjectures and Refutations'; and also ch.1 of *Objective Knowledge* for a succinct statement of his view of induction.
8 For an excellent account of these, see Chalmers, *What is this thing called Science?*
9 Both have been presented forcefully in Putnam, 'The "Corroboration" of Theories'. See also Popper's response in 'Replies to my Critics', pp.993-9, which involves I believe some misunderstanding of Putnam's claims.
10 For discussion of some of the issues mentioned here, see Hempel, *Philosophy of Natural Science*, chs. 2-4; and Quine and Ullyan, *The Web of Belief*, chs. 5-7.
11 See also Chalmers, *What is this thing called Science?*, for a much fuller discussion of falsification.
12 This point is excellently argued in Bohm, *Chance and Causality*, chs. 1 and 5, in the context of a 'process' philosophy of nature, according to which the concept of a 'thing' involves abstraction.

13   Popper, 'Science: Conjectures and Refutations', pp.34-45.
But Popper has a further criticism, on p.38, footnote 3, of the
'theory-loadedness' of clinical evidence, which I do not discuss.
14   *Ibid.*, p.35.
15   See ch. 3, sec. 1, above.
16   Freud, 'Character and Anal Erotism', p.215.
17   Habermas, *Human Interests*, p.266.
18   On transference in psychoanalysis see, e.g., Brown and
Pedder, *Introduction to Psychotherapy*, pp. 58-66. Freud discusses
its central impotance in, e.g. *Introductory Lectures*, lecture 27.
19   Habermas, *Human Interests*, p.261.
20   *Ibid.*, pp.261-2.
21   *Ibid.*, p.269.
22   *Ibid.*, pp.267-9.
23   Cf. Freud's discussion of the prospects for therapeutic success
in his *New Introductury Lectures*, lecture 34.
24   Fay, *Social Theory*, ch.5.
25   *Ibid.*, p.108.
26   *Ibid.*, p.102.
27   *Ibid.*, pp.108-9.
28   *Ibid.*, p.95.
29   *Ibid.*, p.95, footnote 6; see also p.100, footnote 8.
30   *Ibid.*, p.100.
31   Useful accounts of the many post-Freudian forms of
psychotherapy are Kovel, *A Complete Guide to Therapy*, Part
Two; and Brown and Pedder, *Introduction to Psychotherapy*, Part
II.
32   See the discussion of this point in ch. 1, sec. 3, above.

6: THE COMPLEXITY OF NORMS IN PRACTICE

1   I continue to use these terms for convenience, whilst noting the
qualifications to their usual sense mentioned on p.160 above.
2   On behaviour-modification, see e.g. Kovel, *A Complete Guide
to Therapy*, pp.210-20.
3   See, e.g. Belliveau and Richter, *Understanding Human Sexual
Inadequacy*.
4   See Reich, *The Function of the Orgasm*, and *Character
Analysis*. See Lowen, *Bioenergetics*, for one important
development of Reich's earlier therapeutic ideas.
5   See Reich, *Character Analysis*, ch. 14.

6   Such as Southgate and Randall, *The Barefoot Psycho-analyst.*

7   Strawson, 'Freedom and Resentment'.

8   See, e.g. Kovel, *A Complete Guide to Therapy*, ch. 12; and Brown and Pedder, *Introduction to Psychotherapy*, pp.166-180.

9   See Keat, 'A Critical Examination of Skinner's Objections to Mentalism'.

10   Cf. Keat and Urry, *Social Theory as Science*, pp.159-67.

11   See, e.g. Habermas, *Theory and Practice*, pp.25-32

12   See ch. 4, section 1, above.

13   McCarthy, *Habermas*, p.378: see also pp.377-86 for a useful discussion of this issue. One should note also Habermas's espousal of an apparently interest-free form of knowledge in what he calls the 'rational-reconstructive' sciences: on this see McCarthy, *Habermas*, pp.276-79; and Habermas, *Theory and Practice*, pp.22-4, and 'What is Universal Pragmatics?', pp.8-20.

14   See McCarthy, *Habermas*, pp.272-333, for an excellent account of this.

15   See Habermas, 'Theory of Communicative Competence', and 'What is Universal Pragmatics?'.

16   Habermas, 'What is Universal Pragmatics?', p.3.

17   Quoted in McCarthy, *Habermas*, p.292, but with no reference: I believe it is from Habermas's (untranslated) '*Warheitstheorien*' (full reference in McCarthy, *Habermas*, p.443).

18   Habermas, 'Postscript', p.170.

19   Quoted and translated from '*Warheitstheorien*' by McCarthy, *Habermas*, p.299.

20   Habermas, 'Postscript', pp.166-72; but cf. my comments on pp.77-8 above.

21   See McCarthy, *Habermas*, pp.303-04, for some relevant criticisms.

22   Supported, I think, by Habermas's remarks in *Theory and Practice*, p.20, and *Legitimation Crisis*, p.107.

23   Habermas, *Theory and Practice*, pp.25-6.

24   Apel, *Towards a Transformation of Philosophy*, pp.256-85.

25   So we here 'return' to the point at which I left unspecified a possible argument for the normative presuppositions of engagement in scientific practice, on p.48 above.

26   Habermas, *Legitimation Crisis*, p.108.

27   See Freud, 'Character and Anal Erotism'.

28   e.g. Watson, *The Double Helix*.

29   See, e.g. Popper, *The Open Society and its Enemies*, vol. II; and Kuhn, *The Structure of Scientific Revolutions*.

30 Feyerabend, *Against Method*.
31 See, e.g. Nozick, *Anarchy, State and Utopia*, ch. 8; and Sampson, *Liberty and Language*. Cf. my review of the latter, in 'Chomsky's Politics'.
32 See Berlin, 'Two Concepts of Liberty', section VIII, for a classic defence of this view; and cf. pp.191-2 below.
33 Habermas, 'Theory of Communicative Competence', p.372.
34 Habermas, *Legitimation Crisis*, p.107.
35 *Ibid.*, p.108.
36 *Ibid.*, p.110.
37 *Ibid.*, p.108.
38 Habermas, *Communication*, p.184.
39 I shall focus almost entirely on Part One of this book. A helpful introductory account of Rawls's theory is S. Gorovitz, 'John Rawls: Theory of Justice'.
40 See Rawls, *A Theory of Justice*, section 14. I am excluding, however, his claim that procedural outcomes must be 'tested' in relation to what he calls 'considered judgments': see *ibid.*, section 9.
41 See Rawls, *A Theory of Justice*, section 7. On the idea of trade-off relations in political philosophy, see Barry, *Political Argument*, pp.3-8.
42 See Wolff, *Understanding Rawls*, for an interesting account of the development of Rawls's position.
43 See Rawls, *A Theory of Justice*, section 15.
44 See Nagel, 'Rawls on Justice', and Teitelman, 'The Limits of Individualism', for discussions of this issue.
45 Habermas, *Legitimation Crisis*, p.108.
46 *Ibid.*, p.108.
47 McCarthy, *Habermas*, p.428, footnote 37.
48 See Habermas, 'What is Universal Pragmatics?', p.3.
49 See his discussion of the 'separation of powers' in *Legitimation Crisis*, p.111.
50 *Ibid.*, p.112.
51 *Ibid.*, p.113.

CONCLUSION

1 So I am generally sympathetic to Colletti's position, in *Marxism and Hegel*.
2 The title of a paper now forming ch. 6 of his *Theory and Practice*.
3 Quoted by McCarthy in his introduction to Habermas, *Communication*, p.x.

4 See the account of Gadamer's exchanges with Habermas in McCarthy, *Habermas*, pp.162-93.

5 See, e.g. Rose, *The Conscious Brain*, pp.126-34 and 203-18; and Hilgard et al., *Introduction to Psychology*, pp.141-5. Cf. the comments on 'innateness' on pp.122-3 above.

6 See e.g. Gregory, *Eye and Brain*, chs. 11 and 12; and Hilgard et al., *Introduction to Psychology*, pp.145-8.

7 My view here is influenced by Hooker, 'Empiricism, Perception and Conceptual Change'.

8 Cf. pp.19-20 above.

9 Cf. ch. 5, sec. 1, above.

10 On this development in the philosophy of social science, see Apel, *Analytical Philosophy of Language and the Geisteswissenschaften*, ch. 4.

11 See ch. 3, sec. 4, above.

12 See, e.g. Adlam et al., 'Psychology, Ideology, and the Human Subject'.

13 See Hampshire, *Thought and Action*, for an account of these and related contrasts.

14 See ch. 4, sec. 3, above.

15 See ch. 6, sec. 1, above.

16 See ch. 6, sec. 2, and ch. 2, sec. 2, above.

Bibliography

Where there is more than one work by the same author, these are listed in alphabetical order by titles.

Since several of Freud's works are now available in the Penguin Freud Library, as well as the Standard Edition, I have used the former for all works referred to that have so far been published in it, and the latter for those that have not. The dates of the original German publication of each work are included in parentheses.

Adey, G. and Frisby, D. (eds.), *The Positivist Dispute in German Sociology*, Heinemann, London, 1976.

Adlam, D., Henriques, J., Rose, N., Salfield, A., Venn, C. and Walkerdine, V., 'Psychology, Ideology and the Human Subject', *Ideology and Consciousness*, no. 1, 1977, pp.5-56.

Albert, H., 'Behind Positivism's Back?', in G. Adey and D. Frisby (eds.), *The Positivist Dispute in German Sociology*, Heinemann, London, 1976, pp.226-57.

Albert, H., 'The Myth of Total Reason', in G. Adey and D. Frisby (eds.), *The Positivist Dispute in German Sociology*, Heinemann, London, 1976, pp.163-7.

Althusser, L., *For Marx*, Penguin Books, Harmondsworth, 1969.

Apel, K.-O., *Analytical Philosophy of Language and the Geisteswissenschaften*, D. Reidel, Dordrecht, 1967.

Apel, K.-O., *Towards a Transformation of Philosophy*, Routledge & Kegan Paul, London, 1980.

Arnold, M. B. (ed.), *Feelings and Emotions*, Academic Press, New York and London, 1970.

Ayer, A. J. (ed.), *Logical Positivism*, Free Press, Glencoe, 1959.

Barnett, S. A., *'Instinct' and 'Intelligence'*, Penguin Books, Harmondsworth, 1970.

Barry, B., *Political Argument*, Routledge & Kegan Paul, London, 1965.

Beck, L. W., 'Neo-Kantianism', in P. Edwards (ed.), *The Encyclopedia of Philosophy*, vol. 5, Macmillan, London, 1967, pp.468-73.

Beckner, M., *The Biological Way of Thought*, University of California Press, Berkeley and Los Angeles, 1968.

Belliveau, F. and Richter, L., *Understanding Human Sexual Inadequacy*, Hodder & Stoughton, London, 1971.

Benton, T., *Philosophical Foundations of the Three Sociologies*, Routledge & Kegan Paul, London, 1977.

Berlin, I., 'Two Concepts of Liberty', in *Four Essays on Liberty*, Oxford University Press, Oxford, 1969, pp.118-72.

Bernstein, E., *Evolutionary Socialism*, Schoken Books, New York, 1961.

Berofsky, B. (ed.), *Free Will and Determinism*, Harper & Row, New York, 1966.

Bhaskar, R., *The Possibility of Naturalism*, Harvester Press, Hassocks, 1979.

Bhaskar, R., *A Realist Theory of Science*, 2nd ed., Harvester Press, Hassocks, 1978.

Bhaskar, R., 'Scientific Explanation and Human Emancipation', *Radical Philosophy*, no. 26, 1980, pp.16-28.

Boden, M., *Purposive Explanation in Psychology*, Harvard University Press, Cambridge, Mass., 1972.

Bohm, D., *Causality and Chance in Modern Physics*, Routledge & Kegan Paul, London, 1957.

Borst, C. V. (ed.), *The Mind-Brain Identity Theory*, Macmillan, London, 1970.

Brown, D. and Pedder, J., *Introduction to Psychotherapy*, Tavistock Publications, London, 1979.

Chalmers, A. F., *What is this thing called Science?*, Open University Press, Milton Keynes, 1976.

Cohen, G. A., 'Marxism: A Philosophy of Nature?', *Radical Philosophy*, no. 2., 1972, pp.28-31.

Colletti, L., *Marxism and Hegel*, New Left Books, London, 1973.

Dahrendorf, R., *Essays in the Theory of Society*, Routledge & Kegan Paul, London, 1968.

Duhem, P., *The Aim and Structure of Physical Theory*, Princeton University Press, Princeton, 1954.

Duhem, P., *To Save the Phenomena* (trans. E. Dolan and C. Maschler), Chicago University Press, Chicago, 1969.

Edgley, R., 'Dialectic: A Reply to Keat and Dews', *Radical Philosophy*, no. 21, 1979, pp.29-34.

Edgley, R., 'Reason as Dialectic', *Radical Philosophy*, no. 15, 1976, pp.2-7.

Edgley, R., 'Reason and Violence', *Radical Philosophy*, no.4, 1973, pp.18-25.

Ekman, P. (ed.), *Darwin and Facial Expression*, Academic Press, New York, 1973.

Eysenck, H. J. and Wilson, G. D., *The Experimental Study of Freudian Theories*, Methuen, London, 1973.

Fay, B., *Social Theory and Political Practice*, Allen & Unwin, London, 1975.

Fay, B., 'How People Change Themselves: The Relationship between Critical Theory and its Audience', in T. Ball (ed.); *Political Theory and Praxis*, Minnesota University Press, Minneapolis, 1977.

Feyerabend, P., *Against Method*, New Left Books, London, 1975.

Fletcher, R., *Instinct in Man*, 2nd ed, Allen & Unwin, London, 1968.

Frankel, B., 'Habermas Talking: An Interview', *Theory and Society*, vol. 1, 1974, pp.37-58.

Freud, S., *The Standard Edition of the Complete Psychological Works of Sigmund Freud* (trans. and ed. J. Strachey), 24 vols, Hogarth Press, London, 1953-1974. (Referred to here as *Standard Edition*.)

Freud, S., 'Character and Anal Erotism' (1908), in *On Sexuality*, Penguin Books, Harmondsworth, 1977, pp.207-25.

Freud, S., *Civilization and its Discontents* (1930), *Standard Edition*, vol. 21, pp.59-145.

Freud, S., '"Civilized" Sexual Morality and Modern Nervous Illness' (1908), *Standard Edition*, vol. 9, pp.177-204.

Freud, S., *The Ego and the Id* (1923), *Standard Edition*, vol. 19, pp.1-66.

Freud, S., 'Instincts and their Vicissitudes' (1915), *Standard Edition*, vol.14, pp.109-40.

Freud, S., *The Interpretation of Dreams* (1900), Penguin Books, Harmondsworth, 1976.

Freud, S., *Introductory Lectures* (1917), Penguin Books, Harmondsworth, 1973.

Freud, S., *New Introductory Lectures on Psychoanalysis* (1933), Penguin Books, Harmondsworth, 1973.

Freud, S., *An Outline of Psychoanalysis* (1938), *Standard Edition*, vol. 23, pp.139-207.

Freud, S., *Project for a Scientific Psychology* (1895), *Standard Edition*, vol. 1., pp.283-346.

Freud, S., *Three Essays on the Theory of Sexuality* (1905), in *On Sexuality*, Penguin Books, Harmondsworth, 1977, pp.33-169.

Freud, S., 'The Unconscious' (1915), *Standard Edition*, vol. 14, pp.159-216.

Freud, S. and Breuer, J., *Studies in Hysteria* (1895), Penguin Books, Harmondsworth, 1974.

Friedman, R. B., 'An Introduction to Mill's Theory of Authority', in J. B. Schneewind (ed.), *Mill: A Collection of Critical Essays*, Macmillan, London, 1968, pp.379-425.

Gay, P., *The Dilemma of Democratic Socialism*, Collier-Macmillan, London, 1962.

Gerth, H. H. and Mills, C. W. (eds.), *From Max Weber: Essays in Sociology*, Oxford University Press, New York, 1946.

Giddens, A., 'Marx, Weber, and the Development of Capitalism', *Sociology*, vol. 4, 1970, pp.289-310.

Gorovitz, S., 'John Rawls: A Theory of Justice', in A. de Crespigny and K. Minogue (eds.), *Contemporary Political Philosophers*, Methuen, London, 1976, pp.272-89.

Gregory, R. L., *Eye and Brain*, 3rd edn, Weidenfeld & Nicolson, London, 1977.

Habermas, J., 'The Analytical Theory of Science and Dialectics', in G. Adey and D. Frisby (eds.), *The Positivist Dispute in German Sociology*, Heinemann, London, 1976, pp.131-62.

Habermas, J., *Communication and the Evolution of Society*, (trans. T. McCarthy), Heinemann, London, 1979.

Habermas, J., *Knowledge and Human Interests* (trans. J. J. Shapiro), Heinemann, London, 1972.

Habermas, J., *Legitimation Crisis* (trans. T. McCarthy), Beacon Press, Boston, 1975.

Habermas, J., 'A Positivistically Bisected Rationalism', in G. Adey and D. Frisby (eds.), *The Positivist Dispute in German Sociology*, Heinemann, London, 1976, pp.198-225.

Habermas, J., 'A Postscript to *Knowledge and Human Interests*', *Philosophy of the Social Sciences*, vol. 3, 1973, pp.157-89.

Habermas, J., 'On Systematically Distorted Communication', *Inquiry*, vol. 13, 1970, pp.205-18.

Habermas, J., 'Towards a Theory of Communicative Competence', *Inquiry*, vol. 13, 1970, pp.360-75.

Habermas, J., *Theory and Practice* (trans. J. Viertel), Heinemann, London, 1974.

Habermas, J., 'What is Universal Pragmatics?' in *Communication and the Evolution of Society* (trans. T. McCarthy), Heinemann, London, 1979, pp.1-68.

Hampshire, S., *Thought and Action*, Chatto & Windus, London, 1960.

Hare, R., 'Descriptivism', in W. D. Hudson (ed.), *The Is-Ought Question*, Macmillan, London, 1969, pp.240-58.

Harré, R., *The Principles of Scientific Thinking*, Macmillan, London, 1970.

Hayek, F. A., *The Counter-Revolution of Science*, Free Press, Glencoe, 1955.

Heisenberg, W., *Physics and Philosophy: The Revolution in Modern Science*, Allen & Unwin, London, 1975.

Hempel, C. G., *Aspects of Scientific Explanation*, Free Press, New York, 1965.

Hempel, C. G., *Philosophy of Natural Science*, Prentice-Hall, Englewood Cliffs, 1966.

Hilgard, E. R., Atkinson, R. C. and Atkinson, R. L., *Introduction to Psychology*, 6th edn, Harcourt Brace Jovanovich, New York, 1975.

Hinde, R. A. (ed.), *Non-Verbal Communication*, Cambridge University Press, Cambridge, 1972.

Honderich, T., *Punishment: The Supposed Justifications*, Hutchinson, London, 1969.

Hooker, C. A., 'Empiricism, Perception and Conceptual Change', *Canadian Journal of Philosophy*, vol. 3, 1973, pp.59-75.

Horkheimer, M., *Critical Theory* (trans. M. O'Connell et al.), Herder & Herder, New York, 1972.

Hudson, W. D. (ed.), *The Is-Ought Question*, Macmillan, London, 1969.

Jahoda, M., *Freud and the Dilemmas of Psychology*, Hogarth Press, London, 1977.

Jay, M., *The Dialectical Imagination*, Little, Brown & Co., Boston, 1973.

Keat, R. N., 'Chomsky's Politics: Review of G. Sampson, *Liberty and Language*', *Radical Philosophy*, no. 25, 1980, pp.35-9.

Keat, R. N., 'A Critical Examination of B. F. Skinner's Objections to Mentalism', *Behaviorism*, vol. 1, 1972, pp.53-70.

Keat, R. N., 'Positivism and Statistics in Social Science', in J. Irvine, I. Miles and J. Evans, (eds.), *Demystifying Social Statistics*, Pluto Press, London, 1979, pp.76-86.

Keat, R. N., 'Scientific Socialism — A Positivist Delusion?', *Radical Philosophy*, no. 23, 1979, pp.21-3.

Keat, R. N. and Urry, J. R., *Social Theory as Science*, Routledge & Kegan Paul, London, 1975. (2nd edn. due 1981).

Kline, P., *Fact and Fantasy in Freudian Theory*, Methuen, London, 1972.

Korsch, K., *Marxism and Philosophy* (trans. F. Halliday), New Left Books, London, 1970.

Kovel, J., *A Complete Guide to Therapy*, Penguin Books, Harmondsworth, 1978.

Kolakowski, L., *Positivist Philosophy*, Penguin Books, Harmondsworth, 1972.

Koyré, A., *Metaphysics and Measurement*, Chapman & Hall, London, 1968.

Kroner, R., *Kant's Weltanschauung* (trans. J. E. Smith), University of Chicago Press, Chicago, 1956.

Kuhn, T. S., *The Structure of Scientific Revolutions*, 2nd edn, University of Chicago Press, Chicago, 1970.

Laplanche, J. and Pontalis, J. B., *The Language of Psychoanalysis*, Hogarth Press, London, 1973.

Laslett, P. and Runciman, W. G. (eds.), *Philosophy, Politics and Society*, Third Series, Basil Blackwell, Oxford, 1967.

Lessnoff, M., *The Structure of Social Science*, Allen & Unwin, London, 1974.

Lichtheim, G., *Marxism: An Historical and Critical Study*, 2nd edn, Routledge & Kegan Paul, London, 1964.

Lipset, S. M., *Political Man*, Heinemann, London, 1960.

Lobkowicz, N., 'Interest and Objectivity', *Philosophy of the Social Sciences*, vol. 2, 1972, pp.193-210.

Lowen, A., *Bioenergetics*, Penguin Books, Harmondsworth, 1976.

Lukes, S., 'Alienation and Anomie', in P. Laslett and W. G. Runciman (eds), *Philosophy, Politics and Society*, Basil Blackwell, Oxford, 1967, pp.134-56.

Lyons, W., *Emotion*, Cambridge University Press, Cambridge, 1980.

McCarthy, T., *The Critical Theory of Jürgen Habermas*, Hutchinson, London, 1978.

McMullin, E. (ed.), *Galileo: Man of Science*, Basic Books, New York, 1967.

Mandelbaum, M., 'Two Moot Issues in Mill's *Utilitarianism*', in J. B. Schneewind (ed.), *Mill: A Collection of Critical Essays*, Macmillan, London, 1968, pp.206-33.

Manning, A., *An Introduction to Animal Behaviour*, 2nd edn, Edward Arnold, London, 1972.

Marcuse, H., *Eros and Civilization*, 2nd edn, Beacon Press, Boston, 1966.

Marcuse, H., *Negations*, Allen Lane/The Penguin Press, Harmondsworth, 1968.

Marcuse, H., *One-Dimensional Man*, Routledge & Kegan Paul, London, 1964.

Marcuse, H., *Reason and Revolution*, 2nd edn, Routledge & Kegan Paul, London, 1955.

Marx, K., *Critique of the Gotha Program*, in K. Marx and F. Engels, *Selected Works*, Lawrence & Wishart, London, 1968, pp.315-35.

Marx, K., *Economic and Philosophical Manuscripts*, in *Early Writings* (ed. L. Colletti), Penguin Books, Harmondsworth, 1975, pp.279-400.

Maxwell, G., 'On the Ontological Status of Theoretical Entities', in H. Feigl and G. Maxwell (eds.), *Minnesota Studies in the Philosophy of Science*, vol. 3, University of Minnesota Press, Minneapolis, 1962, pp.3-27.

Midgley, M., *Beast and Man*, Harvester Press, Hassocks, 1978.

Miliband, R., *Marxism and Politics*, Oxford University Press, Oxford, 1977.

Mill, J. S., *Auguste Comte and Positivism*, Ann Arbor, Michigan, 1965.

Miller, D., *Social Justice*, Oxford University Press, Oxford, 1976.

Nagel, E., *The Structure of Science*, Routledge & Kegan Paul, New York, 1961.

Nagera, H. (ed.), *Basic Psychoanalytic Concepts on the Theory of Instincts*, Allen & Unwin, London, 1970.

Neurath, O., *Empiricism and Sociology* (ed. M. Neurath and R. S. Cohen), D. Reidel, Dordrecht, 1973.

Neurath, O., Carnap, R. and Hahn, H., 'The Scientific Conception of the World: the Vienna Circle', reprinted in O. Neurath, *Empiricism and Sociology*, D. Reidel, Dordrecht, 1973, pp.299-318.

Nozick, R., *Anarchy, State and Utopia*, Basil Blackwell, Oxford, 1974.

Oatley, K., *Brain Mechanisms and Mind*, Thames & Hudson, London, 1972.

Outhwaite, W., *Understanding Social Life*, Allen & Unwin, London, 1975.

Passmore, J., *A Hundred Years of Philosophy*, Penguin Books, Harmondsworth, 1958.

Philips, D. Z. and Mounce, H. O., 'On Morality's having a Point', in W. D. Hudson (ed.), *The Is-Ought Question*, Macmillan, London, 1969, pp.228-39.

Plant, R., *Hegel*, Allen & Unwin, London, 1973.

Popper, K. R., *Conjectures and Refutations*, 3rd edn, Routledge & Kegan Paul, London, 1969.

Popper, K. R., 'The Logic of the Social Sciences', in G. Adey and D. Frisby (eds.), *The Positivist Dispute in German Sociology*, Heinemann, London, 1976, pp.87-104.

Popper, K. R., *Objective Knowledge*, Oxford University Press, London, 1972.

Popper, K. R., *The Open Society and its Enemies*, vol. 2, 4th edn, Routledge & Kegan Paul, London, 1962.

Popper, K. R., 'Replies to my Critics', in P. A. Schilpp (ed.), *The Philosophy of Karl Popper*, Book II, Open Court, La Salle, 1974, pp.961-1197.

Popper, K. R., 'Science: Conjectures and Refutations', in *Conjectures and Refutations*, 3rd edn, Routledge & Kegan Paul, London, 1969, pp.33-65.

Putnam, H., 'The "Corroboration" of Theories', in P. A. Schilpp (ed.), *The Philosophy of Karl Popper*, Book I, Open Court, La Salle, 1974, pp.221-40.

Quine, W. V. and Ullyan, J. S., *The Web of Belief*, Random House, New York, 1970.

Rawls, J., *A Theory of Justice*, Oxford University Press, Oxford, 1972.

Reich, W., *Character Analysis*, 3rd edn, Pocket Books, New York, 1976.

Reich, W., *The Function of the Orgasm*, Pocket Books, New York, 1975.

Reich, W., *The Sexual Revolution*, 4th edn, Vision Press, London, 1972.

Robinson, P., *The Sexual Radicals*, Paladin, London, 1972.

Rose, S., *The Conscious Brain*, rev. edn, Penguin Books, Harmondsworth, 1976.

Ryan, A., *J. S. Mill*, Pantheon, New York, 1970.

Saint-Simon, H., *Selected Writings on Science, Industry and Social Organization* (ed. and trans. K. Taylor), Croom Helm, London, 1975.

Sampson, G., *Liberty and Language*, Oxford University Press, Oxford, 1979.

Schilpp, P. A. (ed.), *The Philosophy of Karl Popper*, Books I and II, Open Court, La Salle, 1974.

Schneewind, J. B. (ed.), *Mill: A Collection of Critical Essays*, Macmillan, London, 1968.

Searle, J. R., *Speech Acts*, Cambridge University Press, Cambridge, 1969.

Shaffer, J., *The Philosophy of Mind*, Prentice-Hall, Englewood Cliffs, 1968.

Shapere, D., *Galileo: A Philosophical Study*, Chicago University Press, Chicago, 1974.

Sloman, A., *The Computer Revolution in Philosophy*, Harvester Press, Hassocks, 1978.

Solomon, R. C., *From Rationalism to Existentialism*, Humanities Press, New York, 1972.

Southgate, J. and Randall, R., *The Barefoot Psychoanalyst*, Association of Karen Horney Counsellors, London, 1978.

Strawson, P. F., 'Freedom and Resentment', in P. F. Strawson (ed.), *Studies in the Philosophy of Thought and Action*, Oxford University Press, Oxford, 1968, pp.71-96.

Strawson, P. F., *The Bounds of Sense*, Methuen, London, 1966.

Taylor, C., 'Neutrality in Political Science', in P. Laslett and W. G. Runciman (eds.), *Philosophy, Politics and Society*, Basil Blackwell, Oxford, 1967, pp.25-57.

Teitelman, M., 'The Limits of Individualism', *The Journal of Philosophy*, vol. 69, 1972, pp.545-56.

Thompson, E. P., 'An Open Letter to Leszek Kolakowski', in *The Poverty of Theory and Other Essays*, Merlin Press, London, 1978, pp.92-192.

Thompson, E. P., 'The Poverty of Theory', in *The Poverty of Theory and Other Essays*, Merlin Press, London, 1978, pp.193-399.

Thorpe, W. H., *Animal Nature and Human Nature*, Methuen, London, 1974.

Watson, J., *The Double Helix*, Penguin Books, Harmondsworth, 1970.

Waxman, C., *The End of Ideology Debate*, Funk & Wagnalls, New York, 1968.

Weber, M., *The Protestant Ethic and the Spirit of Capitalism* (trans. T. Parsons), Allen & Unwin, London, 1930.

Weber M., *The Methodology of the Social Sciences* (trans. E. Shils and H. Finch), Free Press, New York, 1949.

Williams, B., 'A Critique of Utilitarianism', in J. J. C. Smart and B. Williams, *Utilitarianism: For and Against*, Cambridge University Press, Cambridge, 1973, pp.77-151.

Wolff, R. P., *Understanding Rawls*, Princeton University Press, Princeton, 1977.

Index